T0051516

The Boy Who Sat
By The Window

The Boy Who Sat By The Window

THE STORY OF THE **QUEEN OF SOHO**

DAVID HODGE

MARDLE

First published in 2022 by Mardle Books
15 Church Road
London, SW13 9HE
www.mardlebooks.com

Text © 2022 David Hodge

Hardback ISBN 9781914451744
eBook ISBN 9781914451751

A CIP catalogue record for this book is available from the British Library.

Every reasonable effort has been made to trace copyright-holders of
material reproduced in this book, but if any have been inadvertently
overlooked the publishers would be glad to hear from them.

Design and typesetting by Danny Lyle

Printed in the UK

10 9 8 7 6 5 4 3 2 1

Cover images: Marc Abe
Cover artwork: David Hodge
Cover design: Simon Levy

"Thank you, Zinan Chan,
for 12 glorious years of total love."

FOREWORD

Dusty is a strange bird it's fair to say and, if there is such a thing as 'self-deprecating confidence', she has it. Even in the early days of my noticing and befriending Dusty, there was already an edge to Dusty. The make-up was so carefully done and ridiculously precise and then you had the fashion drag – *not* drag drag – but full on, high fashion Vivienne Westwood (in totality).

She's been everything. Door Whore, DJ, pop star, artist and writer. And now, dammit, a book which was preceded by a podcast. With this book, you see Dusty laying out her past and walking towards the future – or even just the now.

Dusty's life has not followed an orthodox path. She's not the queen you think she is. She's more. She's complicated, she's bitchy, she loves gossip. She pretends not to care, but wants it all. She is deliciously Midlands-ish. She is freak royalty. I remember watching Dusty talking to Pete Burns one night at the *Nag Nag Nag* Club and just thinking... look at those two ridiculously beautiful things.

My Children, My Sisters, Queers, Weirdos, Fashion Junkies, Show-Offs, Attention Seekers, Freak Royalty.

Enjoy this story. I already jumped to the parts about me.

– Boy George

PROLOGUE

I murdered her in the middle of Trafalgar Square.

The whole thing was carefully planned. It would be witnessed in plain sight by thousands of people, though none of them would realise what they were seeing. It would be her last dazzling appearance. The smell of the greasepaint, the roar of the crowd; all that had sustained her for so many years then, once the spotlight had been switched off, the deed would take place. No fuss, no bother, just silently in the shadows. The sudden, swift flash of the blade.

But before that shadow moment came, there would be this final blaze of glory. I owed the old girl that at least. She'd done a lot for me after all. So, the last glimpse her public would have of her must singe the retinas and impress itself there forever.

What would make it even more memorable was that, for some time now, she'd been living in semi-seclusion. Not, like Norma Desmond, in a crumbling mansion on Sunset Boulevard, but in a basement council flat in King's Cross. Nor had she even been a tangible creature anymore, existing only on the racks of shimmering dresses, on the wig-stand, in the make-up boxes among the eyebrow pencils, the foundation and the lippy. But now all of this would come together in a glorious swan song. For one brief, shining moment, she would live and breathe again. Her 'Mr De Mille' moment was upon her. She was ready for her close-up.

Since her public hadn't seen her for a while, there was no way she would emerge from the basement flat looking like some raddled old harridan. In Trafalgar Square, when that close-up was 20ft wide on the big screens, the crowd was going to gasp in wonderment. So the preparation would be punishing. Merciless months of early morning runs, hours in the gym, a ferocious diet till the pounds of over-indulgence were shed and she was back to being a Size 12 again, just as she'd been aged 18. A thousand pounds was spent on a wig alone, a blonde extravaganza that channelled Eva Peron rather than Norma Desmond. The gown, a masterpiece of brocade, velvet, rhinestones and worth a small fortune, would be hidden at first beneath a sweeping cloak which would then flutter to the ground to reveal the goddess underneath.

But most important of all, as it always had been, would be the face. On the day, and as she had done for the past 25 years, she sat down in front of a mirror and, for four solid painstaking hours, performed the ritual of turning herself into what she wanted to see. It was a ritual of technical skill, artistry and even of magic. For that quarter-century, it had been this act of transformation which had excited her. The thrill of it equal to, perhaps even surpassing, the applause and attention which she knew the end result would bring.

She could not do all of this entirely alone. Great ladies had always required the assistance of maids for their *toilette*.

To shoehorn her into the corsets which would provide the infinitesimal waistline desired. To thread the expensive silk flowers into the wig. To generally bill and coo and tell her how absolutely fabulous she looked.

But now, the passing of time had dulled the thrill of the transformation and the small world in which she had moved had itself moved on. So it was time to go. The party was, for her at least, nearly over. But not just yet.

And, within that small world, this was the biggest party of the year. At the foot of Nelson's Column was a huge stage and behind it a large, tented area crammed with the big stars of its firmament. None of it fazed her in the least; she'd done all this a hundred times before and today she'd do it again. When she arrived backstage, the desired effect was achieved. Heads turned, jaws dropped and flashguns flashed. Wow. Look at *her*. Even if some younger people weren't totally sure who she was, they could tell she was *somebody*.

She talked to the press. Where had she been, they asked? What were her future plans? The usual banality. She told them she was here to say goodbye, that after today she wouldn't return, but they didn't believe her for a moment. You'll be back, they told her, you'll never give this up. She smiled sweetly and said nothing and let them take their photographs.

She took a glass of champagne and then the moment came. Lifting the cloak and the gown off the floor, she stepped carefully on her six-inch heels through the tangle of cables and sound equipment. Somebody announced her name and she walked out onto the stage. And there were few stages anywhere in the world to rival this one. The façade of The National Gallery straight in front; St Martin-in-the-Fields to the right. Landseer's lions on either side and the two great fountains playing in the middle. And all those faces looking up at her. Ten thousand maybe. At the sight of this vision, magnified on the screens, a huge cheer ricocheted round Nelson's square. They knew a star when they saw one.

Soon, as always, she had them in the palm of her hand and under her thumb. When anybody jumped into the fountains, she ordered them out and out they came. If anybody heckled, she heckled back better. She'd always been known for her sharp tongue and time hadn't blunted it. As the song went, good times and bum times, she'd seen them all and was, emphatically, still here.

For the next few hours, she strutted her stuff in the hot midsummer sun. The objective the same as it always had been. Trying to make sure everyone was having a good time. Putting a bit of sparkle and glamour into daily lives which might well be dull, deprived or difficult. But, on this one day of the year, it was more than that. On this one day, a community which could still face marginalisation at best and oppression at worst, took charge of the very heart of the capital city and made it their own. Loud and proud and two fingers to anyone who didn't like it.

And then the show was over. Looking out at the rippling field of faces, she told them to remember that they were all one family. Black and white. Gay, lesbian, trans, non-binary or whatever the hell else they might want to be. She told them they were all incredible and amazing and she meant it. And then she took a bow.

Backstage there would be more partying for a while. The flashguns still popping, the eager young faces still jostling to be photographed. And though the great square would gradually empty, the clubs and bars would stay full for hours yet. Soho, that iconic place in which she had spent so much of her life, would scarcely sleep tonight.

But now she wanted none of that. It was time for the shadows and she slipped quietly away into them. A taxi was found and before it had gone more than a few blocks, the assassination began. The thousand quid wig came off; buttons and corsets were loosened. There was no need for perfection now. All of that was done with. In the basement flat in King's Cross, the magnificent dress and the cloak were carefully removed and returned gently to the boxes of tissue paper. The high heels and the padded bra eased gratefully off with a long sigh of relief.

And there I stood in my bathroom. A naked man. Only on my face did 'she' still exist. I ran a bath full of bubbles and sank into it. I let the warm water soothe from my body the marks of the corsets and the dress and the high heels. And then, with nothing more than soap and water, I washed her off my face. I'd gone through that process so many times before, but this would be different. This time, I was washing her out of my life.

I felt some emotion of course. As I said, the old girl had been good to me in many ways. She made me famous, albeit within that small glitterball of a world. She'd certainly made me a lorry load of money in her day. And I could still see the faces and hear the roar of the crowd in Trafalgar Square. But she'd also brought me unhappiness, distorted values and had obscured, behind the sequins and the sparkle, the person I really was. So I felt no guilt at killing her off and I would never mourn her.

I got out of the water, now streaked with the diluted residue of her powder and paint, her lotions and potions and watched her go, literally, down the plughole. The sense of relief was overwhelming. Because if it hadn't been her, it might have been me. Slowly but surely, it had become a question of survival.

'Are you okay?' asked the person that I loved.

'I'm fine,' I replied.

I got into bed and slept like a baby. Rest in peace, Dusty.

he view from the window was not inspiring. A stretch of scruffy grass. Drab school buildings opposite. The backs of the identikit houses in an adjacent street. A canvas devoid of colour, of interest, of hope. But it was to be my fate to be made an outcast and to sit alone by that window for nearly a year. Most of us have childhood experiences that mark us for life. That was mine.

I envy those with rose-tinted memories of their early school years but mine are as dark as a pair of Anna Wintour's sunglasses. It started on the very first day at nursery school. I was four years old, hysterical and begging my mother not to leave me in this strange place, which smelt of cabbage and of other children I didn't know and didn't want to.

In this world, there are people who need to learn how to bite. Or, to be precise, bite back. Sometimes, they're people who belong to minorities: racial, sexual, economic. Sometimes, they're people who, for whatever reason, were never taught to value themselves. Often though, they're just a bit 'different' from the norm. And that's enough to make them a target for abuse, physical or mental. So, if you turn out to be one of those, you eventually learn that, to make life bearable, you need to bite back. I was one of those people.

Much later, I'd learn to do it with my tongue but, on that first day, I actually did it literally. A teacher called Mrs Woolaston was trying to prise me, kicking and screaming, away from my mother's legs, so I bit her on the hand. She never liked me after that and didn't bother to hide it. Those teeth-marks paved the way for a miserable, lonely time at school and for my lifelong struggle to make myself accepted and liked.

But Mrs Woolaston was just the warm-up act for a teacher we'll call Miss Pinchface. I'm changing her name in case the awful cow might still be alive, sitting in some care home watching afternoon repeats of *Midsomer Murders* and I've no wish to add to her woes. There are other false names I might choose: Cruella de Vil, Lady Macbeth and some not printable, but let's go with Miss Pinchface because that's how she always looked. No sign of any enjoyment of life, certainly not of being a teacher. Oddly enough, she was quite young back then. Maybe she'd had a rotten childhood herself and saw nothing wrong in making sure that other kids did too.

I've often thought that everyone who seriously thinks of becoming a teacher should look at themselves in a mirror and ask themselves some very hard questions. Do I really like children? Do I understand them? Do I genuinely want to bring out the best in them and set them on course for a happy and successful future? If you don't, please go and do something else. Because the harm you can do is incalculable and can scar lives forever as Miss Pinchface scarred mine.

For reasons I'll come onto, I coped with my earliest years by creating a fantasy world. Many troubled children do this and it's usually harmless unless it slides over into the real one. And that was my mistake. After seeing the film *'Born Free'*, about a lioness called Elsa, I created a scenario where my father had got a job as a game warden in Kenya and we were all going to live in the bush. I'd convinced myself this was totally true and shared the good news with Miss Pinchface, who for once seemed interested in me. That afternoon, when my mother came to pick me up, Miss Pinchface made a beeline for her and my fantasy was immediately uncovered. Mom just rolled her eyes, but the next day Miss Pinchface took her revenge, calling me to the front and telling all the other kids about my amazing future in Kenya.

'Isn't that wonderful, everybody?' she asked the class.

'Oohs' and 'aahs' came from the rows of little desks, as they struggled to picture me in khaki shorts and a pith helmet.

'There's just one little problem,' said Miss Pinchface, her thin lips pursed tight. 'Can you guess what that might be?'

Silence.

'The little problem is that it's all a complete tissue of lies. Not a word of it true. Lies, lies, lies. And what does that make David Hodge?'

'A liar' came a voice.

'Correct. It makes David Hodge a nasty little liar. And what do we do with liars?'

'Punish them?' said another voice.

'Correct. We punish them. We teach them a lesson.'

And that was what she proceeded to do, though much more than even she perhaps imagined. So I was moved to that side desk over by the window, looking out over the scruffy grass, tarred and feathered with the label of liar, cut off from the others as if I had the plague. During the long, lonely months of my exile, Miss Pinchface said hardly a word to me, unless to find some reason to scold or shame me in front of the rest. Nor was I allowed to join in any group activities, as she claimed I was also disruptive. The other kids followed her lead and I was rarely invited to join in their games. I was a small, sad seven-year-old pariah.

At the time, mercifully, I didn't really understand how evil all this was. In those times, it would no doubt have been seen as justified. Today she'd probably be sacked for her persecution. Anyway, it didn't work. In fact, just the reverse. All it did was to push me further and further inside the bubbles of make-believe that, throughout my life, I would always use to shield myself from things I found unpleasant. If the outside world didn't want to understand me, I would make my own reality.

So, sitting at that window, staring out at the bleak canvas of a dull Midlands town, I painted other pictures. Of worlds more exciting and glamorous than this one. Of how I'd one day make my mark. Of people who'd accept me and value me. In time, in ways beyond even my imagination, I'd achieve much of that. But in the darkest corner of my mind, however hard I fought back against it, I would always be the boy who sat by the window. I still am.

 remember the day they took the animals away. I can still see the big trailer swallow up my father's horse and my sisters' ponies. I can still hear the panicky neighing of the horses and the sobs of my siblings. My mother's prized possession was more easily hidden; a collection of Doulton figurines which she'd managed to ferret away somewhere before her porcelain shepherdesses could be seized and added to the list of saleable assets. The bailiffs and debt collectors had landed on our doorstep and repossessed everything we had, including the doorstep. Our large, lovely farmhouse near Lichfield was gone too. Being too young for ponies and other such luxuries, what the bailiffs repossessed from me was the vital childhood sense of safety and security.

Not long before, my father had been declared bankrupt after his family tiling and kitchen business had collapsed. To say that we went from riches to rags would be slightly melodramatic, but not far off. Though unable to understand just how bad things were, I somehow sensed that nothing would be quite the same again. And it never was.

There were five of us. My parents, Clive and Jean. My older sisters Karen and Julie. And me. We were a Midlands family born and bred and, apart from me, still are. Lives spent in and around Walsall and its satellite towns and villages. My parents had been each other's first and only love, but they had a funny way of showing it. Except it wasn't funny for their children. They argued constantly, passionately and very loudly for most of their years together. Their relationship could go from freezing cold to boiling hot in a matter of minutes. Consequently, their three kids grew up to believe that shouting and screaming was the norm, that all family life was like a scene from *Who's Afraid Of Virginia Woolf?* I don't remember actual pots and pans being hurled, but every insult and expletive certainly was.

My father Clive was a man of excesses. He worked hard, had been highly successful at first and tended to do everything 'big'. He went hunting and shooting with the local nobs, drove a Bentley and bought a racehorse, which proved to be a duffer in every race it ran. My sisters went to the best schools in the area, while I rode around the farm on a little electric buggy and played with the ducks and the chickens. The house always seemed to be full of people; parties, music and corks popping. Unfortunately, my father was particularly susceptible to popping corks and, as his business ventures gradually hit trouble, he hit the bottle. Just as I would later turn out to do, Dad always fled from reality if he could.

Somehow, he managed to hide all of this from my mother so that, when disaster finally struck, it came as a terrible shock from which I don't believe she ever entirely recovered. Suddenly, without warning, the days of wine and roses were over and she faced a return to the near-poverty of her early life. Jean had been brought up in Walsall which was, and still is, a tough industrial town blighted by deprivation. Her father had died when she was 15 and she'd had to sew knickers in a factory for nine hours a day. Later, she'd gone on to be a nurse. But then she'd met and married the ambitious Clive Hodge. Bye-bye to the bedpans and bandages. Hello to the big house, the Bentley, the parties and the ponies. But then, in a nightmare from which she couldn't wake up, it was all gone. Snakes and ladders.

In Jean's case, the bottom of the snake was all too familiar. After being thrown out of the farm in Lichfield, we all moved to her mother's house in a run-down area of Walsall. We literally had nowhere else to go. As is often the case, the people my father had helped or employed in the good times, completely turned their back on him. Worse still, his own mother and his two brothers, all of whom were both financially comfortable, did nothing to help us. No doubt, all these false friends still went to church on Sundays and considered themselves loving Christians.

Nana Edna's house was like stepping back into post-war England. It was tiny with no central heating. The only warm spot was in front of the fire in the sitting-room. The bedrooms were freezing. Mom and Dad moved into what had been Nana's bedroom and she reluctantly moved into a box-room scarcely bigger than a cupboard. My sisters and I shared a single bedroom with three little beds crammed in. The only toilet was a dystopian shed out in the garden, inhabited largely by monstrous spiders; the sight of which certainly helped the bowels to move. The fact that the house was next door to a huge cemetery did little to add to its cheer, though the dead were probably warmer than we were.

As a four-year-old, it was something of an adventure and I made the best of it, as kids do, amusing myself in my self-contained world. One day, Nana Edna came into her teeny garden to discover that I'd cut the heads off every single rose.

'What in God's name?' she spluttered. 'Where are my roses?'

'In there,' I replied, pointing to a bucket of water filled with petals. 'I'm making you some perfume.'

What could she possibly say after that? I'd often remember it in the future when squirting myself liberally with Chanel or Yves St. Laurent. The child is the father of the gay man.

But I wasn't too young not to pick up on the stoic misery of my parents. My father went about with failure hanging over his head like a thundercloud. There was the element of blame too of course and my parents' rows became real humdingers that could be heard halfway down the street. Dad would often say he was leaving us forever, then go out and return even more shame-faced and drunk as a skunk. This was the beginning of the growing alcoholism which would throw an all-consuming shadow over all our lives till the day he died.

Despite this, Dad did his best to build a new life for us all. He got a job as a lorry driver and my mother went to work as a cleaner in a care home. My sisters settled into a new school, though much less prestigious than before. A small degree of stability returned. So, a little money came into the house, but it was still a house of cards. You always felt it wouldn't take much to blow it down.

'Kissed with fire' said Nana Edna, ruffling my flaming red hair. 'You're kissed with fire.'

With my parents out at work and my sisters at school, I was left at home with her during the day, listening to her

Max Bygraves records on an old gramophone. She loved bloody Max Bygraves. To this day, I still remember the words to *Tulips From Amsterdam* and *You Need Hands*. Though she lived in a humble house on a small pension, Nana Edna always made the best of herself. She was still quite a pretty woman, wore powder and lipstick and every week had her pure white hair set, returning with subtle shades of blue, pink or violet; a transformation which I'd begun to find very interesting. Nana tried to paper over the widening cracks in my parents' marriage by taking me out to the Walsall Arboretum, followed by lunch at 'The Golden Egg', where she'd make do with a cup of tea while I ate egg and chips and a strawberry milkshake.

'Don't you like egg and chips, Nana?'

'No, no, love, a cuppa's enough for me.'

I only understood much later that her pension would only stretch to the one meal and not two. She even encouraged me to draw and paint, though money was too tight to provide the proper equipment, so I'd just use a biro pen and doodle on the backs of old Christmas cards.

Nana Edna had a large tribe of sisters, whom she often took me to visit. One sister had a sofa still covered in the plastic it had arrived in, as she didn't want it ruined. Another had a tortoise in a greenhouse with which I became obsessed. I'd sit quietly listening to these game old girls reminiscing about 'the good old days' when they'd all lived together in a terraced house and taken turns in a tin bath by the fire. Even at that age, 'the good old days' didn't sound that great to me. Their memories were certainly on another planet from those I had of our big house with the Bentley and all mod cons.

Nana Edna was never overly affectionate. She certainly hadn't been so to Mom as a child, which probably explained that toughness at the core of her daughter. Yet I knew Nana loved me and I adored her in return. She was a second mother; the sort who believed that family always came first, a belief she'd certainly proved by taking in her devastated daughter, her drunken son-in-law, their three young children, not to mention three messy dogs. In fact, she didn't even like to mix socially with people to whom she wasn't related by blood. It was a definite eccentricity, but we were all the grateful beneficiaries of it. At our lowest ebb, she'd given us all shelter, support and unquestioning love. The little she had, she'd shared with us without thinking. Later in my life, when I came across unkindness or selfishness in people, including myself, I'd sometimes think of Nana Edna and try to reconnect with the sheer goodness and quality of spirit that she embodied. Nearly half a century later, at the launch of the first exhibition of my paintings, I remembered her, the biro pen and the old Christmas cards. Despite all the troubles and self-doubt in my life, I'd somehow always clung on to Nana's faith in me.

Kissed by fire, she'd said.

Eventually, after much hard work, my parents saved up enough for the deposit on a rented house of our own, back in the small town of Aldridge where I'd been born and where we'd once lived before moving to that money-guzzling palace near Lichfield. Aldridge was a quiet, fairly well-heeled place near Walsall, full of retired, conservative people with neatly mown lawns.

It was a spacious house with a big back garden and a huge oak tree to which Dad tied a tyre on a rope to make me a swing. I spent hours spinning and twirling on that rope, spinning fantasies out of gossamer, still lost in my inner life.

Looking back, I don't think we could really afford that house, but at least it allowed my mother the illusion that things were getting better. We lived there for five rocky years, during which there were constant rows about money, plus a long list of other things for my parents to scream about. The rows could go on for days and only end with one of them slapping or hitting the other. Not nice for children to witness. But Clive and Jean never bothered to hide this misery from their kids and we were overexposed to the language and passions of the adult world long before we could properly understand it.

During these years, my father's boozing grew increasingly apparent. The poor man was obviously going through some sort of nervous breakdown, which nobody recognised or diagnosed.

'For God's sake, get a grip on yourself!' my mother would shout, as he sat there pissed as a rat, his head in his hands, rocking to and fro.

'You've got three kids and a wife!' She'd yell. 'You're a man. Start acting like one and pull yourself together.'

One time, I found him passed out on the grass near our house.

'Dad's dead! Dad's dead!' I screamed, running indoors. 'Get an ambulance!'

Awful for a young boy to experience, but in retrospect, Dad was just a desperate man with a young family to feed who'd lost everything he'd worked for; his dignity most of all. My mother was equally desperate; not to return permanently to the poverty she'd grown up in and she just couldn't understand the fragility of his emotional state. Only the rich got much help with mental health problems back then and, though we tried to disguise the fact, the Hodges had now come down in the world with a bang. In Seventies Britain, there was no Prozac, no Cognitive Behavioural Therapy or Mindfulness. It was 'get a grip'. Be a man. Pull your socks up. Stiff upper lip. Poor Dad.

By escaping from reality into the bottle, my father just gave himself a dangerous addiction that would prevent him from ever changing that reality. Double whammy. When he was pissed, he was a different man to the loving Dad I adored. Once, he gave away my highly prized ventriloquist doll to one of his boozing buddies. Another time, he ate an Easter egg I'd been saving up for the occasion. Small things, but huge crimes in the eyes of a five-year-old. There were many more examples of him undermining my trust in him. I was never sure which father would be coming home from work: the amazing one or the drunken one. It was confusing and de-stabilising. He always seemed to let us all down when we needed him so much to be strong.

Naturally, I still worshipped him. When he was sober, he was indulgent in a way my mother never was. If I wanted chocolate, he'd buy me a huge bar which I ate till I was sick. When I wanted a pet mouse, he let me have hundreds of them, housed in special tanks in the garage. He'd take me for long walks in the countryside, teaching me about the flowers and the animals. To my mouse menagerie in the garage, I soon added guinea pigs, hamsters and even a grass snake called Hector. Eventually, my mother freaked out when the mice got into the house and ran across her when she was in bed. The exterminators came the next day and I never saw the mice again.

'Mouse murderer!' I yelled at her and sulked for days.

I think Dad indulged us because he realised that his mental state wasn't strong enough to be much of a father, so he tried to compensate with kindness. Neither then, or as I grew up, did he ever reprimand me or punish me. He seemed incapable of setting boundaries for his children because, in his own life, he had imposed so few on himself.

So Dad, at least when sober, was the 'good cop' and my mother the 'bad'. But the stresses on her, strong as she was, were enormous. My father went from one low-paid job to another and her fear of becoming homeless returned. She'd somehow managed to squirrel away some of the beautiful furnishings from our old farmhouse to make our rented home look good and hide from the prosperous neighbours the truth of our impoverished state.

The house was always immaculate, smelling of wax polish and 'Shake 'n Vac' and my sister's schoolfriends were discouraged from coming round in case it caused a mess. There were no birthday parties or sleepovers at our address. I guess her compulsive tidiness reflected the need to have at least one aspect of her turbulent life under control. She worked hard all day, cleaning at the old folks' home, then came home to clean some more. No wonder she was often too exhausted to play with us or ask about school. Instead, she showed her love by battling to put food on the table, the roof over our head, clothes on our backs and, above all, by trying to keep my father sober.

Luckily, this lack of mothering was compensated for. Apart from Mom and Nana Edna, I had a third. Julie, the younger of my two sisters. Though only four years older, it would often fall to Julie to babysit me when our parents were out working; cooking me beans on toast and keeping me amused. She was clever, artistic and as kind as anyone you would wish to know. When it was all kicking off between my parents downstairs, she'd get into bed with me and reassure me that everything would be okay. She'd read me stories and, like Nana Edna, encouraged me to read and write. She was patient, kind and seemed to understand me.

Knowing that I had almost no friends at school, she invented one for me. An imaginary chum called Icky Bicky, who spoke in a baby voice and would only come to see me when I touched Julie's front teeth. We'd have long conversations with Icky Bicky and I totally believed in the reality of his existence. I'd nag her endlessly to let him come and talk to me till, no doubt bored shitless by the whole nonsense, she broke the sad news that he had died and wouldn't be coming to see me anymore. I cried my eyes out. How ironic that my first experience of genuine loss should be to a non-existent friend.

My other sister Karen, eight years older than me, was the archetypal angry teenager. She'd had the very best of everything as a child and was probably more traumatised by the removal of all that than Julie or me. Like all of us, poor Karen was suffering, but far from silently; her shouting and screaming nearly as scary as that of my parents. As she grew, she started 'going off the rails': boys, drinking, taking the pill, all the usual stuff. She threw crockery and stuck a knife into the centre of my mother's prized mahogany dining table. She hit a boy with a piece of wood and was taken to court. And one day, the tweedy neighbours rushed out onto their manicured lawns to watch my father literally dragging her, kicking and yelling, back into the house as she made another bid for freedom.

Full of anger and disdain for everything and everybody, the polar opposite of my loving Julie, my older sister seemed to hate my very existence. We never had fun or played together. We hardly even spoke. My first clear memory of her was when, in Nana Edna's little house, she stood up in our shared bath and urinated down onto me. Not surprisingly, I've never been close to Karen and never will be. It's just not true that blood is thicker than water. Without love, the blood is curdled and meaningless.

So, Clive and Jean Hodge and their three children were all, to a greater or lesser extent and in their different ways, troubled souls. For us kids, this perhaps derived from one factor above all the others. Though my parents loved their children, their primary emotional involvement was always with each other. Each was the stormy centre of the other's world and their children were unconsciously sidelined. Collateral damage. They may have laboured all hours to look after us materially, but emotionally we were left to fend for ourselves. The tempests raging around us always seemed to trivialise our needs and magnify those of our parents. Our fears and feelings, our hopes and dreams weren't really on their radar. My sisters and I wanted that kind of attention and rarely got it. Looking back now, I see quite clearly that, for the rest of my life, I would be trying to find it.

'O f course,' said Mr Bullock, delivering the school's obligatory 'birds and bees' lecture, 'there are exceptions to the norms of reproduction. Such people are called homosexuals.'

He was standing behind me and, as he spoke, patted me on the head three times. In that moment, he destroyed me.

Mr Bullock was my science teacher and, like most other people, appeared to have a problem with my existence. Like Miss Pinchface, he seemed to hate me at first sight and never missed an opportunity to make sarcastic remarks to or about me. Bullock was a good name for the sort of man he was; probably in his forties at the time and with a penchant for flirting with the teenage girls he taught.

His bubbling dislike of me came to a head on 'birds and bees' day. There was nothing in his spiel most of us didn't already know backwards and I was drifting off into one of my bored trances. When he got to the 'male and female make a baby' bit, he wandered close to me without my noticing. Then the podgy hand landed on my head and made those three pats, like a pope giving a blessing to a pilgrim. Yet this wasn't a benediction, but a crucifixion. A crucifixion in the form of the cruel laughter which now swept towards me, knocking me over with shame and embarrassment. But Mr Bullock hadn't finished yet.

'These unfortunate people,' he declared, 'are destined to lead sad, miserable and lonely lives.'

He walked away from me, seemingly oblivious to the fact that he had just obliterated what little confidence I had in myself and humiliated me in front of my peers which, for a teenager, is just about the worst thing you can do. I was gutted and sat there in red-faced silence. Still desperate for attention, both at home and at school, I'd suddenly got it in the most dreadful way.

As Miss Pinchface had exiled me to the desk by the window, Mr Bullock had now exiled me from my peers by different means. Like her, he'd nowadays be fired for the way he treated me. Like her, he was a teacher, who damaged children rather than nurtured them. Over the years, I've often liked to imagine that macho Mr Bullock was subsequently arrested for cottaging or, better still, that he'd discovered one day that a child of his own was gay and that he'd had to face up to that and deal with it.

Sad, miserable and lonely. I could have wept at those words and I seem to remember that, once safely in private, I did just that...

Devastating as it was, I suppose Mr Bullock's pronounce-ment was hardly necessary. He certainly wasn't the first person to make it.

Back in nursery school, about the time Miss Pinchface had sent me to the desk by the window, I'd become aware of not being quite like the other little boys. I wasn't interested in the stuff most of them enjoyed; football, cricket or pretending to kill people with toy guns. I hated all sports and didn't even want to learn to ride a bike. My parents had bought me one, but I was too scared to remove the stabilisers for years, till my mother blew her fuse.

'For God's sake Clive, teach that boy how to ride that damn bike properly.'

By this time, I guess I'd become increasingly effeminate. I was far more interested in playing with Julie's dolls, drawing pictures and playing with my toy animals. I'd also become very interested in my mother's wardrobe. I'd wear her fur coat and dance around in her high-heeled shoes. I'd pin on her false hairpiece and put on all her jewellery in one go, 'playing ladies' in her bedroom. I sensed by the disapproving looks and comments that I should keep this pastime private, so I started to wait till she'd gone out before indulging in these first cross-dressing games. Julie however was all for it. She loved dressing me up and once persuaded me to go over to our neighbour's house and introduce myself as my own female 'cousin' from America. God knows what they thought when this bizarre vision appeared on the doorstep.

'Howdy folks, I'm Peggy Sue. David's cousin from Chicago.'

Actually, that's not true. I can imagine *exactly* what the neighbours thought and of course they were quite right. And naturally, everyone else around me had come to the same inescapable conclusion.

'I'm not sitting next to you,' said a boy as we gathered in the school hall for assembly. 'You're a poof.'

'What do you mean?'

'My big brother says you're a poof,' he replied. 'And that I shouldn't sit close to you or it might rub off on me.'

With that, he got up and moved away. At that time, I had no idea what a poof was or how one acted. I suppose I should have asked somebody or looked it up in the dictionary, but I didn't. Soon the name-calling spread and I was officially designated as the school 'poof', accustomed to being called the dreaded word every day. I began to learn when to keep my mouth shut and to sense when to move away from situations that would lead to me being mocked, kicked or punched. I'm quite sure that the teachers were aware of what was going on but, in the Seventies, no guidelines from Stonewall existed for them to manage the situation, even if they'd wanted to and I suspect few of them did. So they ignored it and let me sink or swim.

Of course, as I grew, the full meaning of being a 'poof' finally dawned on me. I'd been born in 1967, the very year that homosexuality had been partially decriminalised in the UK. But it's far easier to change a law than to change social attitudes. In the Seventies, it seemed to be perfectly acceptable to say whatever you wanted, however nasty, however publicly. Comedians like Bernard Manning mocked gay people, black or brown people, fat people, the disabled, all women in general and anyone else they could get a cheap snigger from.

'Poofs' in particular were an easy target. We were still freaks and weirdos; to be pitied at best, vilified at worst. The only gay people portrayed on TV or in the media were camp comedians like Larry Grayson or John Inman in *Are You Being Served?*. Nowadays, in far more liberated times, we laugh *with* these characters, but back then, they were laughed *at*.

Even those celebrities whom we'd now say were 'obvious', rarely came clean about their sexuality. The late, great female impersonator Danny La Rue pretended that cross-dressing was just his 'act', though it seems crazy that anybody ever believed it. Nor did the great actor Dirk Bogarde, star of pioneering 'gay films' like *Victim* and *Death in Venice*, ever really leave the closet in his lifetime. Who did these guys think they were kidding? So, back then, being gay was rarely mentioned and certainly not by anyone I knew.

Even before the boy in assembly refused to sit near a 'poof', I'd known that I was different from the rest. This sense of exclusion wasn't helped by my flaming red hair. Nana Edna's lovely compliment that I was 'kissed by fire' was turned into an insult: 'carrot top', 'ginger nut' and a lot of far nastier things. All of which made me feel even more of an outsider than sitting alone by the window already did.

But in parallel with the negative stuff associated with being a 'poof', a more positive thing was beginning to happen. One which would dictate the future course of my life to an arguably greater extent. Even by the age of seven or eight, I was beginning to develop an interest in my appearance or, as I'd call it grandly in the future, a sense of my personal aesthetic.

The fact that my parents were always short of money contributed to my exclusion at school. To save cash, my mother always knitted my school jumpers herself. They were beautifully crafted, but I was always aware that they looked 'homemade' and very different to everyone else's plain grey C&A jumpers. I would beg her not to make me wear them. Tears and tantrums. But to no avail. However I drew the line when I was told to wear a pair of brown baby sandals; probably a hand-me-down from some relative. Round toes with a buckle. Hideous. It was the Seventies and everyone was starting to wear platform shoes. I'd seen a pair of chunky wedgies in the local shoe-shop and I lusted after them. Sure enough, when I arrived at school in the baby sandals, the teasing started at once. I was told they were girl's shoes. My toes were stamped on. I was still back in Miss Pinchface's class at this point and the bitch didn't hide her amusement. Agony.

So I worked out a plan to get those platform shoes. That night on the way home, I scuffed the toes of the sandals against a wall till there were holes in the leather. I sneaked back into the house and found my old school shoes, the only other pair I had apart from pumps. I threw these over into next door's garden, which left only the pumps as alternative wear to my now ruined baby sandals. The next morning, I came down in the wrecked sandals and my mother went ballistic.

'Jesus Christ, what on earth have you done? Do you think I have money to burn on new shoes? Get upstairs and put on the old ones!'

I pretended to search for them and then she tried too, but they were of course somewhere among the neighbour's dahlias. Now late for work, she sent me to school in the pumps, which elicited a sharp note from Miss Pinchface, instructing her never to send David to school again in pumps. My mother, red with anger, ordered me into the car and we drove at supersonic speed to the shoe shop, due to shut at five-thirty. There I was made to try on a very ugly pair of black school shoes, which was not the result I wanted at all. The platforms I wanted so much were right there on a shelf! I could almost smell the leather. If I didn't get them, I felt sure I would die. So I threw the biggest hissy fit of all time. I lay on the floor. I screamed and shouted. I threw the ugly black shoes across the shop floor. It was an Oscar-winning performance. Joan Crawford would have been proud of me. And it worked! I got the little platforms and would literally live in those wedgies till my feet outgrew them.

Being the shoe-shop diva was about more than just getting those shoes. I'd won the first small skirmish in the many battles I'd have with my mother about my appearance. It would be a long, drawn-out war, lasting many years, exhausting the combatants. In the end, Mom would retreat in sheer exhaustion and I would be the ultimate victor, but that triumph was still a long way off.

Now too, I first understood something even more important. Whilst being different could bring very negative attention, *looking* different could be a far more positive experience. And it was positive attention I needed more than anything else. At school the next day, my shoes were the talk of the class. Everyone wanted to try them on and feel what it was like to walk on a half-inch platform, though it was tame compared to the pop stars on TV like David Bowie and Marc Bolan, who were tottering around on three or four inch jobs. Unlike my mother's hand-knitted pullovers, I paraded those shoes with pride and for once felt as if I was included by the other kids, though I can still see Miss Pinchface's sour expression when she saw that happening.

'I suppose you think you're cock of the walk today, David?'

The episode of the shoes matters in my story because it first showed me the power of appearance and how it could even change your life. It was a lesson that would shape my whole future. Little David Hodge, the 'poof', the 'carrot-top', was never going to be a 'plain black shoes' personality. He was going to be a dazzler. He was going to be noticed in this world. He would make his mark far beyond the confines of that bleak classroom, this dingy playground and the narrowed minds of the suburban avenues.

hen, as the bailiffs had once taken away our animals, Dad was taken away too. Well, it didn't happen quite like that. He went of his own volition and 'for his own good', but that was how it seemed to the eight-year-old me. But this was so much worse than the bailiffs. So much more horrible.

'I'll not be gone long,' he promised as he headed for the rehab unit of a local hospital. 'I'll be back before you know it.'

The worst of it was not being allowed to visit him. He was to be shut away from the outside world like a prisoner or a leper. I wrote him long letters detailing every moment of my day and he'd send back postcards saying he was fine and including conkers he'd collected in the hospital grounds.

As soon as he'd left the house, my mother had sat her three children down and given us a strict lecture.

'You're to tell nobody where Dad has gone,' she said. 'Do you understand that? Absolutely nobody. Not at school, not anywhere. But if you do let it slip that he's in hospital, you must say it's for an ulcer.'

Young as we were, none of us kids bothered to ask the real reason. We knew it well enough. Dad had become a car salesman by now and sometimes took me with him to sales pitches if he was working alone. Mom encouraged this in the belief that my presence would make him think twice about drinking. But he'd always managed to dodge me at some point and get in a few slugs of booze; his voice and demeanour changing as the day wore on. I knew instantly when he'd had a drink and I hated it.

How sad it was that we all felt such shame and needed to treat this calamity as a terrible secret. But back then, the stigma of alcoholism was so much worse than now; no real recognition that it was an illness. People's attitudes were far more unfeeling. That old, damaging 'get a grip' mentality at work again. Yet it would be wrong to say there was no compassion at all. One morning before school, Nana Edna took hold of my hand.

'You mustn't worry about your Dad, son,' she said softly. 'He is going to be okay. He's a good man and he loves you very much.'

I already knew he was a good man and that he loved me. After all, how many men going through what must have been the trauma of rehab would have bothered to collect conkers for their kid back home. But sadly, Clive Hodge wouldn't be exactly okay. The rehab was not a total success and, in the years to come, we'd still live through intermittent bouts of heavy drinking, though these didn't seem to last quite so long and getting back on the wagon was a slightly easier climb.

When he came back from rehab, Dad made an extra effort with his children. Long country walks. Trips to Whipsnade Zoo. He even built me a greenhouse in which I grew tomatoes and flowers. A right little Alan Titchmarsh. Obviously, all of this derived from the guilt Dad must have felt. Guilt about his drinking and the pain it caused to those he loved. Guilt about the business that had failed, the posh house that had been lost, the Bentley, the ponies, the whole shebang that had spelt success in his eyes and which had gone with the wind. What a heavy load dear Dad must have carried.

Yet if all this makes him sound like a weak man, at the mercy of his addiction, that wouldn't be quite accurate. Inside Clive Hodge still burned a fierce inner strength, a determination to battle onwards and try, whatever the odds, to win it. And so, time and again he climbed back on that wagon. When once he'd driven that Bentley, now he drove a truck. Where once he'd lived in that splendid house, he now lived in one that belonged to somebody else. And yet, he took it on the chin and fought on.

In my own life, I was to inherit, almost as a carbon copy, both my father's weaknesses and his strengths. I too would hit the depths a few times, but I'd somehow always find it inside myself to rise up again. And that would always be Dad's greatest legacy.

I called them my 'luckies'. A collection of little ornaments, whose heads I touched superstitiously every morning in the hope of having a nice day at school. They were on a shelf in the small bedroom I now had to myself and which, intro-spective as ever, I'd turned into my own private kingdom, away from everyone else.

By now, the Hodge family had had a very welcome bit of luck. My mother landed a job as the warden of an old people's sheltered housing estate. It came with rent-free accommodation and the energy bills thrown in. The down-side was that it was a very small house in a rough area on the other side of Walsall. Despite this, we said goodbye to the tweedy neighbours of Aldridge and took our chances. No more manicured lawns, but more money in the bank.

In my new school, I still had big problems relating to the other children and soon found myself an outsider once again. It was my voice they mocked this time. Walsall had a strong regional accent called 'Yam Yam' and I'd come from a very middle-class school where nobody spoke like that. As a result, to add to 'poof' and 'ginger nut', I was now 'posh' as well. So once again, I turned in on myself, longing to get home to my little room to read my library books or into the garden shed where I'd created a new menagerie of mice, hamsters, rabbits and even a pet chicken.

On Sundays, my mother would take me on her daily round of the old people's bungalows. Most kids would've hated having to visit 45 old folks, but I loved it. I'd been surrounded by Nana Edna and her battalion of sisters all my life and I'd learned to sit quietly, say nice things and listen to their stories of the good old days. Sometimes the oldies would be friends with benefits. The odd 10 pence for being a good boy, multiplied by 45, really added up.

More luck came our way. After three years, Mom was promoted to another site in a better part of town called Shelfield, with a much bigger house and fewer bungalows to look after. Money was much less of an issue, Dad was in a better state and, though the blazing rows continued, my disruptive sister Karen had now left home, taking her temper tantrums with her. For Julie and me, it felt like we had a stable home again at last. Rubbing the heads of my 'luckies' seemed to have paid off. Sometimes a mild case of obsessive-compulsive disorder works wonders.

The boy who sat in the window was now 11 years old. It was time to leave primary school and move on. I said goodbye politely to Miss Pinchface, though what I said to her in my head was a lot less polite. And though I was leaving her, she'd never really leave me.

Going to senior school was a pivotal event. The time when my transformation and growth would begin in earnest and I'd start to develop into a very different kind of adult than, to put it mildly, most of my family had expected me to be.

I saw it as a new beginning. New faces who didn't know me and who hadn't witnessed my isolation and humiliation sitting in exile at that desk by the window. The new school was a maze of corridors and classrooms, a big comprehensive full of big scary kids. But though I was physically small and puny, having lived with my head in books meant that my mind had developed way ahead of my body. I was an intuitive and sharp child who could, when necessary, give verbally as good as he got. The turbulent circumstances at home had at least taught me that.

I was still teased, but not nearly as much as before and at long last I made some friends, whose houses I was invited to visit or who would come home to look at my aviary. Suddenly, everything was far more interesting than it had been before and it dawned on me that I was actually quite clever. In my first year, I got seven 'A' grades. I loved Geography, Art and, especially, History. Whilst my peers in primary school had been kicking a football or wrestling each other, I'd had my nose in an atlas, teaching myself the capital cities of every country. I'd also become a junior Mastermind on the history of the royal family. I'd become fascinated by the monarchy and had rushed to wave my flag at Her Maj when she'd visited Walsall Town Hall in her Silver Jubilee progress of 1977. Walsall must have been a culture shock for her for, as far as I know, she never came back. I became obsessed with other queens notably Marie Antoinette. I devoured historical fiction; loving to read about lives which seemed so much more interesting compared to my own, even if they did end up with their heads chopped off. Little did I imagine that one day I'd be crowned as a queen myself.

Slowly but surely, I gained more confidence and opened out to life, like a flower who'd lived in the shade, at last given the light in which to bloom. I started to have more fun. I became almost precocious and always had an answer to anything the teachers might throw at me. Luckily, this endeared me to some of them and they began to take an interest in the odd little ginger boy with the big mouth and a thirst for knowledge.

So far, I'd had lousy luck with my teachers but now the polar opposite of them came into my life. Her name was Mrs Wall who taught English Literature. She was a massive lady, a bit like Hattie Jacques from the *'Carry On'* films. She wore huge Kaftan dresses, brightly coloured make-up and a wig with a bow in it. She also smoked like a chimney and ate sweets all through the class. Halfway through each lesson, she'd send me to walk her Yorkshire terrier which was left in her car with the window open. I bloody loved her and she seemed to reciprocate. I loved her subject too, so she gave me extra help when I needed it. She encouraged me to join the Drama Club which she ran and often gave me the starring parts. For the first time, somebody made me feel that being 'different' was not a reason for mockery and exclusion but, on the contrary, something to be celebrated and expressed. Much later, I found out that her son was gay. Maybe she'd seen something of him in me and had been trying to help me along the precipitous path. A generous and loving thing to do.

By now I'd understood the simple truth that life was much easier if you were the class clown. The bullies left you alone. The late great Kenneth Williams wrote of discovering this simple fact and now I did too. Like Kenny had, I hit on the wisdom of chumming up with the bigger, tougher boys, as it shielded you from a lot of the name calling. One boy was especially protective towards me. To spare his blushes, I'll call him Pete. Pete was Mr Macho. He was muscular, did Judo and was known as the hardest kid in our year. Aged only 12, he was growing into a man rather quickly with a light moustache and a voice already broken. Nothing remotely comparable was happening to yours truly. I hadn't even started puberty and had no interest in anything sexual, either with girls or boys. I understood the crude mechanisms of sex, but I'd zero interest in trying any of it out. Life was complicated enough, thanks very much.

One late afternoon, I was walking towards the paper shop on my way home. This was always a fright zone as some of the bigger boys who did paper rounds collected their deliveries at this hour and I'd often get a slap or at least mocked. On this day, I'd left it till later in the hope of avoiding them. As I approached the alleyway alongside the shop, Pete popped out of the shadows. He grabbed the arm of my coat and pushed me against a wall.

'Hey, what have I done?' I asked, expecting a thump.

But instead of getting his fist in my face, I got his tongue. I couldn't believe it. Macho Pete was trying to kiss me. It was slobbery and wet, the baby moustache against my skin. Ugh. I didn't like it at all.

'Stop it Pete! Stop it! What are you doing? Let me go! Let me go!'

I struggled and screamed till he finally released me. I ran for it and didn't stop till I got home. I spent the evening locked in my room trying to figure out what had happened. This was way out of my comfort zone. The next day at school he made a beeline for me.

'If you ever tell anyone what I did, I will fucking smash your head in.'

And I never did tell anyone, though I used the incident to my advantage a few times. If things were getting a bit rough for me, I'd call in Pete to warn them off, which he always did very effectively. Through an unrequited kiss, I'd obtained my own mini security service and Pete never let me down. I guess he was shit scared that I would actually spill the beans and his butch persona would be blown to pieces. I suppose this was unspoken blackmail on my part, but what the heck.

I've heard that Pete is happily married with kids these days. And I really hope he's happy. I often wonder if he remembers that stolen kiss or if he's banished it from his mind as a moment of testosterone-fuelled teenage madness, before he returned to the straight and narrow. I reckon there must be thousands of old married blokes around who still flinch at similar memories. Or maybe they don't flinch at all. Maybe they wonder what would have happened if they'd explored that impulse a bit further and even wish that they had.

Anyway, if Pete does remember me, at least he can't think of me as an easy lay.

I went and sat beside her on the sofa, all wide-eyed and innocent. It was a minute or two before she looked down at me and screamed.

'Oh my God. You dirty, dirty boy,' yelled my other grandmother; my father's mother, a woman who, compared to Nana Edna, I didn't like much.

Out of my trouser flies, like a giant penis, stuck a big sausage I'd nicked from the fridge. The moment she saw it, I cut the end off with scissors I'd concealed in my pocket. Gran Hodge was very short-sighted and screamed the roof off, which brought my mother running in from the kitchen.

'Look, I've cut my willy off,' I shouted, rolling on the floor holding up the half sausage.

Gran Hodge was not remotely amused.

'You're a stupid, spoiled, vile boy,' she stormed, 'and a great big cissy to boot.'

Gran Hodge lived in a flat above the shop she owned, which sold fire grates and kitchens. She was a quite well-to-do and snooty old woman who, my mother believed, thought herself 'a cut above us lot' and considered that her son Clive had married beneath him. She was plain-speaking and brusque with a big nose and a stout figure. Unlike my darling Nana Edna, she never wore make-up or had her hair done, regarding such things as vanity. She had a strong opinion on everything and considered any opposing view quite ridiculous. In other words, a battle-axe. She went on a world cruise and on other exotic holidays. Like her two other sons, she did sod all to help my father at the time of the bankruptcy. There had been fat chance of Gran Hodge taking us all under her roof, in the way that Nana Edna had done without thinking.

She certainly didn't like me any more than I liked her. More than once, she called me a cissy and nearly got a slap from Nana Edna for saying it. The two grandmothers cordially hated each other's guts. I exacerbated her dislike by eavesdropping on her private conversations with my father, then repeating it all to Mom and Nana Edna.

By now it was clear to me that it wasn't just other kids to whom I was a cissy; it was adults too, although my own parents had never yet used that word, to my face at least, though they must by now have thought it.

By the time I was 13, my own hormones weren't exactly raging but they were certainly getting a bit more curious, though it was more an academic curiosity than gagging for another tongue down my throat. I just wanted to find out more about this alien 'gay' thing which everybody accused me of being, so once again, I trotted off to Walsall Library. I found a small book of gay people talking about their lives and devoured it in one sitting. Many of the stories sounded so familiar to my own. I was indeed, quite possibly, 'one of them'. I understood however that dealing with this would only make my life a lot more complicated and, as I still wasn't remotely inclined to be sexually active, I decided to put being a 'poof' on hold. I knew enough for now.

Luckily, I found other outlets for self-expression that didn't involve willies in any way, whether real or in sausage form.

'Ooh, you ought to be on the stage,' people said quite often.' You're very arty, aren't you?'

My adored Mrs Wall, my Hattie Jacques lookalike, thought so too. At the age of 14, I made my formal entry into showbiz in the school's annual variety show. In my warbling boy soprano, I sang a song from *My Fair Lady* and delivered a monologue as Puck from *A Midsummer Night's Dream*. I may not have nominally been the star of the show, but I was as close as anyone got. My parents watched with their usual subdued enthusiasm, that strange degree of detachment from their children I've already described. Mom certainly showed no inclination to become a pushy stage mother. There was no 'darling, you were wonderful' or 'you're going to be BIG!'.

But Mrs Wall was pleased as punch and, in a way, that was far more important. In the foyer after the show, just as we were heading home, she heaved her 20-plus stones towards us in her huge kaftan and the wig with the bow in it.

'David, David wait! I've brought a friend who's just dying to meet you. He finds you divine!'

I'd been Eliza Doolittle that night; now here was my Professor Higgins. Someone who would become another mentor, another guiding spirit. But more than that. Mrs Wall had also brought me the best possible present I could have had at that moment in my life. Another homosexual.

5

'd never seen anything quite like him before, except John Inman in *Are You Being Served?* but even Mr Humphreys didn't come close.

Even his name was exotic. It was Alain, pronounced 'A Lane'. No boring Walsall name like Kevin or Reg for this extraordinary vision, though I'd not have been surprised if he'd been baptised with an equally dull moniker and had flatly refused to accept it.

He was fortyish, very short and quite chubby which is not a great combo. But that was where his negatives, at least in my eyes, stopped dead. He wore an all-in-one jumpsuit in bright orange and big black cowboy boots. His hair was dyed an obvious bottled blonde with a cropped 'Noel Edmonds' style beard. To top it off, his eyes were heavily lined and with half a ton of mascara. His voice was both posh and camp; beautifully projected, as if he were always on stage. And indeed he was. Alain was permanently 'on'. Shopping in Sainsburys, changing the cat litter or cutting his toenails, he was never 'off'. Waiting in the wings just wasn't his style. Centre stage. In a solo spotlight. That was Alain.

'Alain is the drama instructor for the Aldridge Youth Theatre,' said Mrs Wall, in slightly awed tones as if he were Cameron Mackintosh and Andrew Lloyd Webber rolled in one.

'And I'd *so* love it if you'd come along and join us tomorrow night,' said Alain. 'You've got talent, young man and we must bring it out. Bring it out!'

I felt sure in an instant that there was little chance of Alain having a lovely wife at home plus a few sweet kiddies and a whippet. My parents felt it too. Dad looked especially dubious.

'If that big poof touches you, then you let me know, okay?' he said in the car going home.

I promised I would, though, had it happened (which it never did) I'm not sure I would have. Maybe it was the use of that word again. The word that had been flung at me for as long as I could remember. I instinctively felt a fellowship with this flamboyant little man in the orange jumpsuit and the dyed hair. This sudden blaze of colour and personality beside which, my parents looked like two-dimensional, monochrome cardboard cut-outs.

The next evening, I arrived early at the purpose-built theatre in the centre of Aldridge. I was greeted by Alain, busy sewing sequins onto a headdress he was going to wear in the next production.

'Nefertiti, Queen of Egypt' he said. 'Fucking gorgeous, isn't it darling?'

'It's very nice,' I said meekly.

That night, Alain's language was rather different from the one he'd used in front of my parents. It was littered with 'fuckings' and 'cunts', which I found fabulously interesting. Alain might have been a cultured aesthete, but he had the mouth of a truckdriver with a haemorrhoid.

From that moment on, we forged a very special teacher/ pupil friendship. In my three years with the Youth Theatre, I attended classes on two weekday evenings after school plus rehearsals on Sundays. Bit by bit, Alain moulded us all into teenage theatricals. In me, he had the perfect pupil.

He recognised at once that I had a proclivity for make-up and showed me the basics of the art which would become my stock-in-trade in later life. Soon, I was the one in charge of the make-up box and designing the face paints for all the productions. This was the real beginning of my fascination with the process of transformation that could be achieved with make-up. You could do almost anything if you knew how. Even the Plainest Jane like me could be recreated as something exotic and glamorous. This realisation would have a profound psycho-logical effect and become one of the major drivers of my life.

Alain was the epitome of the great teacher. The dazzling antidote to Miss Pinchface and Mr Bullock, who were never creative, only destructive. He guided me through the basics of the craft of acting and gave me starring roles in several productions. But he wasn't always patient, nor even kind, and would swear at us all without hesitation.

'That was fucking useless, you stupid cunt!' he'd shout at some poor sod. 'I might as well go home and watch a repeat of fucking *Brideshead Revisited,* because I'm not finding any fucking Laurence Oliviers here, am I darlings?'

And yet we all had a strange, but strong affection for him and I, in particular, worshipped him. Because what he gave me went far beyond the magic of the make-up box.

He once invited some of us to tea at his home in Solihull. It was basically a theatre set in an ordinary two-bedroom flat. His living room looked like the apartments of Madame de Pompadour at Versailles. In his bedroom, he'd created a huge Gothic bed, draped in velvets and *faux* fur. In a spare room, he had an antiquated sunbed under which he lay for hours, developing a permanent tangerine glow, which would then be enhanced by multiple layers of foundation and bronzing powder. He also had a huge fluffy white cat called Bobbins which he stroked like a Bond villain. I never forgot the lesson of that flat and how Alain's sheer style and creativity had made a silk purse out of a very ordinary sow's ear. Years later, I would do my own version of his little palace.

When I was about 15, Alain took a small group of us on a trip to Brighton. Once again, Dad sensed danger.

'If that big poof touches you…'

Incredibly, knowing Alain's taste for velvets and furs, it was to be a camping trip (no jokes please) involving actual tents. He sensed I was shy, so I was given a tent of my own. During the day, he'd take us to the famous nudist beach. My parents would have fainted.

Alain would strip right off without a flicker of embarrassment and lie down like a stark-naked orange whale. The other boys didn't bat an eyelid as they'd known him for years, but it was certainly an eye-opener for me. There were willies everywhere; sausages left, right and centre. It didn't take more than about 10 seconds to rumble that a hefty proportion of these 'naturists' were gay. This was the first time I'd seen openly gay people in the voluminous flesh. Men were lying around on the beach, some in couples, some holding hands. It came as both a shock and a thrill. People like Alain and I were not so rare after all. There were loads of us. Dozens. Hundreds. Thousands even. I just didn't know any of them yet, but I wanted to.

Slowly but surely, though still silently, I had started coming to terms with who I was. I had made real friends at the Youth Theatre. I was invited to all the teenage parties. I no longer felt isolated or any sort of outsider. Knowing that I was welcome and that I belonged somewhere made me feel safe, perhaps for the first time in my life.

Despite his wildly theatrical dress and demeanour, Alain, in charge of young people, had always needed to be very careful. There would be no velvets and furs in a cell at Wormwood Scrubs. He never talked to any of us about sex or sexuality. He certainly never asked me about mine. Perhaps he didn't think it necessary. The closest he came was just before he left the Youth Theatre, when he took me aside.

'David darling, always be yourself and don't let anyone dictate who you should become.'

I've remembered those words to this day and still try to live by them. They're as important to me as the Commandments etched in tablets of stone that hunky Charlton Heston as Moses brought down from the mountaintop. And Number One on the list is the one that Alain gave me as his parting gift.

Among the other gifts he gave me was to think twice before you stick a label onto somebody. For, surprise surprise, it turned out that Alain had once been married, had a daughter and now had a girlfriend called Joan. So, despite the stereotypical flamboyance, the ultimate cliche of the camp gay man, I was never entirely sure of his sexuality. Maybe he wasn't either. Gay, bi-sexual, who cares? Perhaps he just wanted to stand out from the crowd and that was the way he happened to choose. Later, I'd choose a somewhat different one, but I reckon the impulse we both had was the same.

I missed him a lot when he left the Youth Theatre and never saw him again till, two years later, I bumped into him in a Birmingham street. By then, I looked completely different, at the height of my Gothic phase with crimped, backcombed hair and a face swathed in make-up, just as his had always been.

'David darling! You look glorious, darling. Glorious. And fuck anyone who doesn't like it.'

Alain's approval meant more to me than anyone else's ever could.

Our paths would never cross again and I regret it greatly. But maybe he didn't want that. Maybe I belonged to a closed chapter. In recent years, I've tried to track him down on social media, but no luck. If he's still around, he'll be in his eighties now and if, by some chance, he ever reads this, I'd be thrilled to hear from him. Alain (or Kevin or Reg or whoever he'd started out as) changed my life.

I did bloody well in my 'O' levels, which paved the way for me to go to college and do 'A' levels. Though I was sad to say goodbye to my beloved Mrs Wall, I couldn't wait to leave school, and start again as a more confident and authentic 'me'.

During the six week break before college, I took the first steps in finding out more about what I still thought of as 'the gay thing'. With my heart pounding, I plucked up the nerve to buy a copy of *'Gay Times'* from WH Smith. I hid it in a huge bag appropriately shaped like a banana and took it everywhere with me, scared to leave it in my room where Mom might come across it. Again and again, I read it from cover to cover. Every article and advert pondered over. It became like a bible to me. There was one advert that I couldn't stop staring at. It was for a gay helpline on which, it emphasised, you could speak to someone in total confidence. I knew I had to ring it.

In those days, before mobiles or the internet, I couldn't possibly use the landline because my mother had the annoying habit of listening in to my calls on an extension and quizzing me about them afterwards. Any call to London would also show up on the phone bill. So, I gathered every 10 pence coin I could find and went to the local phone box. I was shaking like the proverbial leaf, as thousands of others had no doubt done before me when they'd made the same walk. A walk that terrified them but which they knew they had to make. I had no idea what to expect or what I might say. I only knew that this 'thing' was eating me up and I had to talk about it. But when the call was answered, the words just wouldn't come out.

'Hello, London Gay Switchboard. How can I help you?'

Still nothing came. I guess the warm, quiet voice on the other end was used to this.

'It's okay, take your time. No rush. I'm here to listen.'

But then I did rush. Like a dam bursting, once I started I couldn't stop. I told him everything about me: who I was, where I lived, my hobbies, my family. You name it, I wittered on about it. And then, I finally said the words which would change my life forever. The words I'd never spoken to anyone, not even Alain.

'And I think I'm gay.'

If I'd expected a blast of trumpets or a heavenly choir to greet this epic announcement, I was wrong.

'Me too,' said the warm, quiet voice; the very casualness with which he said it, quite wonderful to my ears. As if it didn't matter at all. As if it was completely 'normal'. And a great weight, one carried for so long, seemed to lift from my shoulders in a split second becoming, as it rose, as light as a feather. The relief was indescribable.

'We're all gay in this place,' said the voice. 'Welcome to the club.'

We chatted on for 10 more minutes; nothing serious, no big stuff. All that mattered was that listening ear, the ear of somebody else just like me. Someone who understood me. It turned out his name was David, too.

'I do my shift on Switchboard at this time every week,' he said. 'You can call me anytime you feel like a chat.'

I left that phone box in a happy daze, feeling better than I'd ever felt in my 15 years of life. I'd made the connection. I'd said it. My name is David and I'm gay. All those years of being called a 'poof' no longer mattered. The word could no longer hurt me because I no longer saw it as an insult. Yes, that's exactly what I was. A poof. A homosexual. And, as Alain would say, 'fuck anyone who doesn't like it.'

he caterpillar had taken a few big steps in breaking out of the chrysalis, but the butterfly was still embryonic.

The next two years would be the most pivotal of my life to date. A time of experimentation and boundary pushing. A time when I explored both my sexuality and how I presented myself visually to the world. It was as if I were travelling on two tracks, straddling both, a foot on each track. Sometimes, the two tracks would be close together, nearly crossing; sometimes they'd be miles apart. But each equally important in creating the person I would become.

At Sutton Coldfield College, studying for 'A' levels in Drama, English Literature and European History, I met the friends who are still among my most important people. The true and real friends, who would stick by me through thick and thin.

When I walked into the Drama Department on my first day, I was a naïve, nerdy student in a pair of Bowie trousers with a bad perm. When I left two years later, I'd look like a cross between Siouxsie Sioux and Hiawatha with a painted face and a mohawk. My interests would be different, my lifestyle completely changed, my previous attitudes upturned and questioned.

I immediately hit it off with a girl called Kim; sexy, cheeky, hilariously funny. She enjoyed my quirkiness and was never judgemental about my offbeat ideas. I suspect Kim saw me as a 'project'; rough clay that could be moulded into somebody interesting. With her encouragement, I tentatively began to risk wearing some mascara, a splash of eyeliner, a bit of foundation, all of which I'd remove the instant I got home, having dashed upstairs before my mother saw me. Kim plucked my eyebrows into a more *femme* shape and I began to buy lots more weird vintage clothing from my £4 a week family allowance, which horrified my mother.

I plucked up the courage to tell Kim I was bi-sexual, which sounded more acceptable than gay. She didn't bat an eyelid and it was soon an open secret in the Drama Department. Nobody seemed to care, although they saw themselves as so iconoclastic that they'd have preferred root canal work to admitting that they did.

Kim and I started playing to the crowd and disrupting lessons. I'd never been 'naughty' before and found it liberating. If Miss Pinchface could've seen me now. At that time, a music duo called Renee and Renato had a massive Number One single, a truly dreadful 'granny ballad' called *Save Your Love;* a total waste of good vinyl. The guy came to sing solo at our annual college show. Kim and I didn't like the look of him much; a short, fat Italian bloke who owned a café in Sutton Coldfield. Before he started his ghastly number, we climbed right up into the lighting rig high above the stage to get a better view. Just before he went onstage, I had an idea.

'Shall I spit on him?' I whispered to Kim.

'Yeah, go on, get him.'

Just as the curtains opened, poor old Renato got a massive slimy gob on top of his head. The poor sod didn't even have time to look upwards and had to sing his whole song still wondering what had hit him. I'd never imagined my aim would be so good and was horrified. I had visions of being thrown out of college, but thankfully nobody found out.

Though my hero Alain had now left the Aldridge Youth Theatre, I was still going along, but had begun to get disapproving looks from the stuffy, middle-class management committee for my ever more exotic appearance. 'Tone it down a bit' they said, but I ignored them, just as Alain would have done. On the plus side was a boy called Marcus. Since my hormones were now wide awake, I developed my first real crush. He was a beauty; wavy brown hair, firm-jawed, quiet and kind.

'Better find out if he's gay first...' said David from Gay Switchboard, who by now must have dreaded my rambling weekly chats.

But how did I do that, apart from asking him directly, which I could never do. Ask if he had any Judy Garland records or did embroidery? For months I searched for clues, found none and was mortified when he started going out with a girl. Heartbreak doesn't start to describe it.

One night, Marcus and I went to see *The Rocky Horror Show* in Birmingham. I'd told Kim all about him and sought her advice.

'Make yourself really pretty,' she said. 'You have a lovely little face and look great in make-up. See what he does.'

I'd raided the costume department at college and borrowed a huge white pirate shirt and bought fishnet tights which I shredded. I wore a big, studded buckle belt and a friend crimped my shoulder-length hair. It was the first time I'd worn heavy make-up offstage and in retrospect I probably looked a right old state. But Marcus seemed to love it. The show was great and later, after a couple of cans of cheap cider, both of us were a bit drunk. And then he kissed me. Or did I kiss him? Not sure, it just happened. My first ever kiss with a boy. Wow. I was on Cloud Ninety-Nine. Kim's tactics had worked.

When we met the next day at the Youth Theatre, I was really nervous. No doubt he'd blush, say he was drunk and my balloon of joy would burst into sad little fragments.

'So what did you think of last night,' I asked, my heart banging in my head, along with the hangover from the cheap cider. He knew I wasn't talking about *The Rocky Horror Show*.

'Oh, I liked *that*,' he said, to my amazement. 'We should do that again.'

And so we did. It was my first sweet and very innocent little love affair. Sexually not much happened, which was probably just as well, but at least I now knew what a man tasted, smelt and felt like. We'd just sneak off somewhere for a snog or send each other little love notes. We went to see Culture Club perform in Brum, because Boy George was my greatest hero, his picture plastered all over my bedroom walls. Marcus and I held hands in the theatre, safe in the knowledge that nobody around us cared. We went to London for another show, then walked along The Embankment, talking a lot, kissing a little. A moon shone down on the Thames that night and I was high above it.

The Idyll only lasted a few months, till I was gently let down and he went back to the girls. I guess he was what we'd now call bi-curious, not sure of his sexuality and I offered the perfect opportunity to explore that with as I was pretty and effeminate and didn't challenge his masculinity as snogging some big hairy scaffolder might have done. I was sad of course, but I was having a great time at college and soon got over it. Marcus was a lovely guy and I remember him with affection. But hey, I'd had a romance with a gorgeous boy. The butterfly was almost out of the chrysalis.

Britain was still in the firm, right-wing grip of Margaret Thatcher. It was a tumultuous time when the miners were fighting for survival while the rich were getting richer. In the mid-Eighties, things were still difficult for gay people. Then the HIV and AIDS epidemic began to bite, giving the bigots a chance to spout hate and demonise us all. The 'Gay Plague' they called it, making people fearful of how the virus might be caught. Would you get it by being in the same room as a homosexual, accidentally shaking his hand or sitting on the same toilet seat? Nobody was sure.

By now, I was 'out' to almost everyone who knew me, but it certainly wasn't the best of times to confess it to my parents, who would make my life hell and maybe even kick me out of the house. But, almost by the week, I was drifting further and further away from a conventional masculine appearance. Mom and Dad's idea of a man was Sylvester Stallone or Steve McQueen, certainly not Boy George. I can only speculate that, for a long time now, they'd had their heads deep down in the sand with their fingers in their ears.

So I decided to save my big 'coming out' scene for a while. If there were to be tears, tantrums, threats of eternal hellfire or my packed suitcase in the hall, it could wait. I'd now reinvented myself visually, accepted myself internally and been accepted by a growing gang of great friends. Even in the frightening face of HIV and that of the old witch in Downing Street, this boy wanted some fun.

The gay scene in Birmingham then was pretty parochial for such a big city; limited to a couple of bars and a club, albeit with a definite underground edge. San Francisco it wasn't. In my second year in the Drama Department along came a young man called Hayden, who was in every way the spiritual son of my beloved Alain. Hayden wasn't just 'out', he was 'OUT!' He wore full make-up and a fur coat. He was also exceptionally clever and had Alain's 'fuck 'em all' attitude. He became my instant ally and soon guided me, like a camp Pied Piper, into the world of the alternative scene in which I was to spend the greater part of my future life.

By now, I'd come to understand that my fascination with the transformative power of make-up wasn't entirely visual; it was also a means of putting me more aesthetically in tune with what was going on in my head. In other words, my painted face was simply a reflection of the development of my teenage mind.

Hayden and I would spend hours getting ready; applying full make-up and the Gothic clothes bought from the kooky market stalls in the city centre. Soon I was dancing to the throbbing disco beats, looking like a Goth girl who just happened to be a boy.

At home, I'd abandoned the farcical rushing upstairs to wipe my face clean. My mother of course freaked out and the rows were endless. Once again, the walls of the Hodge abode shook to the rage of people who just couldn't understand one another.

'While you live in my house, you live by my rules,' she shrieked, 'and my rules say you can't wear make-up.'

'Don't be such a stuffy old cow,' I'd shriek back. 'I don't care if I live in your fucking shit house or not.'

'Fine by me,' she'd reply. 'Excuse me while I go and pack your case.'

She tried to listen in on my phone calls to Hayden, so she could batter me about where I was going and whom I was mixing with.

'Who's he then, when he's at home?' she'd demand. 'Is he older than you? Are you being led astray? I'll have the police onto him. Is he a drug dealer? Are you a junkie?'

And so on. I knew in my heart she was showing her concern for me; worried sick that I was skipping away out of her control. But then came the day when she found my carefully hidden make-up bag and threw it all away. It somehow felt like she'd thrown out the heart of me and the subsequent row was the worst of them all. For the first time, my own mother used the word against me.

'You're just a poof!' she yelled. 'My son the poof. The shame of it. How can I hold my head up in this street ever again?'

'I'd rather be a poof than a boring old bag like you!' I screamed back.

There it was. No need to do the big 'coming out' scene after all. She'd said it and I'd confirmed it. Job done.

It was the cutting of the umbilical cord. But I had seen a new way of living by now and I wanted it. I sure didn't want any more of the sour looks, the catty remarks or the

Hodge family screaming matches, those destructive everyday occurrences with which I'd lived ever since I could remember. I wanted to be free to live as I pleased and no longer be drowned in their world of negativity where I had to pretend to be something I was not. I wanted a new 'normal'.

It all came to a head the day after I got my very average 'A' level results. I'd been told I could have scored top grades if I'd worked harder, but by now I'd decided life was for living and not for studying. My parents had already said they couldn't afford to send me to university or drama school and that I'd have to get a job. My mother had the local newspapers laid out on the dining table with rings around the jobs she thought I should apply for. Shop assistants, gardening jobs, that sort of stuff. I laughed and pushed the paper away. No way. I wanted to be a make-up artist or a pop star. Again came the statement that while I lived under her roof... blah, blah, blah.

'Okay,' I said, 'I will go.'

'Oh really?' she sneered 'And how are you going to support yourself? Where are you going to live? You're living in cloud cuckoo-land. You're a joke.'

And so, in the end, Mom didn't need to pack my suitcase. I packed it myself. Except it was actually black bin liners into which I stuffed my records, my clothes and even my duvet, stashed it all into the back of Hayden's car and drove away to a new life.

I still loved my parents, but I could no longer live with them. I had to be free to do what I wanted, dress how I pleased and allowed to be my authentic self at last. I was 18 years old. The little bird had outgrown the nest. Fly high or fall to the ground, it would be up to me and nobody else.

If it was a choice between food and lipstick, the latter would always win. Crazy I suppose, but true.

I now lived with Kim and another friend in a flat in Edgbaston which was hardly fit for human habitation. I got by on a pittance; one of the four million unemployed in Thatcher's Britain. Yet somehow, I still managed to hit the town at least three nights a week.

Though Brum still wasn't exactly a gay Mecca, the alternative scene had perked up a bit. It was the post-Romantic period and bands like Culture Club, Dead or Alive, Soft Cell and Spandau Ballet were huge. Throw in a large, extreme Goth scene and you had a tight knit underground world of escapism, big hair and heavy make-up. For the next two years, I was one of its most enthusiastic inhabitants.

On leaving home, one of the first things I did was to dye my hair. My mother had strictly forbidden it while I lived under her middle-class roof. Maybe because she'd given birth to a carrot-top baby, she found my rejection of that physical fact somehow painful. For me though, changing my hair colour was an important step away from my troubled childhood. It was a constant reminder of the boy who sat by the window and I was determined he wasn't coming with me on my exciting new journey.

All of a sudden, I had long, blue-black locks. I spent hours crimping, backcombing, plaiting it into tiny braids or adding huge hair pieces. I used extensions to make it even bigger and at one point shaved the sides to create a giant mohawk. I shaved off my eyebrows to give me space for a bigger, more dramatic eye make-up area, adding tiny faux diamonds around my eyes with false lashes and glitter. I'd happily spend several hours getting ready to go out, sitting so long in front of a big mirror that my legs would go to sleep and I'd find it hard to stand up. I didn't care. There was nothing I wouldn't try. Sometimes I looked great, other times I must have looked distinctly dodgy. But I now regarded what Kim called my 'pretty little face' as my own personal work of art, creating it with as much skill, flair and originality as I could muster. For the next 25 years, that process would be at the very centre of my existence.

Though I'd left home, I wanted to keep relations with my parents as good as possible. When I went to visit, I'd brush my hair flat and pencil in light brown eyebrows in the hope of avoiding a row with Mom. No such luck. She still went ballistic every time, so I'd just walk out and get the bus back to Birmingham. That happened again and again till she finally realised that the less she said, the longer I'd stay. I think she just hoped that I'd grow out of it all. Years later, at the height of my notoriety as Dusty, she'd admit as much.

'I did hope at one time that you'd grow out of all this dressing-up stuff. You didn't, did you? You actually grew more *into* it.'

By that point in time, we'd be able to laugh about it, but back then it was still a war between us: raw red wounds that would heal after a while before fresh wounds were inflicted which would open the old ones up again.

My father, in contrast, never said much at all. That curious detachment thing again. Back then, it was probably even tougher for a man to accept the fact of a gay son than it was for a woman. Wondering if some flaw in their own masculinity had surfaced in the fruit of their loins. But I never really knew; Dad and I just didn't have the conversation and never would. And that was a shame. But I did know he'd not stopped caring for me entirely.

'Here's a tenner,' he'd say. 'Hide it quick before your mother sees.'

Little did he know I'd spend it on hair spray and eyeliners, but Mom was much more savvy. She'd never give me money, knowing I'd spend it on things she disapproved of. But before leaving her house, I'd always be given a grocery box full of food and my washing done, all fresh and ironed, even if she didn't like what she was ironing. Because by now, my addiction to make-up had spawned a parallel obsession, this time with clothes. I'd scour all the second-hand and charity shops for clothes and jewellery, always searching for anything that was imaginative, individual or just plain weird. Old dressing-gowns in black satin. Big smock dresses, tied round the waist with a bit of rope with tassels sewn on. Silk scarves to wear round my neck or in my hair or, by pinning two together to make an off-the-shoulder top.

Like the make-up, the clothes became both a sort of 'armour' against people's small minds and another way of saying something about who I was. And being able to do that far outweighed the deprivation of living largely on dried Vesta curry and beans on toast.

The other 'journey' I was on wasn't taking me very far. I've never been one of those gay men driven by sex, so the lack of it wasn't a huge problem. And the alarming spread of AIDS continued to stoke fear and distrust of the gay community. Occasionally, when a bit pissed, I'd 'cop off' with some punky lad but it never amounted to much. I think

I still found the physical act a bit animalistic. I certainly wasn't keen on the grubbier aspects of it. If I'd spent every last penny on some exotic bit of clothing, the last thing I wanted was some drunken oik to shoot his load all over it. And there was one brief encounter that would have put anybody off sex for life.

One night, I took a guy home who'd taken too much speed. Halfway through the proceedings, he started to convulse and go stiff, but not where I wanted him to.

'I think I'm ill. Get an ambulance,' he muttered.

'Really? Are you sure? I'll have to go out to the phone box and it's raining,' I said selfishly.

I'd already taken my make-up off and didn't want to go outside without it, so I sat and waited to see if he'd recover. But he didn't.

'Please get the ambulance,' he said. 'Now.'

I sighed and begrudgingly drew my eyebrows back on before going out to the phone box. I was just too young and silly to realise that there was a poor guy on my floor in a near coma. In the end, he was rapidly okay again and I met him in a club a few nights later.

'Let me buy you a drink to say thanks for the other night,' he said nicely.

'No need to say thanks,' I replied. 'But I'll keep the studded belts you left at my flat instead.'

He didn't look happy about it, but I was having them and that was that. Shamefully my narcissism at this point had become all-consuming and my priorities a bit askew. After all the years of repression, I think I'd got a bit drunk on my freedom, determined to do exactly what I wanted and that included how I interacted with other people. I'm not sure that Nana Edna, Mrs Wall, Alain or any of the other people in my life who'd supported me and wished me well would have liked me much that night. Looking back, I certainly don't like myself.

he flat in Edgbaston I shared with Kim was breaking up but, before it did, we threw a huge party. Everyone from college came and some of my new freaky friends. As with any good party, the neighbours called the police, who were quite surprised when they forcibly entered the place. Most of the guests were of indeterminate genders: transvestites, punks, rockers and Goths. Not to mention some of our more conventional friends like Kim's middle-aged mother, who still talks of it to this day. Needless to say, my own Mom would have helped the fuzz to arrest the lot of us. In her view, a night in the cells would've done us all the power of good.

But it was a memorable night, not least because three of the guests became my greatest friends and would remain so for life.

The first was a guy called 'Curtain Mark', so called for his ability to transform any old curtain into a floor-length duster coat in the space of an afternoon. A talent not to be sneered at in my world. Despite the image this description might give, Mark was far from being a delicate flower. He was a fearless character with a razor-sharp wit, bossy, acidic, sometimes even cruel and not somebody to get on the wrong side of. He'd think nothing of getting on the bus into town in full drag, day or night and God help anyone who started to take the piss. Sometimes, he'd even slip into 'leather drag' with a huge dreadlock wig and five-inch stilettos on legs that went on forever. But underneath the attitude, there was a pussycat aching to get out and we bonded at once.

The second was 'Twiggy', real name Chris, who'd been dressing up since he was 14. Unlike mine, Twiggy's mother had a liberal attitude to most things and he'd started club life very young. He was expert on anything involving make-up, knew how to put in extensions and how to make a corset. His make-up was Goth with some cyber-punk thrown in. Like me, he was slim, quite small and could easily pass as a woman. Like Curtain Mark, he was fearless, with a wild temper. A tiny pit bull in drag. No one messed with Twiggy. Yet he was also incredibly loyal and kind. One of the most creative people I've ever met, he would be a lifelong inspiration.

The third musketeer, Stan, was a delightful oddity. From a posh house in a wealthy suburb of Solihull, his parents had also been very liberal. Like Twiggy, he'd started dressing up and had come out as gay at a very early age. Unlike me, Stan had never lived in the shadow of disapproval and was incredibly confident as a result. I felt jealous of that and wondered what I'd have been like if I'd grown up not surrounded by my parents' negativity. Back then, Stan had the fire-red hair that I'd so eagerly got rid of. It was huge, backcombed, adorned with flowers and rhinestones and sometimes a winged dove. He wore ballgowns and long Sixties-style tube dresses over tight black jeans and winkle-picker shoes. His make-up skills were brilliant and he'd later become a well-known professional make-up artist, though by then he'd dropped the drag entirely and become a muscle queen covered in tattoos rather than rhinestones. More than a few actors must have flinched when he/she saw Stan's muscles and tattoos approaching them, only to drop their jaws when they saw his make-up box come out.

There were lots of outlandish people I met at this time, but those three were my main influences and the people I looked to for advice and support. We'd gossip and bitch and sometimes fall out, but that never lasted long as we all got to need each other and we knew it. They've never let me down in nearly 40+ years and our friendships will only die when we do.

On our nights out, we'd gather at Twiggy's flat as, for the bus ride into town, there was safety in numbers. When we were all together, we could literally stop traffic. But not all of the attention was benign. One night we took a short cut through a rough estate, accumulating a growing number of local teenagers who couldn't believe their eyes. In no time, their number grew to about 40 and their attitude gradually got more aggressive; throwing rubbish and the usual tired insults.

'Fucking poofs. Fucking bent bastards.'

'You lookin' for a shag darlin'?'

'D'you want it up the front or up the back, luv?'

The vocabulary of those who abused us was rarely original or high-flown. The prose of Marcel Proust or Henry James it definitely wasn't. But still it's not nice to have either insults or rubbish hurled at you as a symbol of how other people evaluate you and, though our hearts were racing, we kept our heads high and passed through the yobs like pearls through swine. We left them behind on their scruffy grass verges, doing drugs, scratching their arses or in whatever pointlessness that passed as their suburban lives. There was little chance any one of them would ever turn anyone's head. But the four of us were different and proud of it. We were heading into the bright lights and the big city. And we'd turn every head that saw us.

Sadly, the hostility didn't always come from bigoted heterosexuals. Drag queens, transvestites, punks and Goths would always be a minority within a minority. At that time, the mainstream gay look was what was called 'the Clone'. This was a sort of lumberjack image: short hair, handlebar moustaches, checked shirts and blue jeans. Ironic really, as 99 percent of the clones couldn't have cut down a tree to save their lives. Like the rest of us, they probably worked as hairdressers, or in Boots or the soft furnishings department of John Lewis. This didn't stop them looking down their noses at those of us who, in their judgement, looked 'weird'. They seemed to feel that our shameless effeminacy somehow let the side down, reinforcing the stereotypes and stoking the anti-gay prejudices of Joe and Joan Public. Many of the checked-shirt brigade wanted to be able to 'pass for straight' when it suited them; perhaps in their careers or in the company of parents and family. That was their right of course, though the joke was that, before too long, the public was no longer fooled and the 'Clone' look screamed 'gay' just as much as my wigs, frocks and high heels.

Despite that slightly sour aspect, me and my freaky friends usually managed to con our way past the bouncer on the door and strut our stuff on the dance floor under the disapproving eyes of the 'Clones'.

Though the Birmingham scene was limited and incestuous, there were still some interesting characters. The main gay club was The Nightingale, the entrance to which was guarded by a queen called 'Doris' who had a huge set of keys dangling from his belt, which we imagined might have some sinister connotation – like a torture chamber somewhere in the bowels of the premises. 'Doris' made regular patrols of the club, jangling his keys to make sure nobody was up to anything he didn't like. A rumour persisted that 'Doris' had a wooden leg and had taken a rent boy home to his high-rise flat, where the boy had robbed him and thrown the wooden leg out of the window so 'Doris' couldn't give chase.

Shameful as it is to admit, the prejudices my gang suffered from the Clones, we ourselves inflicted on another sub-group within the community. A group with which, to those uneducated in such nuances, we were roughly synonymous. These was the hardcore transvestites. We considered the way we looked as being pretty, fashionable and dramatic, but this lot all looked like Mrs Doubtfire, Tootsie or Les Dawson in a wig. A delicate androgyny was completely missing. There was no mistaking they were 'cocks in frocks'. They all drank pints, talked about football and, bless them, still resembled the welders and truck drivers they probably were. For some unknown reason, this group always hung out in the pool room which you had to pass through to reach the toilets. We therefore decided to take the piss. We were gobby and bitchy and they didn't stand a chance.

One of them called Lolita had her own pool cue, kept on brackets on the wall, which no one else was allowed to touch. For some reason, Curtain Mark took a dislike to Lolita and squirted a whole tube of superglue onto where the cue was held by the bracket. When Lolita arrived, she pulled a huge hole in the plaster trying to extricate it, while we looked on from the corner, helpless with laughter. Lolita had a pretty good idea who'd done it but, luckily for Mark, she couldn't get the cue off the wall or she might have rammed it where the sun don't shine.

Another of the hardcore transvestites was called 'Mrs Mangel', in homage to the then-famous busybody character in the Australian soap *'Neighbours'*, which starred the young Kylie Minogue and Jason Donovan. Our Mrs Mangel was a bit ancient and shrivelled, with a brassy Barbara Cartland style wig. Unlike Barbara, she never carried a handbag but kept her lipstick and purse in an old plastic bag hooked onto her belt. One night near Christmas, we were dancing in our little group when she decided to come and bop along with us. We were horrified. Young and elitist, we were far too cool to be seen dancing with a grotesque like Mrs Mangel. How dare she?

Twiggy encouraged her to have a sniff of his 'poppers', the drug amyl nitrite, on which the old thing soon became quite giddy. But Twiggy gave her more and more and began to jive with her really fast. He crowned her with one of the Christmas holly wreaths and spun her round and round the dance floor more or less by her neck, until she spun off the dance floor and into the nearest wall. We were helpless with laughter but, when she'd recovered, the poor old thing was furious and reported us to 'Doris' who banned us for three months. Because we were young and pretty, I guess we were mocking old age and ugliness, which was good fun but not very edifying. No doubt Mrs Mangel is now in that big pool-room in the sky and I send my apologies up to her.

'All right,' said my mother. 'You can come back home. But you'll have to cut that hair and tone down your appearance. While you live under my roof...'

It was a drastic decision, like taking a step backwards. But I was struggling to exist on my own and needed more money to, as the saying goes, 'live in the style to which I had become accustomed.' In other words, going out on the town several nights a week. It'd be great not to have to worry about the expense of food and heating bills. I could always put in earplugs to cancel out the worst of my mother.

Anyway, the hair cut didn't matter. I'd been planning to cut it for a while. By the late Eighties, my Gothic look was starting to be a bit passé; a concept which simply couldn't be allowed. A more 'fashion' type of look had come in. Boys began to look more like boys, so I followed suit and let Curtain Mark cut it into a bowl shape; no longer looking like a 'trifle', as some snooty queen had once described me. Now it was a sort of 'lesbian chic'. Like a trendy girl with no boobs. A vast improvement in my mother's eyes.

I dreamed of Gaultier and Westwood, but still no chance on my income. But now, with a little bit more money, I could buy some nicer clothes and put them together in the most imaginative ways I could dream up. Mandarin-collared jackets with matching wide-legged trousers. Enormous shoulder pads. Denim jackets covered with pins and key rings and, ever the narcissist, laminated pictures of myself. With the jingling of the keys and chains, you could hear me coming before you saw me. Clothes were now a kind of craving. As I've said, they had become, and even now still are, like an armour against the 'normality' I had come to so loathe.

Somebody offered to do some 'professional' pictures of me and they turned out really well. A very slim cross between a 1930s lesbian and Karen from Bananarama. Like all these old Hollywood divas of the golden age, I was starting to know my angles, how lighting worked and which positions I looked best in. In these pictures, I saw the someone I wanted to be. Not the boy who sat by the window. Not the toothy redheaded 'poof' of my youth. Seeing myself looking quite beautiful at last gave me a huge injection of confidence; that essential quality for a happy life that had always eluded me. The power of appearance had got me in its grip. In the years to come, this would be both a blessing and a curse.

'I think perhaps it'd be a good idea if you reappraised your approach to interviews such as this one,' said the woman at Boots.

'In what way?' I asked.

'Well, I don't want to be rude,' she replied, 'but it's your appearance. It's not what we're looking for or what most other employers would look for either.'

Boots was the one and only interview I'd landed in my feeble attempts to find gainful employment. A window dressing/merchandising job. I turned up in full face make-up and a big black hat. Well, they sold make-up, didn't they? Surely, they'd like someone who knew how to use it. Some sort of inspiration to the customers maybe? Not a bit of it. In their view, I'd be too much for the average folks buying their cough mixture or suppositories.

So I had to create my own job instead. Around this time, I'd met a wonderful guy called Andrew who became a firm platonic friend and a real soulmate. Both of us unemployed, together we decided to take a stall selling Seventies gear in a fashion market in downtown Brum called Mega Active. Andrew had some money put aside and I borrowed some off my Dad, no doubt relieved that his strange, 20-year-old son might possibly be embarking on some sort of career. We even got a small grant from The Prince's Trust, so God bless Prince Charlie.

The stall was called 'Trojans' and that was exactly how hard we worked to get it up and running. To get stock, we scoured every local second-hand shop and warehouse in the vicinity, eventually expanding from purely Seventies gear to Sixties and Fifties as well. The stall, decorated in Chinese wallpaper with blow-up animals and toy airplanes hanging from the ceiling, soon became a social hub for many of the fantastic freaks from the club scene and we began to make a profit. Life seemed to have developed a purpose. I'd even become slightly less narcissistic and a bit more 'grown-up'. The seeds of ambition had been sewn within me. And it was at least a job I loved doing. A far cry from filling shelves at Boots or any of the other crap jobs my mother had once ringed in the newspaper. It was around now that I began to sniff the vague possibility of making some sort of 'career' out of the things I loved doing.

I was also about to 'grow up' in another way too. After my brief idyll with the gorgeous Marcus, my 'love life' had been, like the Wandrin' Minstrel's, a thing of shreds and patches. But suddenly, in the way that these things go, that changed.

His name was Lee. He was shortish with blond curly hair, almond eyes and a very cheeky grin. He worked in a bakery, a manual job which had given him a very nice body. We didn't have that much in common, but we hit it off quickly. Then, as we were leaving a club, Lee kissed me goodnight. Wow. Cupid's Arrow. This was what I'd wanted so badly for so long. Usually, it'd always been me having a crush on someone, which wasn't reciprocated. But now it was the other way around. Andrew advised caution, not to let my imagination run away with me after just one kiss. So the next time I saw Lee, I played it very cool, in fact almost frigid.

'May I ask what exactly your intentions are?' I asked, like some prim Victorian spinster.

'Intentions? How d'you mean?'

'That kiss,' I replied. 'Are you just messing about? Cos if you are, I'm not playing that game.'

'I'm not messing about,' he replied, looking a bit hurt. 'I'm falling in love with you.'

Gosh. The words everyone hopes to hear at least once in a lifetime. Words nobody had ever said to me. It was like water falling on the desert and soaked up joyously. In no time, I too fell hook, line and sinker.

Soon, my new 'friend' Lee was allowed to stay at my parents' house, sleeping on the floor of my bedroom. In reality, we were 'at it' like very silent rabbits on the other side of the wall from where, only feet away, Mom was, hopefully, fast asleep. Quite a difficult feat. All the usual endearments and instructions having to be whispered.

'No not there. A bit further down.'

'I can't hear you.'

'I said a bit further down. No, not up, down.'

'You're going to *what?* For fuck's sake, bite the pillow then.'

Lee hated hiding the person he really was from his family and colleagues, but he just wasn't ready to deal with that yet. The AIDS pandemic was now at full throttle, so it was the worst possible time to come out. I still faced almost daily insults from total strangers in the street and once, on a bus, a gang of idiots set fire to the back of my hair. I could have been seriously hurt or even killed – I managed not to become the Brummie version of Miss Havisham. But only just. I used to wonder if these morons ever thought through the possible consequences of their actions. Oh, they'd have said, it was just a laugh.

To my great surprise, Lee turned out to be almost as handy with a needle as Curtain Mark and could knock up a respectable looking shirt or pair of trousers in a couple of hours. So Andrew and I asked him to join us in the business, invest some money and take over another stall which would sell new, off-the-wall pieces for which we could charge much more than for the second-hand stuff. For cool, alternative Brummie club kids, 'Trojans' became the 'go-to' place to buy rave gear.

A year or two passed and things seemed to be going great. Lee now had a council flat of his own, so we could shag like rabbits without worrying about my mother pressing her ear to the wall. I'd now become even more confident of my place in the world and started to behave accordingly. If Lee did something I didn't like, I'd fly at him with the temper tantrums and screaming rages that I'd learned from my parents. I just thought that was the norm. I could be petulant and even cruel and, after a while, Lee had had enough of this diva nonsense. He said he wanted a few weeks' break to work out how he felt about me now. I was quite cocky, felt sure he'd soon get over his wobbles and that everything would soon revert to normal. But it didn't. I went to London for a while to stay with Curtain Mark who'd moved down there the year before and who I really missed. When I got back to Birmingham, Lee said he wanted to finish. Heart-broken now, I begged him to think about it for a bit longer. That weekend, the gang was due to go back down to London to see my hero, Boy George. In Andrew's car, the atmosphere was tense, like the distant crackle of electricity in a thundery sky.

Boy George was fantastic as usual, as he began to sing *Do You Really Want To Hurt Me?* I reached out and took Lee's hand.

'I love you.' I said, the words tight in my throat.

Lee pulled his hand away and turned to look me directly in the eye.

'Well, I don't love you. It's over.'

So that was it. As Boy George kept on repeating those lyrics, my little world came crashing down around me, as if the walls of that theatre itself had caved in. It was all my fault, though I was still too up myself to understand that. I'd been offered somebody's love, a love which I had returned and I'd screwed the whole thing up with my infantile self-absorption.

And then it got even worse. Lee and I had a mutual friend called Darren who, in the past, had come onto me quite seriously too, saying he wanted us to be together, though I hadn't felt Darren was the right one for me. Like a game of musical beds, it turned out that Lee and Darren had now become involved. One night, they drove slowly past me on the street and laughed. It was cruel, but probably no crueller than some of the things I'd done and said myself. We were all young and the young can behave very badly as they try to find their wings as adults. But their mockery was the final humiliation. For the first time in my life, sadly not the last, I experienced heart-breaking pain which just wouldn't go away.

For the next six months, I stopped eating and went down to eight stone. I looked appalling.

'David, I beg you to eat something. Anything!' said my mother, who knew quite well that something bad had happened, though I never discussed it with her. Having little sense of anyone's privacy, she came into the bathroom one day while I was taking a soak. She was shocked at how emaciated I'd become and sat down on the loo seat beside me.

'You have to stop this now son,' she said. 'Whatever has happened, it's not worth doing this to yourself. It really isn't.'

She said no more, asked no questions, but I knew she'd guessed the essence of it. Let's face it, most people go through something similar at least once. Maybe it had happened to her, before she met my Dad. But from that day on, the subject of my sexuality was never mentioned again. The years-long battles between us, about the way I looked, where I went, who my friends were, all stopped. Ceasefire. Maybe, when she saw her stick-thin son lying in the bath like a broken reed, she knew at last that she had to accept me as I was and to support me when I needed her. And that is what happened. From that day to this, I have never lied to my mother again. I've never needed to.

Eventually I tried to pick up all those broken bits of me. But it was tough. Friends encouraged me to have a fling or two, but when I did at last try to 'do the deed' with somebody new, I burst into tears and asked him to leave. I just wasn't ready. For two whole years, I would stay celibate as I was still so painfully in love with Lee.

In the end, I realised that the answer to my heart-break was a motorway. The M40 that led to London. The alternative club scene in Birmingham had curdled on me. It was such a small world in which everybody seemed to know everybody else and all about their business. Like those villages in Jane Austen novels. The best thing now was a place where almost nobody knew me. A fresh start. A bigger stage. I'd stifled in Brum long enough and was desperate to escape. To paraphrase Norma Desmond's famous line. 'I was always big. It was the place that was small.'

By happy chance, my best buddy Andrew felt the same. So, with some sadness, we closed down 'Trojans'. We reckoned the remaining profits from it would last us about three months in London after we'd paid rent. Andrew had already found us a double room in a flat and we'd worry about getting jobs when we got there. So I packed up my belongings and got into Andrew's car. The big adventure had begun. The thought of failure was zero. I had huge confidence in my own abilities and felt no fear about the move. What Mom and Dad felt, I don't know. I probably didn't ask. On their side, I guess there might even have been some relief. From now on, for richer for poorer, in sickness and in health, they could focus entirely on each other, which was how, in their heart of hearts, they had always wanted it. And by now, they must have understood that their timid little boy had evolved into a different creature altogether. One largely outside their comprehension.

Like two Dick Whittingtons, though without the cat, Andrew and I saw the towers and pinnacles of London rise before us. If everything went tits up, we could always head back up the M40 with our tails between our legs. But

I somehow knew that would never happen. I sensed this city was where my future lay and I was determined to make that future dazzling, however long it might take.

f anyone imagined I'd spend my first night in London, unpacking my toothbrush and arranging my knickers in a drawer, they didn't know me. Andrew had found us a double room in Barnes, a prosperous suburb just south of the river. A more chic version of Aldridge with the manicured lawns and the old dears walking poodles. Not what I'd come to London for at all. I couldn't wait to get my arse back over the Thames and into Soho.

We headed for *Kinky Gerlinky*, a monthly bash that had become London's go-to place for drag queens, club freaks, Muscle Marys and hedonists in general. We'd been there before, as night-trippers from Brum, three long hours there and back in a cramped minivan, but tonight we'd be there as new-born Londoners. I was foaming at the mouth with anticipation.

And it didn't disappoint. That night I met the enigmatic Marilyn, Boy George's on/off best mate. He was very beautiful but capricious and, from what I'd heard, not always very nice to people. But I grabbed my balls in both hands and went up to him.

'You look great,' I gushed. 'Would you mind if I took your picture?'

Long pause as he eyed me up and down.

'Oh, all right,' he replied, rather churlishly. 'One condition though. You're not in the picture. Just me.'

This deflated my balloon a bit. In Marilyn's eyes, I'd clearly failed some test of style or cool. Oh dear.

'He's snooty, isn't he?' said Andrew, 'considering he's not had a hit for a decade. Who does he think he is? Madonna?'

I'd come across Marilyn in the years to come. Sometimes a good experience, sometimes not. More of that later.

That night, I stayed at *Kinky* right until it closed and they started putting the bins out. On the night bus back to Barnes, I felt so elated that I'd finally broken away from the small-town mentality of my upbringing and was in the city of my dreams.

In the morning, I came down to reality with a bump. The search for work started there and then. Economically, things were improving in the UK. Unemployment was down to below two million for the first time in nearly a decade and the all-pervasive gloom of those years seeming to be receding. I got lucky at once and landed an interview as a shop assistant in a Japanese gift shop off Oxford Street. I followed the advice of the woman who'd interviewed me at Boots back in Brum and wore no make-up, no big hat and somehow talked my way into a job. It turned out to be a bummer. Long hours, boring work, the pay well below today's minimum wage. Worse yet, I was expected to wear what they called a 'Happy Coat', a cheap nylon kimono in muddy green, a vile monstrosity of a thing. Did this sour-faced Japanese manageress know I'd been schmoozing with Marilyn a few hours before? By 10 o'clock on my first day, I'd decided that selling chopsticks and noodle bowls wasn't for me. I went out for a sandwich at lunch time and never went back. But I nicked the 'Happy Coat' and gave it to our landlady's daughter, who loved it. No accounting for lack of taste.

Then things looked up. I got myself onto the books of an agency who provided retail staff cover for the big West End department stores. At the agency, I'd been grilled about my knowledge of cosmetics by another sour-faced dragon, a very officious old duchess in horn-rimmed specs. Her own make-up looked like it'd been applied by an earthmover. I longed to point out that I obviously knew a lot more about make-up than she ever would, though I managed to bite my increasingly sharp tongue.

My first gig was a few days on the Lancôme counter in Selfridges. Not a bad start. But here I was to be vetted by yet another elderly *grande dame*, who kept telling me that Selfridges was a 'high end' department store and how honoured I would be to work there. She reminded me of Mrs Slocombe from *Are You Bring Served?*. Luckily, we never got round to discussing her pussy.

It wasn't a taxing job, though the requirement to stand bolt upright at all times meant my feet were killing me by the end of the day. As a temporary skivvy, I got the boring tasks, like cleaning out the lipstick boxes. The women I worked with were all ageing princesses with thick orange foundation and pale pink lipstick, who considered themselves experts on the beauty industry. I began to wonder if London shops were populated entirely by these old girls, embalmed in far too much slap.

But I stuck it out for the lolly. I'd not realised how expensive it was to live in London. The streets weren't paved with gold, but they were certainly paved with temptation. My Mecca was Hyper Hyper in Kensington, a high fashion marketplace of designer boutiques with row after row of cool fashion brands, selling things you just couldn't buy anywhere else in Britain. I'd dress myself up to the nines and spend a whole afternoon sipping coffee and pretending to read a magazine, but secretly studying the super trendy types who hung out there. Educating myself in what was what and who was who. Building up an awareness of the world in which I so desperately wanted to be a part.

But gradually the lolly was diminishing and I had to do something about it. Andrew and I were paying £60 a week for a shared room, he snored badly and the sleepless nights were driving me insane. Boring Barnes was nearly an hour's journey from the West End and I just didn't like its middle-class smugness and the memories which it evoked of my troubled childhood. It was time to move on.

They called themselves 'The Mummies.'

It was not an appropriate name. There was nothing very maternal about the two butch lesbians in whose 18th-floor council flat in <u>Deptford</u> I soon found myself living. Leafy Barnes it wasn't.

Curtain Mark, my bosom buddy from Brum, was living in the flat next door to the Mummies who, he'd discovered, were looking for a new lodger. The room was grim, but it was £20 a week instead of £60 so I took it. Andrew moved in with Mark and I moved in with the girls. Big mistake.

My new landladies were not kind or pleasant people. One worked in a garage where she no doubt loosened hub caps with her teeth. The other was a shop assistant, though she described herself as a fashion designer and artist. The only thing I ever saw her make was a pair of polka dot, square-legged flares; the only thing I ever saw her paint were the half-finished murals on the walls of the flat.

The place they seemed happy to call home was a hellhole and stank of the shit from their 'children'; three poor felines who rarely seemed to have their litter trays changed. The Mummies sat their enormous arses on bean bags placed on old plastic bread pallets. The coffee table was a piece of broken glass supported on bricks. If my own house-proud mummy had seen it, she'd have freaked. The only thing that made it bearable was the friendly presence of Curtain Mark and Andrew in the flat next door.

The Mummies kidded themselves that they were bohemian and arty but were just extremely pretentious and not very bright. They certainly never clicked when I was taking the piss.

'What d'you think of the work of Kevin Turner?' I'd ask.

'Oh yes, awesome,' one would reply.

'I like his earlier stuff best,' I'd say. 'I think the more recent work is, well, maybe a bit derivative.'

'Oh yes, definitely. Definitely derivative.'

Kevin Turner did not, of course, exist. I never got tired of that little game. Once, the arty one did actually paint a picture. It was a vision of hell. Like a sicked-up chicken curry.

'What d'you think?' she asked.

'It's right up there with Hieronymous Bosch,' I said, sarcastically.

'Wow. Thankyou. Thankyou.'

I was still working as casual labour in the posh shops of London; once for the Seventies fashion queen Zandra Rhodes in Mayfair. Unfortunately, on my first day left alone in the shop, somebody came in and stole a £4,000 frock. So it was bye bye Zandra and back to the beauty counters and the Mrs Slocombes. But there was one compensation. I'd now worked out various ways of nicking the free samples, so my make-up box was heaving with goodies.

The fragrant scents of the beauty counters were a nice contrast to the cat shit of the Mummies' Dickensian flat. But the money just wasn't good enough. I spent almost all of it on partying and clothes, with little left over on which to live. If I wasn't careful, I'd soon find myself heading back up the M40 to Birmingham and the 'told you so' look on my mother's face. Something had to change – and it did. Soon I'd find myself dealing with odours almost as challenging as those from the litter-trays.

Curtain Mark had landed a social care job with Southwark Council doing day-to-day care work for a group of people with learning difficulties, but now living back in the community as Mrs Thatcher had declared they must, having closed down the state facilities in which they'd lived till then. The job paid well by our standards and I was very jealous of the excess cash Mark had to spend on lovely Westwood clothes and trips abroad.

I knew nothing of the complexities of such work, but they took me on and, after just one week's training, I was allocated to one of their 'supported houses', joining an existing team of eight carers and three residents. The only bottom I'd ever wiped was my own and having to give 'personal' care to elderly men was a shock to the system, I can tell you. For a couple of days, I even wondered about fleeing back to the Mrs Slocombes in Oxford Street. But I didn't and I was soon very glad of that decision. The residents were all very sweet and, from somewhere deep inside my narcissistic depths, I summoned up some empathy and began to really enjoy the work.

I was assigned as key worker to a tiny little man called Billy and we soon became great mates. Billy had a totally incomprehensible way of speaking and most people couldn't understand a word he said. But I somehow managed to pick up his wavelength so, as well as being his carer, I also became his mouthpiece, his connection to the world. He was a very kind, truly gentle man and would make me roar with laughter. One day I noticed he had brown powder on his face which was also smeared on the kitchen cupboard doors. Inside were several opened Oxo cubes.

'Billy, have you eaten those Oxo cubes?'

'Well, I just ate two chocolates, but they weren't nice,' he replied. 'So I thought I'd try these instead. They're really good.'

Billy loved the Fifties era, the music of his youth, and knew every Elvis lyric by heart, plus those of countless other rockers he'd swear he'd been chatting to only recently.

'Elvis was here again yesterday.'

'Oh, that's nice, Billy,' I'd reply. 'Anybody else?'

'The Everly Brothers,' he'd say. 'Rosemary Clooney was coming, but she had a cold.'

I helped him to buy an old-fashioned record player and together we'd raid the local charity shops, looking for vinyl of the music he knew and loved so much. Then we'd go home and spend hours singing along to them, just like I'd done as a child with Nana Edna and her bloody Max Bygraves albums. Of course, Billy knew the lyrics far better than I did and got very upset if I got the words wrong.

Amazingly, Mrs Thatcher, or one of her civil servants with a much larger heart, came up with the readies to take Billy on the first holiday he'd ever had in his life. And not just a weekend in Bognor or Torquay, but a week in Gran Canaria and I went with him. We must have made an odd combo, this tiny little man in his seventies and me, the fashion-conscious pretty boy with the Brummie accent and the hint of eye-liner. People at the hotel kept asking if he was my grandfather, so it became easier just to say 'yes'.

I suppose there was a fragment of truth in it, too, because I'd come to love Billy as if he really were my grandad, neither of whom I'd ever known. That week was both heart-warming and heart-breaking. It was wonderful to see Billy loving every moment of something that so many people take for granted every year, but which he'd never known before; the hot sun on his face and the sand beneath his feet. And at the same time, so sad to think about the difficulties and hardships that he'd faced in his life. Yet, despite everything, he remained sweet and affectionate and went on singing *Jailhouse Rock* and *Love Me Tender*.

The contrast between the blue skies of Gran Canaria and the clouded gloom of Deptford was hard to take. So was the contrast between the loveliness of a man like Billy and the ugliness, in every sense, of my two landladies.

During this time, the Mummies had gone off for an extended trip to Australia; their absence from the ghastly flat quite blissful. On the dreaded day of their return, they walked in with not just a suntan and a stuffed Koala, but with a new Australian girlfriend, too. I didn't like to ponder on exactly what the situation was, but the three of them set up camp in the living-room, so the place became rather crowded and tempers frayed. The flat became even more of a pigsty than ever and they seemed to think it was my job to clean up after them. I've never minded a bit of light housework, but trying to clean up after three strapping lesbians with messy habits was more than my delicate sensitivities could handle. If I hadn't recently clocked up quite a ridiculous debt in the Westwood shop, I'd have walked out there and then, but I needed every penny, so I sat tight.

Things came to a head the day I brought my lovely old Billy home, since he'd often asked to see where I lived. The visit was short, the Mummies clearly furious. On the way out, and in front of Billy, the one who worked in the garage accosted us.

'You seem to have forgotten that this is my flat, not yours,' she said.' Never ever bring anyone like that in here again.'

'Like what?' I asked, my hackles rising.

'Like that,' she repeated, glaring at Billy.

Poor Billy stood there humiliated and upset. He was so helpless, so gentle and so good. Christ, he'd suffered enough indignities in his life without this neanderthal woman adding to them. I could have swung for her at that moment. But back then, it was common practice to laugh at anyone who was different and/or give them demeaning or insulting names. They simply saw nothing wrong in doing that. I'd been a victim of it my whole life and knew only too well the pain it caused. And there in front of me, I saw that pain in Billy's eyes. I gave her a month's notice to quit and took Billy home.

Out in the street, he'd gone very quiet and withdrawn. He'd been so looking forward to coming to where his friend David existed when I wasn't looking after him. A tiny event for most people, but for somebody like him, a big excursion. I could have wept.

'How about some fish and chips then Billy?' I asked, trying to put a smile back on my face.

'Oh yes,' he replied.

Billy loved fish and chips. And sure enough, before too long, a bit of battered cod, greasy chips and the sharp tang of vinegar did the trick. And my dear old Billy perked up. But I remained disgusted and furious. At how these two awful women could treat their cats like human beings and a poor old man like an animal.

The Mummies had the gall to be cross that I was going, but only because they'd be hard pressed to rent out the horrible little room to anyone else. With my old friend Hayden, I found a lovely little flat in Catford which we could just afford between us. On the day I moved out, having loaded my stuff into Hayden's car, I remembered I'd left my ghetto blaster and dashed up to get it. On the flat's internal stairs, I was met by the Mummy who worked in the garage. She had a leather tool belt strapped round her waist and was brandishing a large wrench, no doubt the property of the garage. And she was blazing mad.

'You're not taking your ghetto blaster until you clean this flat,' she said.

'Excuse me, but I've not used the communal parts of this flat for over a week,' I replied, 'and I've done more than my share of cleaning lately. So kindly move out of my way.'

'I will not,' she said, crossing her arms like a Sumo wrestler to whom she bore more than a passing resemblance.

'Please let me pass,' I repeated.

'No.'

On the stairs behind me was a huge pile of her cherished *ID* magazines which she'd collected from the first edition, yet had ignored any fashion advice they may have contained. I picked up as many of them as I could and hurled them down at her. At this, the Mummy lost it completely and attacked me with the wrench, screaming language that would make Jim Davidson blush. I was standing on a higher step than her and was taller anyway, so it wasn't difficult to deflect the chubby little arm that held the wrench and to punch her smack in the face. She responded by grabbing a handful of my beautiful, twisted dreadlocks that I'd only put in the week before and yanked several out. This was too much. You can insult me, punch me and wave a wrench in my face but if you touch my hair, you're a goner.

I let rip and literally kicked her down the stairs. I grabbed my ghetto blaster and left that shitty flat, never to see or speak to those bitches ever again. Curtain Mark, alerted by the commotion, had witnessed everything from the open front door.

'Go back and give her another one from me,' he called after me.

I was shaken up, but at least I'd stood my ground. Never was I going to be bullied in adult life in the way I had been as a school kid. Those days were over. I wasn't exactly proud to have hit someone but, in this case, I wasn't sorry either. And perhaps this nasty incident wasn't really about the ghetto blaster or even about my precious hair. Because just before I raised my hand to punch her in the face, I'd seen, in my mind's eye, the sad, hurt face of Billy. That punch was one for him.

an I buy you a drink?' he said, as I stood in a gay bar in sunny Barcelona, watching men dance flamenco together (strange how erotic castanets can be).

Not exactly an original line and I suppose if he'd been dog ugly I'd have turned away in haughty disdain, but he wasn't. He was tall, blond and drop-dead gorgeous and, as we all know, the gorgeous can get away with almost anything in life, including corny pick-up lines. He was a fair bit older than me, but I'd always believed in equal opportunities, so that wasn't a problem.

His name was Dietmar. A German, so I didn't mention the war and for the next week we were inseparable. Apart from being a dish, Dietmar was clever and charming. He also had an unusually large penis. I've honestly never been a size queen but when one comes along, you just have to grit your teeth (or rather you don't), make the best of it and think of England.

I shouldn't really have been in Barcelona at all. Yet again, the problem was money. I'd always sort of felt that the credit card had been invented especially for me. Live now, pay later. What a wonderful idea that is. You buy whatever it is you want, wallow in the pleasure of possession and only panic when you really, really need to. This time however, I'd overdone it and now owed £2,000; a *lot* of money back then and the interest kept piling up. I was worried sick but decided that this great black cloud hanging over me could only be dissolved by me and Hayden taking a short holiday in the sun. After all, you might as well be hung for a sheep as for a goat. And there were certainly a lot of very pretty sheep in this town, strolling up and down The Ramblas, half-naked, strutting their suntanned pecs. Something you rarely saw in Catford.

For those seven days in the sunshine, Dietmar and I had a lovely time apart from one odd thing. He was always rather coy about what he did for a living and indeed his life in general. Naturally, I imagined an international drug dealer or a gangster. But, on the last day, he opened up a bit, explaining that his father was a German aristocrat who lived in Madrid and was buddies with the King and Queen of Spain. So it seemed that the blood which engorged Dietmar's huge willy was actually blue. He lived off an allowance from his father which he supplemented by doing escort work, for which he obviously had the major qualification.

I knew several escorts in London and had never been judgemental about that way of earning your bread and butter. My motto had always been 'you gotta do what you gotta do.' Nevertheless, I asked him loads of questions about the, er, ins and outs of his profession and he seemed surprised that I should be so fascinated. On my return to London we stayed in touch, and he invited me back to Spain a few months later. This time, I'd be staying with him at his apartment in central Barcelona from which, he told me, he worked with a few friends. I packed my bags at once.

When I reached the apartment, I discovered that it was in fact a full-on male brothel and that Dietmar's 'friends' were actually his employees. My handsome, aristocratic German was a male 'madam'. It didn't worry me in the slightest, in fact quite the opposite. I'd always yearned for broader horizons and now here they were.

That evening Dietmar took me out to dinner. But it was soon apparent that I'd not been invited back to Spain just to re-kindle our holiday romance. Dietmar had something quite different in mind.

'Have you ever considered doing escort work yourself, David?' he asked very casually.

'Ha! Who would pay *me*? I'm a skinny ginger queen,' I laughed.

'But you are in Spain, David. And you may have noticed that everyone here has black hair. They really love a ginger. Opposites attract and all that.'

I laughed again and declined, but he wasn't giving up.

'Okay, but somebody's off sick. Could you maybe help out tomorrow, just as a "maid"?' he asked. 'Show the clients in and out, serve drinks, put the washing in the machine. That sort of thing? I'll pay you.'

For the millionth time, I pictured that big black cloud of Visa card debt still looming over me. I had hardly any cash and it would at least help pay for my food while I was there. I wondered if there was a maid's uniform and pictured myself in a little short black number with a frilly white apron, fishnet tights and a feather duster. Though the image of putting the washing into the machine didn't appeal. In a brothel, the stains were likely to be a bit more of a health hazard than spilt coffee or tomato ketchup.

In the event, it was easy enough and I quite enjoyed it. To my surprise, some of the punters were even quite attractive. I'd been expecting Zimmer frames, saggy boobs and acres of sprouting nasal hair. In retrospect, I was of course being groomed for the role which Dietmar really had in mind for me. And it was a starring role, not just a 'walk-on' as the maid.

'David, you have an admirer,' he whispered. 'One of the clients who has seen you serving drinks has made a special request for you. Do say yes. As a little favour to me?'

The pay would be 10 thousand pesetas, about £75. Not to be sniffed at in my present circumstances.

'What would I have to do?' I asked nervously.

'Well, he's a little bit kinky, that one,' replied Dietmar. 'He likes rubber gloves. Just give him a quick wank and that'll be it.'

I thought of the money and glanced over at the man, who wasn't too ghastly.

'Bugger it,' I thought. 'Nobody will ever know and I need the dosh.'

Dietmar sent the man off to one of the rooms and handed me a pair of yellow Marigold gloves. I'd been expecting something black and pvc, not a pair of ordinary washing-up gloves... But maybe these were easier to rinse off afterwards.

I followed this guy into the room, feeling like a bit of a twerp. Things weren't helped by the fact he spoke no English. By now, I knew a few words of Spanish, but the line 'shall I just toss you off then?' hadn't yet made it into the Collins Phrase Book.

So I just pointed at the man and gesticulated at him to undress and he did the same to me. I had absolutely no idea

THE BOY WHO SAT BY THE WINDOW

what I was doing, but I'd seen Julie Walters in *Personal Services*, the movie about Cynthia Payne who ran a famous brothel in Streatham, so I tried to channel Julie. My drama training at the Aldridge Youth Theatre was coming in handy again.

'Just do it, David,' I heard Alain's voice in my head. 'Don't worry about motivation, darling.'

So there I was, stark naked, in a small room in a male brothel in Barcelona, wearing a pair of yellow Marigolds with a bare-arsed, erect Spaniard lying on the bed in front of me and waiting for the business. As my sense of humour is highly developed, I suddenly started to laugh. From the little I'd heard about kinky sex, many perverts take their little fetishes very seriously and laughter is the kiss of death. Though it's beyond me how anyone could keep a straight face when they're trussed up like a chicken or with their goolies smothered in raspberry yoghurt. Luckily though, this guy laughed when I did and after that it was easy.

It was also very fast.

An old Diana Ross song was playing on the sound system. *You Can't Hurry Love*. But there was no need to hurry this guy. He was finished and dressed before the end of the song. I got my 10 thousand pesetas in cash, of which I had to give Dietmar 200, presumably for the use of the gloves which, as I'd expected, rinsed off lovely. I spent some of the cash on a slap-up meal for one in a posh restaurant.

The same man came back several times that week for more of the same and we got through quite a bit of Diana's back catalogue. As Dietmar had said, this guy loved the ginger hair that Nana Edna once said had been 'kissed with fire'. Being a 'carrot top' had been used as an insult for most of my life, so it was rather nice that it was now assisting people to get their rocks off. Among Dietmar's regular clientele, the word soon got out about the ginger delight awaiting them and I returned to London with a less terrifying debt than I'd left with.

I repeated this scenario three times that year for a week at a time. I expanded my repertoire a little as I wouldn't have made enough money with just the Marigold method. Anyway, higher fees could be charged for other personal services. It was a learning curve. I never felt debased or humiliated in any way and never did anything I wasn't happy about doing. Nor did I ever risk my sexual health. But a career as a tart with a heart of gold was definitely not for me. I paid off the credit card debt, cut up the Visa card and stopped taking calls from Dietmar, which I suppose was a little bit ungrateful.

I often imagined him and his big willy out scouring the gay bars of Barcelona for some other red-haired tourist to replace me. I wonder if the Marigolds are still in use these days or perhaps, with the more widespread use of dish-washers, they've lost something of their erotic charge.

Despite these weeks of wild success in Barcelona, I was still riddled with insecurities and truly believed I was ugly. Yet when I look at old pictures from those days, I realise how pretty I actually was. Maybe it was the lingering trauma of my break-up with Lee which had knocked my sense of self-worth for six. So many times in my head, I replayed that awful night at the Boy George concert when he'd said, so coldly, that he didn't love me anymore.

Since then, I'd only had two brief flings of no importance. The 'wham, bam, I'll give you a ring sometime' sort of thing. I deeply missed having real affection and a special someone in my life, so I decided to answer a few of what were then called 'lonely hearts' adverts in the gay magazines. These adverts now seem like dinosaurs from the past but, before the days of Tinder, Grindr and dating apps on phones, those funny little ads were a lifeline to many. A way of meeting people who were perhaps not on the gay scene or lived out of town and a couple of letters or phone calls exchanged prior to meeting in person was a good way of sorting out the wheat from the chaff, the weirdos from the possibilities. By today's standards, it was all very long-winded, but the norm at the time.

These ads often painted tempting pictures that were very far from the truth. 'Hunky' could mean that not even a gastric band operation would remove the 10 stone he needed to shed. 'Often in London' could mean he lived most of the time in Shetland. 'Not out' could be translated as a wife, three kids and a golden retriever. You get the picture. So when I answered an ad from a man in Oxford who described himself as 'tall, masculine and handsome with Latin looks', I sent him a note, a snapshot and half-forgot about it. So I was surprised to receive a letter back with a picture of a truly gorgeous man.

His name was Martin. He'd once been a racing driver but now, somewhat less glamorously, drove lorries instead. We spoke on the phone a few times and he seemed nice; quiet and shy, well-mannered and very complimentary about my picture. We met and it went well. For the next year, we would see each other almost every weekend. He'd come to stay in Catford or I'd go to Oxford. At first it was great fun. He told me he was falling in love with me, just as Lee had once done. I lied and said the same, but it wasn't true. I'd only 'fallen in like' and, as the months rolled by, I realised that, Latin looks or not, we had nothing at all in common, except both being lonely and wanting to find a Mister Right. Martin played football for his local amateur team so, having zero interest in football, I'd go and watch from the warmth of his car, reading the Sunday papers or just falling asleep. Every time he scored a goal, he'd look over at me for congratulation, but my head would be in the news or lolling on my chest. It was a lesson learnt. A relationship that works in the sack isn't enough, it's also got to work with your clothes on. A meeting of bodies is exciting, but if there isn't also a meeting of minds, it's ultimately a dead duck.

I finally broke things off, though we stayed friends. So I was back on my own; something I was more and more used to. On the surface, I was a crazy, hedonistic club kid, but inside I just wanted what most people do, whether they'd admit it or not. A loving relationship with someone who cared about me and to whom I could reciprocate that feeling.

Apart from my little jaunts to Dietmar's brothel, I was still gainfully employed in my caring job. I was very fond of clients like Billy, but 'personal' care was tough work and burned you out. At the same time, my addiction to clubbing had become ever stronger and my face was getting known around town. I'd even been offered hosting and promotion jobs in various venues, but could never commit to it because of my day job, which I wasn't in a financial position to give up. Still, I yearned for a change. There are only so many old blokes' bottoms you want to wipe in one lifetime.

And by a little miracle, that change came to me out of the blue, as these things often do. Something that would come to mean so much more to me than just a job. Something that would make me grow up emotionally.

For the first time in my young life, I would have to look death in the face and appreciate just how short and fragile life could be. And it would mark me forever.

t was a beautiful building, just off Ladbroke Grove in Notting Hill. Converted from an old school, it was light, airy, modern and stylish. With contemporary art on the walls, comfy sofas and big potted plants, it might have been the reception of some trendy boutique hotel. But it wasn't. It was a sanctuary for people dealing with one of the worst crises that had hit the world in the twentieth century. It was a place filled with sadness, struggle, death and grief. But at the same time, a place of tenderness, love and even laughter. There had never been anywhere like it before and probably never will be again. Its name was London Lighthouse.

It was the early Nineties, the height of the HIV/AIDS pandemic. Many lives were being upturned, shattered and lost. HIV hit men, women and children all over the world, regardless of age, ethnicity or sexuality but, in the popular mind and certainly in the popular press, it was seen as the 'gay plague.' So, for gay men in particular, it was a frightening time. Not simply because of the incurable disease itself, but because of the discrimination, ostracism and loneliness it often brought in its wake. As its name suggests, London Lighthouse existed to be a beacon of hope in these uniquely dark times. It was, quite simply, a miraculous place.

A job had come up in its Centre Support Services team and a friend who worked there encouraged me to apply. I worried that my bizarre appearance might put them off, but she assured me that my appearance was utterly irrelevant. Lighthouse, she said, wasn't Boots or Selfridges. I got the job.

Being at London Lighthouse was perhaps the most profound and worthwhile experience of my working life. It opened my immature, blinkered eyes to the reality of what was happening around me. Real life was about far more serious things than going to clubs, buying designer clothes and making up my face. Real life was about so many brave souls, most of them young, struggling to cope with an incurable virus which would probably kill them decades before their time. And it was about the massive effort mobilised by others to help and support them in that fight to the death.

Sadly, it was also a fight against ignorance and bigotry, often stoked by the calculated nastiness of Britain's virulently homophobic right-wing media. For nearly a decade, people had been spoon-fed lies and ignorant rumour by those with a prejudiced agenda. Mrs Thatcher had also introduced the despised Section 28, which demonised gay people still further by making it against the law to teach the truths that might 'promote' homosexuality. She saw the explanation of simple facts as proselytising for what she saw as deviance. When the Lighthouse project had first been revealed, there had been local outrage and ferocious opposition. At angry public meetings, local residents worried that property values would drop and that all sorts of 'low life' would blight their streets. Compassion seemed to be in very short supply. Anyone who got AIDS had brought it on themselves, the dirty buggers.

When I walked into London Lighthouse on my first day, I felt at once that I had connected with something that really mattered. This would be work that I could genuinely care about. On a personal level, I had never so far lost anyone to AIDS. I knew *of* lots of people who had died, but my own back catalogue of grief was pretty limited. But it was soon to be filled to overflowing.

Lighthouse ran a very tight ship and you had to know what you were doing, so my first month was mostly taken up with training. I needed to have a good knowledge of all the many services available at Lighthouse (and in the UK generally) and at least some understanding of the virus and the ways in which it could impact on people's lives. I soon realised the job wasn't for the faint-hearted; this was serious stuff.

My job was to be based around the reception and 'drop in' area of the building. The reception desk was the first point of contact for both service users and other visitors. We also handled the switchboard, directing calls to the right person as quickly as possible. In an organisation with over 250 paid employees and 500 volunteers, this was no small task. The phones rang constantly. People needed fast and efficient service and that's what I had to give them. Often callers were distressed or anxious and there wasn't room for error.

I was also part of the team that provided 'drop-in' services, such as our thrice-weekly tea parties, held to help limit people's isolation, give them somewhere to hang out and meet others facing the same situation. A place where their voices were heard and where what they had to say mattered. A sanctuary from the outside world, which didn't always feel either safe or supportive.

In time, I'd also organise excursions to give people a change of scene and even the odd bit of in-house entertainment. But probably my most valuable role was simply in being the first face encountered by those who'd recently been diagnosed with the virus and who were coming to Lighthouse for the first time. Dipping their toes into this new and frightening world of which their diagnosis had just made them citizens. From my seat at the reception desk, I'd look out the window and see them approaching our front door. I tried to imagine what I'd feel like if it were me. So to each new, nervous face, I gave a big smile, a cheery welcome and a clear explanation of the many ways in which Lighthouse could help them. Above all, I tried to make them feel that they weren't alone with this nightmare from which there was no waking-up.

In those anxious expressions, I saw young people just like me, just like my friends. And when the families of those being cared for in our residential unit, often very sick or dying, came through the front door, I'd see in their heartbroken, disbelieving faces, the faces of my own Mom and Dad.

It helped that I was naturally gregarious and even a bit of a chatterbox, so it was second nature to me to talk to people. That attribute backed up with the rigorous training and support Lighthouse gave me, helped me to be good at my job. I was so proud of what we did and knew how very important it was.

Of course, the day inevitably came when the whole thing got very personal.

'Where's Michael?' I said one day when I arrived for work and looked around for one of my favourite colleagues.

'He's in the Middlesex Hospital,' sighed somebody. 'Not at all well.'

'But I was chatting to him yesterday,' I replied. 'He was laughing and joking as usual. What's happened?'

'Ah well, that's the way it goes,' sighed my colleague, who'd seen a lot more of it than I had.

And that was indeed the way it went. I'd no idea that Michael even had the virus as there was a 'don't ask' policy. People could live with the virus for a considerable time, coping with the various infections which arose from it, then bouncing back for a time. But then, almost out of the blue, they'd be struck down by something really fierce that they couldn't fight off. This was years before today's medications and when the doctor's diagnosis went from HIV Positive to that of full-blown AIDS, you knew you had to start saying your goodbyes. After a week or so in hospital, Michael came back to Lighthouse; not to his seat beside me on reception but to the residential unit where the kindness and help he'd given to so many others was now returned to him in full.

Up on the top floor of Lighthouse, the residential unit was where people could come for palliative care, to rest after time in hospital and get over a particular bout of illness. It was the only part of the building to which the word 'hospice' could be applied; otherwise it wasn't a term much used because the work of Lighthouse was far more wide-ranging than that one narrow definition suggested. The privacy of the top floor was firmly guarded. On the odd occasions when an errand took me up there, what you noticed was the intensity of the silence, in sharp contrast to the other floors which were often quite buzzy. On that top floor, desperately sad though it was, the atmosphere of loving care which permeated all of Lighthouse was at its strongest and most inspiring.

Within weeks, the happy-go-lucky Michael went from being an attractive man in his twenties to a skeletal and very sick guy. I was shocked at the change in him but, by now, I'd learned never to let that show to anyone who was terminally ill at Lighthouse. Inside you though, it was always another little stab to the heart. Nothing more could be done for Michael, apart from to make him as comfortable as possible and wrap him in love. One day, when I came into work, a candle was lit on the reception desk.

'Michael?' I asked somebody at once.

'Afraid so.'

Whenever any service user of Lighthouse died, whether in the building or in a hospital, a candle was lit with a name card beside it. Sometimes, there was just the one, sometimes it was like a Buddhist shrine. So we wrote Michael messages of love in the Remembrance Book that was kept in the Quiet Room, a space put aside for people to pray or just to remember those who'd died. We went to his funeral and cried and said goodbye.

Too many candles, too many funerals, too many lost lives, too many of them young.

One day, a pair of beautiful young men with Manchester accents came up to the desk and asked for more information. I gave them the guided tour and a run-down of what we offered. One was much chattier than the other, who was very sad and withdrawn, and I assumed he'd recently been diagnosed. The chatty one was called David like me, though everyone called him Dids; the quiet one was Peter. Dids asked me if he could return the following day for another chat and when he did, it turned out it was he who was HIV Positive. The look of fear I'd seen in Peter's eyes had been for Dids, not for himself.

I could hardly believe it; Dids was so vital and brimming with life. A young, handsome man, tall and well-built with light blue eyes and long dark eye lashes. He wore tight jeans and checked shirts with braces and a baseball cap. He also had lots of beautifully applied tattoos which he was proud to show off at any opportunity. In short, a man who should've had the rest of his life to look forward to, but who was instead reaching out to a stranger like me for help at his darkest moment.

He told me some of his story. He'd never been particularly promiscuous, though by now we all knew you only had to be unlucky once. He'd been going out with Peter for a couple of years before they'd moved down to London together. They'd both decided to take a test but, because they were both totally healthy, never imagined either of them would be positive. Peter wasn't, Dids was.

'But I'm feeling great,' he said. 'I'm going to the gym. I've got bags of energy. I'm really hopeful I can survive this thing. I'm not done for yet.'

I prayed that he would survive, but knew in my heart the odds were against him. The power of positive thinking rarely conquered this bloody awful virus. But in these grim circumstances, an extraordinary friendship developed between Dids and me. He'd come in to see me every day for hours at a time. He seemed to understand me and to enjoy my company as much as I came to adore his. Gradually we opened up to each other, telling the tales of our different lives. As I rarely did to anyone, I shared the pain of being the boy who sat by the window. I told him of Miss Pinchface and Mr Bullock, but also about Alain and the nudist beach at Brighton, about Lee and my damaged heart, about my obsession with the clothes and the make-up and the freaky clubs. And Dids told me of his own stories; the good and the bad, the hopes and the dreams for the future which now had an unspoken question-mark looming over them. In no time, we became each other's emotional support.

He applied for and got a job in the beautiful Lighthouse café, which meant we were able to spend even more time together. He began to come with me to the clubs and loved that I was doing drag. As he was always very affectionate to me in public, most people assumed we were a couple, but that wasn't true. There was no sexual dimension whatsoever to our friendship. Peter knew that and never seemed threatened by the closeness of my relationship with his partner. Peter was never left out or not invited anywhere we went. I think he understood that it was good for Dids to have fun and be taken out of himself by a mad thing like me. But it was Peter who was his ultimate rock. I knew where the boundaries lay and never crossed them.

Dids soon got to know my chums from Brum like Curtain Mark and Stan. We all went on holiday together and became very close. For my birthday one year, Dids bought me a beautiful gold velvet suit from Westwood that cost £800. I still have it to this day and I intend it to go into my coffin with me when I leave this mortal coil. I want to look my best in case I'm ever exhumed.

Despite all the good times, there was obviously a huge shadow over the lives of Dids and Peter. Sadly, but maybe not surprisingly, this caused some tensions between them and they eventually decided to take a break from each other.

Dids moved into a council flat in the basement of an old house in King's Cross and asked me if I'd like to live there too. It was a perfect arrangement for us both. The flat was so central that cabs to and from the clubs were cheap. As Dids was now on disability benefits, I could be classified as his carer and therefore have no rent to pay. Amid the bustle of King's Cross, the little flat soon became a warm and welcoming sanctuary. Thirty years on, I still live there. It has seen many changes and several other flatmates, but I intend to stay there forever, or until I win The Lottery and can move to Belgravia or Beverly Hills. It holds so many memories, mostly good ones, and especially of Dids. Even now, whenever I put the key in the door, his face flashes through my mind. He haunts the place and I'm so pleased that he's still around.

One morning at Lighthouse, I was on the early shift at reception, feeling like shit, my eye make-up still on from the night before. It was only eight and nothing much happened till the staff arrived at nine, so I had my feet up, drinking a coffee and reading *Mapp & Lucia* by E.F. Benson. If you're gay, you've really got to read at least one M&L novel, if only because it contains, in the character of Georgie Pillson, one of the most memorable screaming queens in popular literature. If somebody tells me they don't like M&L, I begin to doubt if they're really gay. Like not liking Judy Garland or the opera.

I was deep into the doings of Tilling-on-Sea when the bell rang for admittance to the car park. Assuming it was a delivery, I buzzed open the gates. A black car drove in and parked in one of the bays reserved for ambulances. It was a woman at the wheel. Irritably, I banged on the window and gesticulated that she needed to move it, which she then did. Stupid cow, I muttered under my breath and went back to Tilling-on-Sea. A minute or two passed and when I heard somebody enter the building, I looked up to find none other than the Princess of Wales standing in front of me. Christ.

'I'm really sorry,' she said. 'Parking in the wrong space. Idiotic.'

She was dressed very casually but looked quite beautiful, even at this hour of the morning. I was like a rabbit in the headlights. I just sat and stared and muttered that it was okay. I didn't know what to say or where to look. I didn't even stand up. Eventually I managed to ask if she wanted me to ring upstairs to the residential unit and tell them that she was coming up.

'If you wouldn't mind,' she said.

When I called upstairs, I felt totally lost as to how to announce her.

'A lady is here to see you.' I said to the nurse on the other end. 'Can I send her up?'

'Who's the lady?' said the nurse. There were ferocious privacy protocols around anyone going up to the unit.

For some reason, I couldn't bring myself to say 'Princess Diana'. God knows why. All I could really think about was that I wished I'd had my hair done properly which, at that time, was a lime green, spiked Mohican. Not the sort of look you'd find in Kensington Palace.

'A special visitor,' I said to the nurse.

'Yes, but *who is it?*' replied the nurse, a bit irritable now.

I was obviously stumbling, but the princess reached out to touch my hand.

'Just tell them it's Diana, it's okay.'

This kindness confused me even more and for some reason I'll never fathom I said,

'It's Lady Diana'.

'Ooh, nobody's called me that for years,' giggled the princess. 'It's just Diana these days.'

By this point, her marriage to Prince Charles was over and The Queen had recently stripped her of the title of 'Royal Highness'. But that had done nothing to diminish her role as the most famous woman on the planet. People were literally obsessed with her. Everything she wore was copied, her every move made front page headlines. She had the precious gift of being warm, friendly and able to show emotion which the Royal Family were not exactly famous for. They tended to be stiff as statues whilst Diana was just the opposite. Real. One of us. And that's why she was so loved.

She was certainly loved at London Lighthouse. She'd made it her goal to help shatter the myths around transmission of the virus and to do whatever she could to help in this dreadful crisis. That help was gratefully received. She'd often arrive in secret, just as she did that morning, and be whisked up to the residential unit where she'd chat and drink tea with the service users, many of them extremely sick or close to death. She'd also give support and encouragement to the staff, who were having to deal with many challenges, both physical and emotional.

Most of us never actually saw her when she visited privately. It was all choreographed to avoid press intrusion and nobody was ever given prior notice of her coming. She came in secret many times. She came simply because she was needed and because she had a big heart.

So I was lucky to have actually encountered her at all. But I was still discombobulated as I escorted her to the lift.

For some reason, I took my book with me. There was quite a long wait for the lift and I couldn't think of a thing to say. Or maybe you had to wait for them to speak to you?

'What are you reading?' she said to fill the silence, so I showed her the book. 'Oh yes, I've read that. It's *very* camp isn't it?'

I was amazed that a real-life princess actually knew what 'camp' was. She took the book from my hands and only then did I realise that I'd left the bookmark in, which was poking out of the top. A huge cardboard cut-out of a penis.

'Oh, I love your bookmark!' she said.

When the lift came, I held open the door for her.

'Someone will be waiting for you at the top, your Royal Highness,' I said, consciously using the title taken from her in such a mean-spirited way. As her brother would famously say at her funeral, she needed no royal title to impress the world.

When she left again a few hours later, she waved goodbye to me through the window of reception. A month or so later, she came again on an 'official' visit, which was a very different ball game. This time, she was to give an important speech, which would be covered and photographed by the national and international press. The police had closed the road and literally thousands of people had come to see 'The People's Princess' doing what she did best. There was screaming and cheering as she arrived, this time in a chauffeur-driven car. The cameras went crazy. It was total mayhem and almost scary to be part of. Way beyond anything I'd seen as a kid when I waved my little flag at The Queen when she visited Walsall. It struck home to me how much Diana meant to people and how much of an impact her support for HIV/AIDS was having on society. She was a beautiful lady, both in body and spirit. What an amazing queen she would have made. What a loss.

Diana wasn't the only celebrity who visited London Lighthouse. Elizabeth Taylor, who'd done so much for AIDS charities in America came to see our state-of-the-art centre. And Sir Elton John who'd raised vast funding in the UK. Princess Margaret too, who'd been an official patron of Lighthouse, the film star Julie Christie and plenty more. But there was nobody quite like Lady Di for sitting on somebody's bed, holding their hands and having a natter. Not just because she was a princess, though of course that was an extra thrill, but because she was kind and humble and showed that she cared. As Elton sang that sad day in the Abbey, her candle burned out long before her legend ever did. Sentimental maybe but, to everyone at Lighthouse, it was bang on.

As the treatments for HIV gradually came on stream in the late Nineties and into the new century, the illness became something people lived with rather than died from. The need for the residential unit gradually disappeared and, bit by bit, the services of Lighthouse were wound down. Ultimately, the costs of running the building were too great and, to the distress of many people, it was sold and is now, bizarrely, a museum of brands (whatever that is). This sale caused considerable distress at the time, not least because the ashes of many people were buried in the beautiful gardens. Luckily, this has been respected and the garden is still cared for and accessible to anyone who wants to go there.

I was to work at Lighthouse for nearly eight years. It was a long haul and eventually I burnt out, as many people did. But what an honour to have been part of that unique and remarkable place. It changed me forever. It made me grow up.

The Pushca Posse

It's time to talk about 'Dusty O'.

Dusty, the drag queen who would take over my life for the next 25 years. Dusty who would make me famous, even if mostly within London's clubland. Dusty who'd make me lots of money and give me the entree to a glamorous life, far removed from the workaday suburbs of Birmingham. Dusty who, for a time at least, all the punters loved. Dusty who I would love too but also sometimes hate, often at the same time. Dusty who was so much more than a frock, a wig and lots of make-up. Dusty who was, in part at least, me.

The future 'Queen of Soho', that work of art, that epitome of 'fashion drag', was born in a very modest way in the flat in Catford to which I'd moved with my friend Hayden. Her first 'gowns' were simple, handmade creations, though very sparkly and feathery. I cringe when I look at those pictures now. Not quite like Cinderella before the Fairy Godmother got to her, but you get the picture.

Her full name back then was Dusty St. Moritz. I called her Dusty because I was a huge fan of Miss Springfield and her iconic black eyeshadow – unlike the Mummies, she was my kind of lesbian. And St Moritz after the posh fags I liked to smoke (I'd never been a Woodbine or a Players No. 6 girl. I was better than that).

This was what I now think of as my 'baby drag' period. My first faltering steps in the exquisite art of dressing-up. As the Eighties morphed into the Nineties, drag had become incredibly popular on the gay scene. Ru Paul had her huge hit record *Super Model*. Boy George dragged up for a video, though I'm not sure anyone noticed, because he didn't look that different from how he usually did. Suddenly everyone was doing it. Drag was no longer seen as a bit naff or something you just saw in dingy pubs that smelt of stale beer and grubby toilets. Dressing-up was back in vogue, injected with the fresh vitality of a new generation.

Maybe that was a reflection of the wider mood. Mrs Thatcher, that witch on a broomstick, was soon to be swept from power by her own ruthless party and the 'nasty' years seemed to be coming to an end both politically and socially. Though the IRA was still committing its acts of violence, unemployment was drastically down and the country felt on the cusp of something better. Out with the old and in with the new. I was determined to be part of the latter category.

In the years I worked at London Lighthouse, I was continuing my exploration of London's club scene. Obviously, the contrast between the two worlds was spectacular and maybe that fuelled my desire for that latter. After a tough day at work, at the cliff face of life and death, mindless frivolity was the perfect antidote. Yet my interest in these things was never really mindless. I took them very seriously indeed. The transformative power of make-up and high-end clothes still obsessed and fascinated me.

On these outings into clubland, people began to take more notice of me and I was often asked my name. As David didn't quite match the Westwood-clad vision of faux femininity, I started to use Dusty. One night, I was introduced to 'Mamma Yvette', the then-reigning Queen of London nightlife, the drag host and doyenne of The Fridge in Brixton, a massively popular gay venue. 'Mamma Yvette' said I looked great and that she might have a job coming up soon as a 'door whore', the customary name for working at the entrance to a club, checking tickets and generally welcoming people in. So I gave her my phone number on a scrap of paper, writing 'Dusty' with a heart symbol after it But Yvette couldn't see too well without her specs, so I was suddenly christened 'Dusty O' and that's how I got my drag name. Later on, the name would evolve further, growing into 'The Very Miss Dusty O'. I'm not sure I remember why.

It was at London Lighthouse that I became friends with a man who'd have a massive influence on me and my future on the club scene. Philip Stevens ran the stylish café and his catering pedigree was impressive, having worked for the famous hotelier Anouska Hempel at Brown's Hotel. He was 10 years older than me, well educated, well-spoken. He dressed in Westwood and Gaultier and had style and swagger in spades, entering a room as if he were on a catwalk. He was also sharp-tongued, a dangerous gossip and people tended to either like or loathe him.

But he seemed interested in the new curiosity who was working on reception and we formed a close bond, chatting for hours in the café; me like a sponge soaking up his instructions on things I'd not previously cared a jot about. Things such as social etiquette, where to shop, the clubs to be seen in. All very fake and shallow, but great fun and an antidote to the challenging stuff going on all around us. I suppose he became my Svengali, but I was a very willing Trilby.

Arguably the most glamorous and exclusive club night in London at that time was called *Pushca*, held once a month, the creation of a couple of very cool metropolitans called Debbie and Rick Ramswell. These were very expensive rave parties, held in some unusual venue with no money spared in dressing it up to match whatever the theme that month. The difference with *Pushca* was the exceptionally high standard to which every aspect of the event was done and the calibre of the people working to make it the wild success which it had soon become. The entrance fee was high, but a couple of thousand people rushed to pay the price every month, so *Pushca* was a financial success too. Philip, my Svengali who seemed to know everyone in town, showed them some pics of me in drag as Dusty and I was hired as a 'door whore' (though since *Pushca* was far too posh to use a term like that, it was probably something like 'Welcome Coordinator'). The job was easy and though the money was rubbish, it was a free night out and somewhere very 'happening'. It was the start of my club career. Dusty now lived and breathed. In a million years, I'd never have imagined how long her life would be.

'It's all right luv, we'll look after you,' the bouncer said. 'You just feel those biceps.'

Standing in drag in a club doorway in the early hours of the morning wasn't always the safest thing to do. Those 40 kids on the rough estate in Brum who'd pursued me and my friends, threatening and insulting us, were still lodged in my memory. Worse, I'd been beaten up quite badly when, for a short time, I'd lived in a Brixton flat where the neighbours took a similar dislike to having a bunch of drag queens living in their macho midst. Throughout my life, I'd always have to be aware of the impact of my appearance on other people. It was like two sides of a coin. On the one side, that appearance would bring me admiration, plaudits, a measure of fame and a decent income. On the other, it could release the potential for violent aggression – sometimes life-threatening – in some people who felt threatened by difference in a way they could not articulate and so responded with their fists instead. This dichotomy was always to be a basic fact of my existence and had to be taken seriously. When I didn't, when I got careless, there was usually a price to pay.

So having a couple of gorillas guarding me at the door was always very reassuring. If any of the punters gave me any lip, they'd not be let in. The sight of a grumpy brick shithouse dressed in an M&S suit and tie, was usually enough to silence most troublemakers.

Working at *Pushca* for a few months had got me noticed. Another club promoter hired me to do the same work at a straight venue in Mayfair and my income got a very healthy shot in the arm. For once, I didn't have to worry too much about my credit card. I certainly didn't need to toss anyone off wearing Marigold gloves. Unfortunately, even if you take the boy out of Westwood, you can't necessarily take Westwood out of the boy. Every extra penny I earned would go back into the pot to purchase more clothes, wigs, make-up. I had a horror of becoming the person who 'always wears *that*', even if 'that' had cost a month of most people's wages. The more I went out, the more important this became. The pursuit of an image that was always fresh, new and flawless was to become my trademark and the reason why many promoters would consistently employ me in the years to come. In my eyes, this wasn't just indulgence, this was a business plan.

A quick word here about the old dear who's had such a vast importance in my life. Right up there with Mom, Nana Edna and Mrs Wall. Dame Vivienne Isabel Westwood DBE. From the moment I first discovered her wonderful designs, I've loved everything she ever created. La Westwood was the first designer to emerge from club culture as opposed to the marbled halls of Parisian *haute couture*. Along with Malcolm McLaren, she was the mother of the punk scene, in which fashion, design and music all intersectioned in a fresh, original, even aggressive way. The long-established, snooty fashion houses like Chanel and Dior didn't know what had hit them. Vivienne Westwood was suddenly where it was at and I became her dedicated follower. I still am. Over the years, I've blown money on Viv in the way that others do on cocaine, the horses or high-class hookers and never regretted a single penny. As I've already mentioned, I'm going to be buried in Westwood. There's simply no other way to go. A shroud in a class of its own.

Meanwhile, the *Pushca* people decided to open a new weekly night in the West End to be held at the ultra-cool Viper Room, co-owned by the actor Johnny Depp. This one was to be called *Bambina*. I'd be the door whore and Svengali Philip would be taking care of the guest-list. It was only a small venue in club terms, holding about 400 punters, but definitely big in snob appeal. People queued round the block, trying to get past Philip who had extremely high aesthetic standards and absolutely no qualms about turning more people away than he let in. Like the Emperor Nero at the Colosseum, he had the power of life or death. Thumbs up or, more often, thumbs down. Sometimes my heart ached for them as Philip blocked them and their little painted faces fell. I used to wonder how many of his style rejects would need years of therapy for low self-esteem.

Bambina attracted high-end fashion types, media people, drag queens and those club kids pathetically desperate to be noticed. I was in my element. I was hosting The Party in town and suddenly became The Person to know. It was heady stuff. Everything I thought I wanted at the time.

More than once, I asked myself what Mom would have thought. But then she lived in another world with no connection to this one. Or so I thought.

'You've got to be joking,' she said when I called her up. 'You want me to do *what?*'

'It'd be fun,' I replied. 'Getting your face in the papers.'

'It might be your idea of fun, but it certainly isn't mine,' she said and the phone slammed down.

As *Bambina* was a club crammed with drag queens, *The Sun* newspaper had approached Debbie and Rick Ramswell about finding participants for a planned feature. Christ knows what twisted mind had dreamed this piece up, which was to be about drag queens and their mothers. Their *mothers!* Debbie and Rick thought it would be good both for me and the club's profile, but they'd not met Jean Hodge, who didn't give a shit about the club but who did give one about the neighbours back home. I was a bit disappointed, as it might have been a further signal of her acceptance of me and my way of life. But though we'd made some progress in that direction, this was clearly a step too far. My Mom would sooner have been on Page Three with her tits out, than on Page Eight with a drag queen son.

But I was buggered if I was going to let this chance of 15 minutes of fame slip away, so I had the wheeze of asking Rick's mum if she'd pretend to be my loving, totally accepting mother and, game for a laugh, she turned up on the shoot and we told the reporter a pack of black lies about our fabulous imaginary relationship.

'David does all my make-up, don't you dear?' she coo-ed into the tape machine. 'What he doesn't know about foundation isn't worth knowing.'

'I've taken 10 years off this woman,' I replied. 'Before I got my hands on her, she looked like Hilda Ogden.'

'He chooses all my outfits now,' my 'Mum' chipped in. 'Don't you dear?'

'You just needed to know there was life beyond Dorothy Perkins,' I bitched back.

'Oh, isn't he a scream?' she asked the reporter.

And so on. To my absolute delight, we ended up on the cover of *The Sun's* free magazine, much to the absolute fury of my own mother. Not that I'd dumped her for a stand-in, but that the neighbours would see her drag queen son on every newsstand in Birmingham, not to mention nearly five million readers from John O'Groats to Land's End. I didn't give a toss. It was my first taste of notoriety and I bloody *loved* it.

Back then, there was a wide range of free gay magazines and papers available in most gay bars and clubs. In those pre-internet days, they were of the utmost importance if you wanted to promote your name and your club. The biggest of these was *BOYZ* with a distribution of a hundred thousand copies every week. On the back of my new-found fame in The Sun, Svengali Philip persuaded them to do a big fashion feature starring me and styled by himself. Philip had connections everywhere, including at Jean Paul Gaultier and fixed the loan of some gorgeous outfits from their latest collection. It was decided that some 'eye candy' was needed alongside me, so I modelled them with my old friend Stan, now spending more time in the gym than on his make-up and a stunning Mexican called Carlos. They had the name 'Dusty' written in lipstick all over their hairy arms. The pictures came out beautifully and *BOYZ* made me their 'cover girl' alongside the three-page feature. My clubland profile rocketed and the phone rang with all sorts of offers. Dusty was starting to go places.

One of these offers was an interview with another gay mag in which I talked about my time with the Marigold gloves in Barcelona. Mistake. At this point, I was still juggling this glam stuff with my day job at London Lighthouse and my brothel revelation caused consternation from certain people there. Not quite the image they wanted to promote, they sniffed. Philip flew to my defence, reminding them that Lighthouse was supposed to be an equal opportunities employer and that no judgements should be made about people's past lives as long as they did their job well. As I did my job very well, and people knew it, that little storm in a teacup was dealt with pretty quickly. But even a place as wonderful as Lighthouse harboured a few 'tossers'.

* * *

'Come on, pretty thing. Get your ass up here,' said Grace Jones.

As the TV chat-show host Russell Harty had famously found out when she'd boxed his ears on live TV, Grace could be a bit scary, so when she ordered you to get your ass up there, you got it up there.

'There' was on top of the bar in the V.I.P. room at *Bambina,* where our Gracie was dancing like a dervish and now demanded a partner. It was pretty sexy stuff of course and I suppose a straight man might have got a stiffy, but I was merely dazzled – though by this time, I was almost blasé about all the celebrities who now boogied into my orbit.

After those spreads in the gay mags, Dusty had really emerged into the spotlight. Invitations to parties, invitations to fashion shows and the openings of exhibitions. It was a scene where there was an endless hunger for new faces and Dusty was suddenly flavour of the month. However, to many of the old guard on the club scene, I noticed that I'd become something of a threat, having come from nowhere so quickly and knocked a few of them off their wobbly pedestals. It was that *All About Eve* scenario. They were the ageing 'Margo Channings' and I was 'Eve Harrington'. Never did I imagine that one day in the future, the roles would be reversed.

Then came the night I found myself catapulted into an unexpected new side to my career in clubland. The DJ who played in the V.I.P. room at *Bambina* didn't turn up and, as I lived nearest, I was sent in a cab home to pick up my record collection and step into the breach. After about three minutes of rudimentary instruction on how to use the record decks, I gave it a go. I decided to play exactly what I'd like to hear myself and within minutes the room was crammed with dancing queens bopping to my collection of Seventies and Eighties classics, plus a bit of Bassey and even a Danny La Rue track. Whenever I screwed up mechanically, the punters just cheered and whistled. The regular DJ was fired and I took over the decks in the now re-christened 'Dusty's Room'.

Suddenly, totally untrained and almost incompetent, I was a DJ in London's coolest venue. Eventually, this new string to my bow would take me not just into every big club in the country, but around the world. Most of the well-known club DJs of that time, masters of the art of mixing, were horrified that this dragged-up creature, who didn't give a fuck about any of that, was being touted as the next big thing.

Apart from Grace Jones up on the bar, I did the grind with Kylie on the dance floor and hung out with Debbie Harry, Cyndi Lauper, Pamela Anderson and The Pet Shop Boys. By now, I was most definitely a *West End Girl* and a very long way from Walsall. Maybe the biggest thrill was the night I met the incomparable Mr Pete Burns of the band Dead or Alive, who had been my icon for years, right up there on the bedroom wall beside my beloved Boy George.

'Have you seen La Toyah?' Pete said, coming up to me at the bar. 'Was supposed to be meeting her here.'

'La Toyah who?' I said, as if I didn't know.

'How many fucking La Toyahs are there?' said Pete quite reasonably.

I never knew if this was true or not. Certainly, Miss Jackson never turned up. But anything was possible with Pete Burns, who said what he wanted when he wanted and, if he believed it to be true, then it kind of was, to him at least. If he'd have told me he was meeting The Queen Mother here, then he'd probably have been quite sincere.

That night, Pete was wearing a jet-black Cleopatra wig, which made him look just like Elizabeth Taylor entering Rome in the movie. In those days, Pete was arguably just as beautiful. He was also charming and intoxicating and seemed to have taken to me, a brother in androgyny. I offered to get him a drink. He said he'd have what I was having; something lethal called a Jager Bomb shot – an alcoholic 'bomb' of 35 percent-proof spirits dropped into a glass of Red Bull. We did a shot together, then another and another. I soon used up all my complimentary drink tickets and had to beg more from the management. But this was the great Pete Burns after all, and I'd have taken in washing to buy this guy as many drinks as he wanted.

When I had to do my DJ set, he came into the box too and we chatted on while I spun the decks. His favourite subject seemed to be cosmetic surgery.

'Have a look at this,' he said suddenly, pulling back the Cleopatra wig to show me the staples behind his ears, which were pulling the skin back to lift up his face.

For some reason, he swore blind the wig was his own hair, which it palpably wasn't cos I could see the join. But, being Pete, he'd no doubt convinced himself that it really was. God knows what his real hair colour was because Pete probably didn't know. But he was funny and bitchy and I loved him.

The next week he came back to the club and offered to perform for us for £2,000, which he insisted was a lot less than he was used to and that he therefore wouldn't perform his mega-hit *Spin Me Round*. Debbie Ramswell wouldn't wear any of this. £2000 was pretty much the door takings, which paid the wages. And *Spin Me Round* was the only song the customers would really want to hear. After much haggling, Pete agreed to £200 and to include the big hit. I doubt he was remotely bothered about the cash, but just wanted his star status recognised.

A bit more diva-like behaviour followed. Pete now decided he needed to change his outfit and hijacked Stan, my old friend from Brum, as a minder to escort him back to his home in Notting Hill, apparently warning Stan on the way not to steal anything from his house. When they eventually returned to the club, Pete seemed to be wearing pretty much the same outfit and had just backcombed his hair/wig a bit, hopefully without dislodging any staples. The next drama was that he'd broken the kitten heel on one of his boots, so Stan had to be sent out to the late-night corner shop to buy superglue and stick it back on. My other old friend Andrew, a big chap, was recruited as security to escort Pete and prevent anyone touching him as he made his way through the expectant crowd towards the stage.

This surprise personal appearance by a big star went down a storm, though Pete hadn't finished toying with us yet. After a couple of songs, he stopped in mid-flow and demanded his 200 quid before he'd carry on. Debbie made a frantic dash for the till. Pete rolled up the bank notes and stuffed them in his boot before restarting the show. In the end though, the performer in him took over and he delivered far more than just those three songs. At the end, he just walked off the stage and vanished into the night without saying goodbye to any of us. I didn't care about the diva stuff. In the end he'd delivered. In the years to come, I'd get to know this enigmatic man better and would continue to worship him, no matter how many wigs he wore or how many staples would be needed to hold up that beautiful face. Pete Burns was the real deal.

That night in the now famous 'Dusty's Room' was memorable for one other reason and one a lot less glamorous. It was the first time I ever tried drugs. I'm sorry to say that, in the excitement of that moment, I took the cocaine that a customer offered me in the toilets. As is usual with coke, I soon wanted more and, as I was now earning quite good money, I could afford to buy the £45 wraps from the dealer who operated from the club. I'm ashamed to confess that I loved it. It let me remain the life and soul of the party for hours on end, which was essentially my job description. For those few short but intense hours, it made me feel the star of the show and a million miles away from the boy with the ginger hair in his hand-knitted jumper, worrying if his Dad was going to come home drunk that night. If only Miss Pinchface could see that boy now. Now he hung out with Pete Burns and danced on a bar-top with Grace Jones. Fuck Miss Pinchface.

By now, I acted and dressed as someone very different from that boy, even someone of a different gender. I was a DJ in the hottest club in the West End of London, mixing with celebrities and fabulous freaks who all thought that Dusty O was the bee's knees. What could possibly go wrong?

But just like the massive, remorseful hangover that very first hit of cocaine gave me, the real world outside the clubland doors had a way of breaking into my magic bubble. And the worst of these instances was about to hit.

Dusty
1/3/94 +
David

David with 'Dids' at London Lighthouse

My friend Dids had started having more serious problems with his health. He was admitted to hospital with one ailment, then released and admitted again a few weeks later with another. It was the usual cycle that I'd witnessed so many times at London Lighthouse and we all knew what it meant. Each time things got a little bit darker and Dids suffered a little bit more. Positive thinking and trips to the gym could only do so much. He'd lost a lot of weight and muscle mass and, as the damn virus got a tighter grip on him, had begun to look very frail. The handsome, fit young guy had begun to fade away before my eyes. Most days he wouldn't leave the sofa. It was pretty obvious that he was feeling terrible, in spite of his brave attempts to hide it from me.

With Dids, bravery was always the operative word, as it was with so many of the very sick people I knew from Lighthouse. The famous definition of the word courage is 'grace under pressure'. And Christ, I witnessed so much grace.

'Wouldn't it be nice to have Peter round?' I said one day.

'Yes,' he replied. 'Yes, it would be nice.'

I knew he'd missed Peter and Peter had missed him just as much. So gradually they started to fix what had gone wrong between them; the bond only fractured but never broken. Poor Peter. I saw in his face the same deep sadness I'd seen so often in the faces of family and friends at Lighthouse. Clinging to the memories of the good times gone by and struggling to picture a world without that person in it. None of us wanted to think about our lives without Dids.

Dids himself was under no illusions anymore. He'd certainly not be one of those who made a pilgrimage to Lourdes for a chat with St. Bernadette or to adopt some bizarre diet as so many did in those days, in the hope of a miracle. Dids knew he had to put his house in order. He'd grown away from his family in Manchester and hadn't seen them for several years, but he contacted them now and his mother and sister came down. As with Peter, whatever the reasons for the estrangement, all that seemed so trivial now, so ridiculously unimportant when there was so little time left to heal the wounds. Ever mindful of what would happen to me when he died, he made me the legal co-tenant of the flat, so that I'd not be out on the street after he'd gone. Typical Dids, thinking of other people when he had every reason to think only of himself.

After one of his regular hospital stays, he decided to go into the Residential Unit at Lighthouse for some aftercare. At least there he'd have constant attention and a bit more company. Peter could visit him there more easily and I'd see him during the day when I was at work. Svengali Philip was kindness itself, organising all his food requirements personally, providing a diet designed to help get his strength back. He also got nonstop attention from the nurses and from his erstwhile colleagues in the café who'd pop up to keep him amused. Amazing, the restorative power of a bit of gossip about the doings of mutual friends. Dids was incredibly popular with everyone and, for a while, rallied a little.

But only a little. When he came home, Peter and I took it in turns to stay with him at night, changing his sheets several times as he suffered from horrendous sweats that literally soaked the bed. Depriving him of the balm of a deep sleep, it was exhausting for him and for us too, but there was nothing in this world we wouldn't have done for him. He was soon in a lot of pain and discomfort, which broke our hearts to witness. Any hopes we'd clung to were long since gone. Gradually his vital organs could take no more and had shut themselves down and he suffered immensely.

Another visitor came to see Dids in his last days in hospital. Somebody he'd heard all about but had never met before. My mother Jean and I were finally enjoying a better relationship now. I'd raved to her so often about my friend and she seemed to understand how much I loved him.

'I'd like to come down and see him,' she said on the phone one day.

'But you never go on the train!' I replied.

For some bizarre reason, Mom had only been on a train twice before in her entire life and then it had been with my Dad. I'm not sure why. Possibly because they rarely left the Midlands and always drove whenever they did. So, getting on a train by herself was a really big deal; like Christopher Columbus setting out to discover America.

'I just want to come,' she said again. 'So I'm coming.'

And she did. She got herself on board a train at Birmingham New Street and came to London on her own. We went to the hospital together.

'Hello Dids love,' she said to him, lying there on his pillows like a ghost; half there, half not. 'I hope you don't mind me dropping in on you without an invite.'

Bless her, she sat there the whole afternoon, held his frail hand, chattering away about fuck-all. It was beautiful to see. Before she left, she gave him a long, gentle hug and was obviously very emotional. I was so very proud of how she'd managed to move forward in her outlook and make some positive changes to how she viewed the world. Now there she was, sitting in an AIDS ward, visiting a dying young man with her cross-dressing son who obviously adored him. It was a million miles away from everything she knew, yet she'd found the courage to show kindness and support to somebody who needed it. Mom had been through so much in her lifetime, so many hard knocks, and she'd become blocked and guarded as a result of all that stuff. But now, she managed to reach out to a stranger and show the very best of herself. On that day, beside Dids' bed, there was no woman on earth I'd rather have had as my mother.

There was another visitor I brought to Dids' bedside during those last days. In recent times, I'd met and got to know Boy George, my great hero. I'll write more about George later, but I want to record here how kind he was to Dids, whom he'd met once in our flat when Dids had given George a tarot card reading, a skill which Dids liked to pretend he possessed. In the years to come, George and I would have more than a few queeny tiffs but, when it really matters, he never lets you down.

The doctors in the Middlesex Hospital hadn't hidden from Dids that, his organs having failed, he was close to the end of his journey. Sunken and shrivelled on his pillows, Dids took it in his stride and stayed calm. He made detailed plans for his funeral so that it would be just as he wanted it. He asked George if he'd sing at his funeral and George of course agreed. Through all of this, I was still working in 'Dusty's Room' at Bambina. The week before he died, Dids asked me to call in at the hospital on Saturday night before going on to the club, which I did with George in attendance.

The two of us must have made quite a sight: me in drag, George in full face make-up and his trademark hat, holding the hands of the ghost on the pillows. The nurses were agog. After we'd gone, Dids told them that his famous friend would be singing at his funeral so they should all get there early to get a decent seat. It was, he said, a great way to ensure a good turnout for his finale.

I thought how hard it must have been for Dids to see George and me, all dolled up, heading out for a night on the town. Bright lights, booze, dancing, the buzz of being young and alive. All the things Dids had once been able to take for granted, but which had now been snatched away. That night, at the club, I probably drank more and partied harder than ever but, in my mind's eye, all I could really see was the face of the half-ghost on the pillows.

The following Saturday evening, the phone rang as I was getting ready for work. It was Peter from the hospital. Dids had just gone, he said. It had been very peaceful and without pain. Peter asked if he could come round. I washed the make-up off my face and arranged another DJ to cover for me at the club. Peter came and we cried and hugged together, still somehow in disbelief that Dids had been stolen from us, even though we'd been preparing ourselves for long enough.

Later that night, alone in the flat that Dids and I had shared, it felt so strange to think that he'd never again come through the front door. I was glad that he was no longer suffering, but so incredibly sad that he was gone from my life. He'd been my beloved best friend. The brother I'd never had. Even a sort of guardian angel, always there for me with help, advice and love whenever my road had been bumpy. He'd put up with my tantrums and silliness and encouraged me to be what I wanted to be. He was totally irreplaceable.

On the reception desk at London Lighthouse, the new candle duly appeared. As usual, both staff and service users walking past would stop and glance at the name card beside it. There were many long sighs and murmurs of 'oh no!'. The funeral was beautiful, exactly as he'd planned it and filled to the rafters with people who had cared about him. Boy George sang a song called *Il Adore* which he'd written about another friend of his who'd died of AIDS. In the gardens at Lighthouse, where Dids and I had spent so many happy hours chatting away, his friends attached loving messages onto balloons and watched them float up into the city sky. He'd wanted just a cardboard coffin, decreeing we should spend the money saved from a wooden one on a party instead.

And so we played his favourite music and remembered him as he would have wished; a wonderful, sensitive man with a huge and loving heart. In a sad twist of fate, it wasn't long after his death that medical advances came onstream which would soon turn this deadly virus into a treatable illness like diabetes. Oh Dids, I often thought, if only you'd been able to hang on a little longer.

Still, all these years later, whenever I hear George's moving song, it's Dids I think of.

'Here in this cold white room
Tied up to these machines
It's hard to imagine him as he used to be
Laughing screaming tumbling queen
Like the most amazing light show you've ever seen
Whirling swirling never blue
How could you go and die?
What a lonely thing to do.'

('Il Adore'. Lyrics Copyright: George Alan O'Dowd, John Themistocleous.

Used by kind permission.)

And now it's time to talk properly about George (sorry it's taken this long, darling).

Back in Walsall, I'd never imagined that I'd ever meet the guy whose pictures were plastered to my bedroom wall, let alone call him a friend. But, as my crazy life unfolded, that's what happened.

The first thing to say about Boy George is that he wasn't/isn't 'normal.' For as long as I can remember, I've had a horror of 'normal'. I'm not exactly sure how to define the word, but I know it when I see it and I still run from it sharpish when I do. So, when I first laid eyes on George Alan O'Dowd I was smitten. That fantastic freak. That massive talent. The Karma Chameleon who changed his image whenever he felt like it, always original, always breaking the mould.

As well as having him up on my wall (plus a few girls like Sade and Bananarama to put my mother off the scent), I pasted his pictures into scrapbooks and ended up with no less than 15 volumes. I played my Culture Club albums over and over till they nearly wore out. Above all perhaps, I wondered how, looking as he did, he went out shopping for a pint of milk and did the 'normal' things. He'd have been murdered if he'd lived near me. I loved his fearless attitude of no apology or explanation. He looked the way he wanted to look and sod off anyone who questioned it. I also loved his intelligence and how he gave short shrift to some moronic interviewer who questioned his sexuality or how 'appropriate' his latest look was. 'Appropriate' wasn't really a word in George's lexicon. Fuck 'appropriate'.

'What d'you like *him* for?' my father once sneered.

'I like him, because he's not like *you!* That's why!' I spat back. Cruel of course, but partially true.

The other pop idols of the time simply passed me by. Stevie Wonder, Paul McCartney, Phil Collins had zero chance of being pinned to my wall. Boy George was the business. Boy George was who I wanted to be. His very existence gave me the courage to take the first steps in achieving that seemingly impossible dream.

Our first real-life encounter was not memorable. Certainly not to George, since he was completely off his face.

It was 1986. He was taking part in the huge anti-apartheid Freedom Festival on Clapham Common. I was just 18 and still living in Birmingham then. Borrowing the fare from my father, my friend Susan and I went on the train. Culture Club had just released a new album and George was sporting yet another new look; less androgynous more 'fashion', shorter hair and less make-up. There were rumours he was on drugs, but I refused to believe my icon had even the smallest flaw. I never doubted for a second that he could walk on water or do that loaves-and-fishes thing.

It was a massive event; a quarter of a million people came to see artists like Sting, Sade, Peter Gabriel and The Communards. Somehow, Susan and I managed to push our way right to the front of the stage. We waited an eternity for George to come on and, when he finally did, we were horrified. He looked emaciated and had some sort of face pack hanging off one side of his face, that looked like candle wax. He sang incoherently and it was all a bit embarrassing. We were shocked, though we still screamed our tits off, much to the annoyance of a gang of girls behind us who were waiting for Maxi Priest. Insults were traded; they dared to call George a washed-up old queen and we called Maxi Priest a waste of space on a good stage. This escalated into a cat fight from which we were rescued by one of the security guards, who hauled us over the railings to save our skin from the band of vicious harpies.

We now found ourselves backstage and suddenly came face to face with George himself, who'd just come off to boos and catcalls from a quarter of a million people. He was in a complete state and obviously very high indeed, but this didn't stop us flinging ourselves at him and gushing.

'You were wonderful. Just amazing. We've come from Birmingham.' All that unctuous fan-crap.

There were cameras everywhere, MTV was filming a behind-the-scenes piece. Maybe that was why, even through the fog of whatever he was on, the performer in George suddenly kicked in. He hugged and kissed us.

'Come with me,' he mumbled, taking my hand. Oh my God. I was holding the hand of my hero.

He stumbled into his trailer and we followed. He could hardly speak and seemed to be falling asleep. I was sitting next to him, half in ecstasy, half in total shock at the state of him. He started signing autographs, but his head fell forward onto the marker pen he was using.

'You got ink marks all over your nose,' I said.

He mumbled something in reply, but I had no idea what it was. At this point his management suddenly arrived like the cavalry and we were all evicted from that trailer in five seconds flat. I managed to hang about long enough to watch a photo line-up of all the star performers. George appeared, threw himself onto the grass and began to roll around like a dog on a beach.

'He's totally fucked,' I heard Sting say to Sade.

George was quickly bundled into a big limo and driven off at lighting speed before he could do his reputation any more harm. Somehow his management kept the press footage off TV and MTV never broadcast the car crash 'interview'. Back in Brum, most people seemed to think I was attention-seeking as usual and making it all up. But the following week '*The Sun*' ran the headline *Boy George has eight weeks to live*, breaking the news of his chronic heroin addiction. At that time, I'd been so naïve, without any experience of drugs, and had just thought he was drunk.

I worshipped him so much that I got really worried. I couldn't bear the thought of my hero in an early grave, turned into one of those gods who died young and were turned into mawkish legends – James Dean, Buddy Holly, Brian Jones etc. I wanted George to go on creating great music, being my inspiration and my guide and never ever being 'normal'. And thank God he did. Somehow, he got on top of his troubles, rose like a phoenix and had a huge No 1 hit the very next year.

I never imagined I'd ever brush against George's world again. But I did when, against all the odds, it became my world too.

'Yeah, I'd love to come over tonight,' she said, 'but can I bring George?'

'George who?' I replied.

'Boy George. He's a singer.'

Bloody hell. Yes please. Amanda Ghost was a friend of Svengali Philip. A would-be singer too, she was loud and brassy with her eye on the social ladder, but she was friendly, good fun and we'd hit it off. I'd asked her over so that Dids could read her tarot cards.

It was mega flap in our flat. I took down all my George memorabilia from the living-room so as not to embarrass either of us. When the doorbell rang, my heart was racing. He was looking fabulous and was so sweet and unpretentious. It can't have been that often that an international superstar found himself in a basement flat in King's Cross, but he never let you feel he was slumming it.

'Love this place,' he said. 'So original.'

By now, it certainly wasn't much like your average council abode. IKEA, Habitat and even John Lewis found no space here. The Very Miss Dusty O, dazzling jewel of London's alternative nightlife, required a far more exotic setting than the bland emporia of Oxford Street could provide. I'd always remembered the exotic abode of my camp mentor Alain back in Solihull and with that as inspiration, I gave Dusty the palace she deserved. A gilded Baroque fantasy, a miniature Versailles just off the Caledonian Road or, as I liked to call it, Liberace on a budget. It wasn't just over the top, it had absolutely no idea where the top was. Eventually it appeared on a Channel 4 documentary called *Britain's Weirdest Council Homes*. I wasn't too keen on that adjective; 'fabulous' would have been better.

Anyway, it was right up George's street. We had a lovely evening with Japanese food shipped in from the local take-away and Dids doing his daft thing with the tarot. As he left, George told me to get his number from Amanda, saying it would be nice to hang out again. I was thrilled and more than a bit starstruck. My teenage idol wanted to hang out with me. OMG. I decided to leave it for a few days, so as not to seem too much like a fan, but the very next afternoon, George called and asked me over to his place for a chat and a cuppa. Never in my life did I spend so little time in getting myself ready. Just as well; if I'd had a week's notice, I'd have spent every minute of it in front of the mirror.

I jumped in a cab and went up to Hampstead. And wow, there it was. The famous mansion I'd seen in *Smash Hits* magazine as a teenager, a vast Gothic fantasy of grey-black stone that sat on the edge of the Heath like a bat with its wings folded. Creepy, fabulous, unforgettable. I felt a bit like Pip in *Great Expectation's* on his first visit to Miss Havisham. As usual, there were a few fans hanging around at the gate, mostly teenage girls. I swanned past them and was buzzed through the gate, trying not to look too cocky. Dream on, girls.

Inside, George's mansion wasn't at all like Miss Havisham's gaff. Quite a few candles admittedly, but no cobwebs or rotting wedding cakes. It was stylish, eclectic, filled with good art and interesting *objets*. George, Amanda and I picked up where we'd left off the night before in King's Cross, nattering away about all sorts of stuff. Sometimes, it's an anti-climax when people meet their heroes. They turn out to have pimples or bad breath, or they're a foot shorter than in their photos, or they're just plain dull and uninteresting, the product of a little bit of talent and a lot of promotion. But the opposite was the case with young Mr O'Dowd. George was exactly the person I'd imagined him to be; funny, intelligent, wildly original, an artist to his fingertips.

On my tour of the house, I'd admired three beautiful Versace make-up brushes with crystal handles kept in his dressing-room. A cut above mine from Boots No.7. As we left with his two dogs to walk me up to the tube station, he had a present for me.

'Here are those brushes you liked,' he said.

'Oh wow, I couldn't possibly...'

'Yes, you could,' he said.

For about a year after that, we saw each other regularly. He took me to the recording studios where he was working with Mica Paris and to several showbusiness events. He loved my drag and encouraged me to get bigger and bolder with my looks. That was wonderful for me. So often in my past, I'd been told to 'tone it down'. My mother of course. People at job interviews and so on. Now, instead of saying 'less, less', here was somebody saying 'more, more.'

When George went to Australia, to perform at the Mardi Gras, he brought me back a huge crown of faux diamonds. Then he asked me to appear in the video for his track *When Will You Learn* in which I wore the crown and he took me to Italy to promote it. It was all heady stuff for the boy from a small Midlands town who'd wondered if his life would ever amount to much.

George was a sweet, generous but also quite demanding friend. When he wanted your company, you jumped to it or got the cold shoulder for a couple of days. Things went very much at his own pace and in his own way. It wasn't meant unkindly; it was just what a star had grown to expect from those around him. When somebody reaches that level of fame, they're surrounded by people wanting a piece of them. The stresses are enormous; creating, performing, promoting, staying at the top of the greasy pole they've worked so hard to climb and which they could so easily slide down again if their star wanes, if fashions change, if fresh new faces appear at their heels. All of which I'd one day discover for myself, albeit at a much less exalted level. So I never minded if George sometimes did the diva thing a bit. Anyway, I reckoned he'd deserved it, after everything he'd done for all us freaky gays in the Seventies and Eighties; all those teenagers with his picture on their walls, so relieved to know that they weren't the only person in the world who was a bit 'different'. George was a brave ground breaker for so many people. Respect.

But though people often try to feed off famous personalities, it can also happen in reverse. George always needed new things and new faces to stimulate his incredibly active mind. He himself had always challenged the norms with his looks and his music, and maybe he recognised a fellow traveller in me. On the same wavelength. With the same attitudes. And so a lasting friendship took root and flourished.

I was always amazed how hard George still worked. By that point, he'd sold 75 million albums, had the Gothic mansion on the hill and more than a few bob in the bank, yet still he worked tirelessly. But then, that was simply what a creative artist had to do. To create and go on creating.

Once he was to appear on a Vanessa Feltz show called *A Day With Vanessa* in which she hung out for the day with a celebrity. George asked me if I'd like to be included in the shoot, so I rushed out and bought a new white faux fur jacket and had a new wig in a huge haystack style with George's crown on top. The filming in George's Gothic mansion was fun, with me pretending to be his housemaid and serving them coffee.

I didn't greatly take to Vanessa, who I overheard being bitchy behind his back, though I suppose that's a bit rich coming from me. Pot and kettle. That evening we all went to a millinery fashion show being hosted by Christopher Biggins, a sort of male version of Miss Feltz, but without the dress sense. Vanessa made a bit of a spectacle of herself by insisting on getting up and modelling a hat, once they'd found one big enough to fit her head. Frankly, I found her terrifying.

'I've just been offered a huge TV show in the States' she whispered to me, as if it were a state secret. 'But my husband said, "Oh Vanessa, how much *more* famous do you really want to be?"'

Not long afterwards, I read in the media that her husband had left her and that she was on the lookout for love. Though I reckon that she'd already found it in her own reflection and no bloke could possibly compete.

On Christmas morning, George called in on his way to his Mum's place in Shooter's Hill to bring me a present. A bright orange Westwood coat. He'd worn it in the video for *The War Song* and, knowing I was a Westwood addict, wanted me to have it. It was a beautiful item but a little too big for me and orange wasn't really my colour (it would have suited Vanessa better). I stored it away like some magnificent treasure. Several years later, when George and I were having one of our periodic tiff-ettes, I sold it to a designer clothes dealer for £800 and bought myself a Westwood sheepskin jacket that actually fitted me.

A decade after that, I sold the sheepskin for £1,000 to the same dealer. That orange coat was the gift that kept on giving.

Dusty Dj-ing at Heaven

he death of my beloved Dids had ushered in another chapter in my life. The pain of his loss had almost broken me and, to numb the grief, I threw myself into nightlife ventures with even greater passion. But whilst it was fine for David Hodge to mourn quietly, the Very Miss Dusty O didn't 'do' sadness or grief. Dusty had to be the life and soul of the party. After all, that was the whole point of her. To hell with reality. Life is a cabaret, old chum.

The first venture looked good on paper. Svengali Philip and I decided we were ready to start our own midweek club night. We'd watched how the *Pushca* and *Bambina* people operated and felt it wasn't exactly rocket science. As usual, we were high on ideas, but low on funds.

We found a chic little club in Mayfair called *Ormonds*, that was relatively cheap to hire on a Tuesday night. We called our new event '*The Love Lounge*'. It was all quite ambitious, but Svengali Philip bulldozed ahead, spending money like water. With his obsession for perfection, he soon exceeded our agreed budget on things which I saw as superfluous, like silver cushion covers and tablecloths. He also imposed quite a high entry charge to keep out what he called the 'riff-raff'; a serious mistake as the 'riff-raff' made up the core audience in most commercial clubs. Thinking he knew what he was doing, and still very much under his influence, I was too cowed to speak out. In our double act, he was very much the senior partner; something I found increasingly irksome as my own self-confidence grew. But though Philip could afford to lose a few thousand pounds, I certainly couldn't.

But credit where it's due, he did pull out an ace for our opening night party. At that time, Jean-Paul Gaultier and the French TV presenter Antoine de Caunes hosted a very popular and hilariously tacky show called *Eurotrash*. A tie-in book was being published and we landed the launch. So there I was, sipping champagne with Jean-Paul Gaultier. As one does. The press were all over us like a rash, flashbulbs popping whilst we were being filmed for a popular TV show. The nightclub royalty was there, all dressed-up and blowing kisses into the air. Mayfair venue. What could possibly go wrong?

That night was a roaring success and all over the papers, both gay and mainstream too. It seemed like we were onto a winner. But it wasn't quite that simple. Most of the customers at the launch had only come because of the TV cameras and lots of them had got in free of charge as well. Basically, we'd ended up providing the club scene with a fabulous party and didn't even cover our costs.

But I held my nerve, hoping the first-night freeloaders liked us enough to come back the next Tuesday. They didn't. Nobody loved '*The Love Lounge*' quite enough and we closed after just four weeks. A slap in the face from the airy-fairy clubland population. An even bigger slap for my credit card, which audibly groaned every time I hit it with another invoice.

But it was a useful learning curve. What seems easy from the outside is most definitely not from the inside. Despite my affection for him, I also decided to pull back a bit from the influence of Svengali Philip and to trust my own instincts a lot more. As for all the silver cushions and tablecloths I'd paid for, I never saw any of them again. Philip took them all home.

Bubble burst. The Very Miss Dusty O needed to think again.

The Nineties saw a rebirth of club culture in London and the UK. Many new clubs, both straight and gay, opened and business was thriving. DJs were being turned into celebrities, which always seemed weird to me. Excess, often fuelled by drugs, was the order of the day.

The London gay scene, as it so often did, led the field with nights like 'Trade', 'Fruit Machine' and 'Crash' – names that can still bring a tear to the eye of gentlemen of a certain age. It had now moved away from the semi-underground venues it had long inhabited and was establishing itself very visibly, especially in Soho, with swanky new venues. The seedy old gay pubs with flock wallpaper, grotty toilets and beer-stained carpets were on the way out. Old Compton Street became the high street of a gay village with gay cafes, restaurants and shops of every kind. It would have been no surprise if somebody had opened a gay shoe-repair shop, exclusively devoted to mending six-inch diamante heels.

But the truly important thing about the gay village was less tangible. For so long, there had always been an element of fear in being visibly gay in the streets of British cities; especially for people in drag. Now, that fear was vastly diminished by the sheer volume of people who had taken over these Soho streets as our own space. It was a small kingdom of course, but it was ours. Within it, and for the first time, I felt both physically safe and part of a greater community; emotions so long denied to gay people and which the straight population could always take for granted. Simple things like showing affection for friends or partners on the street is, even today, mixed with a tinge of apprehension for many of us. But now at least we had our own stomping-ground, where we called the shots and where visitors were welcome, but had to play by our rules and not the other way around.

Out in the wider UK, things were still not equal, but progress was being made. Tony Blair's Labour Government implemented legislation that brought the age of consent for gay men down from 21 to 18. Above all, Margaret Thatcher was history by now and her vile 'Clause 28' was repealed. Ding-dong, the witch was dead, at least in a political context.

All these flash new bars and clubs were the rocket-boosters under the clubland career of the Very Miss Dusty O. I was offered lots of work and my name was soon a familiar fixture on flyers and adverts in the gay rags. Even people who'd never seen Dusty in a club began to know who she was. I was still the front person at *Pushca* which, despite all the new venues, remained a very high-end gig. My DJ skills were still pretty ropey and one bitchy writer described my mixing as being like that of a 'deaf amputee'. Despite that little drawback, Dusty always gave the punters a great show and she became extremely fashionable, so none of that mattered a damn.

These were the years when some wildly extravagant parties were thrown. At *Pushca's White Party*, Dusty was going to make the most spectacular entrance of her career.

One of those memories I'll take with me to the grave. The venue was dressed spectacularly. Billowing white sails made of acres of fabric floated among crystal chandeliers and it felt like you were dancing on big white clouds in heaven. Dusty would arrive in a white stretch limousine which would drive right inside the venue and onto the middle of the huge dancefloor. The white-clad security men would help me out of the limo and escort me to the DJ box. It was my Madonna moment. Flashing lights, the crowd applauding. There was an Arabian-style VIP tent, in white of course, in which I entertained the various celebs who pitched up, including the boys from *Take That*. There, I held court on huge white floor cushions plying Robbie Williams and Gary Barlow with champagne.

'A top-up, Robbie?'

'Don't mind if I do, love.'

'Gary?'

'Oh go on then. Just this once.'

The whole thing was gloriously over the top and I loved every second of it. Wouldn't you? No more cans of cheap cider on the back of a bus for this queen. No more dangerous journeys being called names or having my hair set on fire by local chavs. I was a scene star now. I wondered what Alain from the Aldridge Drama Club would think if he could see me now. How I wished I'd still known where he was and invited him here tonight.

'David darling, always be yourself,' he'd said. 'Don't let anyone dictate who you should become.'

Well, I'd done that, hadn't I. Through thick and thin. Through all sorts of opposition and derision. Whatever my faults and shortcomings, nobody could deny me that.

In particular, not Mr Bullock, that teacher who'd tried to humiliate me in front of the class. Homosexuals, he'd said, would always be sad, lonely people. Well, not tonight mate.

As I gazed into the handsome face of a slightly pissed Robbie Williams, I had almost forgotten about the boy who sat by the window. Yet I knew quite well that, somewhere deep inside me, he still lived and breathed.

If you've never been inside a skip, I don't recommend it. It's certainly not one for the bucket list.

The glamour of the *'White Party'* certainly went to my head. As did far too much champagne and, I'm ashamed to say, cocaine. Not to mention the limo, the security guards, the Arabian tent, Robbie and Gary.

After I'd finished my DJ set, I started to dance on the huge white podium behind the DJ box. I was high as a kite and drunk as a lord, but I felt so beautiful and lucky and that atmosphere of total joy carried me to a dangerous place. The technicians shone a spotlight on my crazy antics, so I gave them all something to look at. Craig Revel Horwood would have given me a 10. Salome would have given me 11.

But that podium was very high and I was getting very hot. I was wearing enormous six-inch, elevated 'prostitute' shoes with a thin spiked heel that was notoriously difficult to balance on. Way down below the podium and hidden from public view was the reality behind the glitter – a massive skip full of used cans, plastic cups and waste from the bar. Not a pretty sight. Sure enough, it was only a matter of time, before the booze, the drugs, the heat and the six-inch heels caused me to slip and fall backwards, headlong into the skip.

The crowd must have thought this dramatic departure was all part of the show. Dusty was well-known to be up for anything. So the band played on. The lighting guy didn't notice either; maybe he'd gone for a pee. Whatever, the result was that I lay unconscious in that skip, half buried in cans and plastic cups for *two whole hours*. Eventually my prolonged absence was noticed by Svengali Philip and a search ensued.

'Christ Dusty, what the hell are you doing in there?' I vaguely heard somebody say.

'Where?' I mumbled, still pissed, still higher than any kite could ever hope to fly.

'In the fucking skip!'

'What skip?'

I was totally unable to clamber out of the thing, but somehow the security men managed the task. They brushed me down. They'd get me a taxi to take me home, they said. The limo that had brought me seemed to have gone back to the garage.

'I'm not going home!' I said. 'What do I want to go home for?'

So I stayed and partied on for another two hours. Madness. By the time I got home and undressed, I was black and blue and could hardly breathe. The next morning, I had the mother of all hangovers and had plummeted down into my usual depressive state after taking cocaine. After a while, the pain had got so bad, I took myself off to the hospital.

'You're lucky to be alive,' said the doctor. 'You've got two cracked ribs and severe concussion. If your head had hit the metal side of the skip, you'd have probably been killed.'

'Right.' I said, casually, as if he'd told me I had an ingrowing toenail.

'What on earth were you doing?'

When I told him, I'm not sure he quite believed me, but I still like to think I brought a bit of levity to his hectic day in A&E. A bit of glamour to his usual round of road accidents, scalds, double pneumonia and strange items inserted into orifices. I pictured him in the doctors' pub that evening telling his medical mates about the drag queen who'd been drinking bubbly with Robbie and Gary and had fallen into a skip.

And that's how I handled the whole episode. Extremely serious as it was, I made light of it. I treated it as Dusty herself would have treated it; turning it into a hilarious anecdote that was soon devoured by the clubland gossips and spread around town. By this point, I'd come to believe that all publicity was good publicity, even if acquiring it could have killed me. It would certainly have made a good story for whoever gave my eulogy at the crematorium.

In retrospect, I know that the death of Dids had been way more traumatic for me than I could admit even to myself. Recovering from it was seriously hindered by my ongoing job at London Lighthouse, where the amount of grief and sadness that I had to internalise daily had begun to wear me out. I'd started to feel emotionally incapable of coping with any more and that clearly meant I could no longer do a good job there. I loved the place, it had meant the world to me for eight whole years, but the time had come to leave.

In truth, all I really wanted was to have a good time. That sounds so shallow, but having spent so long learning to live with loss and death, and at such a young age, I just yearned to escape from it all. And the Very Miss Dusty O was my escape route. Dusty took my hand in hers and led me gently away from the cruelties of the world into a bubble

David and his
sister Julie ▾

▲ David aged 17
with his mum Jean

...and aged 19 ▶

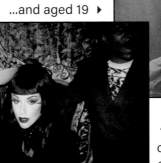

◀ With Boy George
on the set of the
Culture Club video
shoot for *I Just
Wanna Be Loved*

◀ David with Pete Burns, early 2000s

...and with Steve Strange mid-2010s ▼

David and
Boy George
for *Boyz*
magazine
cover ▶

With Karl Lagerfeld ▼

▲ With Boy George at a private member's club for the Pride parade

In The Music Hall Menagerie in Leicester Square, London ▼

▲ Pride London: hosting the main stage in 2015 at his last drag appearance

◀ David with mum Jean and sister Julie at Jean's 80th birthday lunch

▲ David painting in his early days

Sitting by his own window ▶

David and Marc

of hedonism. For the next two decades, I would allow myself to live in that bubble. I would be one of the West End's 'rent-a-freaks'. I'd travel the world, do exciting things and make lots of lolly. I would even become the creature who the press liked to call 'Queen of Soho.'

But bubbles, however glamorous, are fragile things. They are easily blown about. And they can easily burst.

Over the next few years, Dusty's reign as Queen of Soho became well-established. She had the crown on her head and carried the mace, which she sometimes used to whack any challengers for her throne. She wasn't always, if the truth be told, terribly nice. Nana Edna would not have approved.

Being a bitch is a tired gay stereotype, but I'm afraid I was born to be one and when somebody offered the chance to be bitchy in print it was irresistible. A new gay magazine called *DNA* was about to hit the scene and the editor wanted a witty, satirical column that would pull no punches and respect no egos. Dusty was the girl for the job. She grabbed her pen in five seconds flat and, for about a year, wrote a scathing critique of clubland, slagging off everyone she knew. It was very cruel, but extremely amusing — at least to me. *DNA* was essentially a huge piss-take of the silliness and vanities of the contemporary gay scene, so there was no shortage of material.

One of our regular targets was an ageing drag queen called Yvette (why are so many geriatric drag queens called Yvette?)

'Tragic news! Dear Yvette has been attacked by a pit bull terrier,' Dusty wrote. *'But don't worry.The pit bull is fine and Yvette is so ugly that nobody has noticed the difference.'*

We also ran an Yvette puzzle. A bit like snakes and ladders, but every snake and every ladder led to a square that said, *'Yvette is a talentless old man in a wig'.*

It wasn't exactly the wit of Oscar Wilde, Noel Coward or Dorothy Parker, but was lapped up by most of clubland London, who rushed out to get a copy to see how vile Dusty had been that week. It upset poor Yvette greatly and I look back on it with a slight sense of shame. But I had no shame back then. Years later, when I became the victim of an online bully who said similar things about myself, I too was deeply hurt. Tit for tat. Sorry Yvette. But it was a scream at the time.

I was getting plenty of gigs by now and making a healthy income. On a good night, if I was doing two gigs on the same evening, I could trouser £1,000 (considerably more in today's money). What club DJs and drag queens always tried to land were 'residencies' i.e. a regular date at a club. However humble the venue, these were a necessity for a reliable income. The big gigs in glam places were great, but they were the icing on the cake. You had to be prepared to 'slum it' a little in order to pay the rent. Naturally, I always wanted to be in the company of the seriously dressed-up, made up, fantastic freaks of cutting-edge clubland, but the 'Jeans and T-shirt brigade', the ones Svengali Philip regarded as 'riff-raff', were the mainstream population of gay London and often had just as much money to spend as the Westwood, Versace and Gaultier crowd.

At my peak, I had a string of residencies. One of these was *'The Gay Tea Dance'* at The Limelight Club, a beautiful-converted church on Shaftesbury Avenue. This ran from six till 11 on Sundays and attracted people with 'proper' jobs, who had to work on Monday mornings and couldn't afford to get home at 5.00am, totally wasted. It was generally untaxing as the crowd was more relaxed than my usual *Pushca* types who tended to be a lot more demanding.

The other nice gig I hooked was at the legendary gay night *BANG*, which had moved to the vast gay club Heaven, under the arches of Charing Cross Station. *BANG* had been a huge hit in past years but was way past its iconic best now and would only get three or four hundred people on a good night. But it was great fun to do and let me get to know all the bigwigs at Heaven who'd later employ me on other nights.

Both these residencies would last about five years and were the foundation on which I could build my other, higher profile work. Apart from the lolly, they kept my name in the gay press, something that was really important to any clubland career. Once the spotlight was on you, you needed to keep it there.

But I was still hosting 'Dusty's Room' at *Pushca*, which fulfilled my need for high glamour, famous faces and a skip-free zone. The *Pushca* parties had now moved into the prime Saturday night slot at Ministry of Sound which at that time was the most renowned club in the whole of the UK. It was also the most technically advanced and if you were a Ministry DJ, even if it was via the back door, as in my case, you were taken very seriously by other club promoters. In clubland terms, it was like being a Knight of The Garter. So ironic, since the only thing I was much good at mixing was a gin and tonic.

One Saturday, there was a grand event with an 'Evening Dress' theme.

'What are you going to wear?' somebody asked me.

'A ball-gown of course.' I replied, baffled by such a stupid question.

Whilst I might not be able to stretch to a carriage drawn by plumed white horses, I was determined to be Cinderella that night. Having spent thousands that year at the new Westwood shop in Conduit Street, buying something almost weekly, I reckoned they owed me a favour for plugging their brand so hard. Luckily, they agreed, providing me with a stunning corseted, silk gown with layer after layer of tulle petticoats. It was extremely valuable and delicate. Not the sort of frock you'd eat fish and chips in and certainly not risk a cup of coffee. It really was one of dear Vivienne's absolute stunners.

On the night, I made my spectacular entrance as planned to a satisfactory amount of 'oohs' and 'aahs'.

'Dusty, you look fabulous.'

'Is that M&S, dear?'

'But how did you get *into* it, darling?'

It was quite a big night at Ministry of Sound because *Kiss FM* radio were transmitting some of the DJ sets live across the nation. I'd not expected to be asked to do a set because my stuff was quite camp and not at all the seriously credible house music that Ministry was famous for. But suddenly, without notice, I was sent into the DJ box to do my thing. The problem was the dress. Joan, my driver, had to help me squash the gown into the DJ box, not much bigger than a phone booth. My set was to last two hours as it usually did.

When you watch a Cinderella movie, what you don't see is that she has to go for a dump halfway through the ball, just as the handsome prince is coming round with the glass slipper. You don't see her hoiking up the huge crinoline, trying to get her knickers down and her arse onto the loo seat. Halfway through my DJ set, this is what happened to Dusty. Out of the blue, she became desperate. Onto the turntable went the mega long version of Donna Summer's *I Feel Love* with another equally long track lined up to follow.

'Just press play when Donna finishes, if I don't make it back,' I said to Joan and made my dash for the loo before there was a nasty accident.

But manoeuvring a 4ft-wide ballgown through a packed, heaving nightclub took time. So did ramming myself into a tiny cubicle. So did getting my panties down under the layered petticoats of priceless tulle. By this point, my arse was in such a panic that instead of letting itself go with a grateful sigh, it clamped up on me. In my experience, the clamping reflex is an occasional hazard at the moment of intrusion, but rarely at the moment of extrusion. Oh God. I reckoned that, back in the DJ box, Donna Summer would now have finished feeling the love and the second track would be well underway. I talked to my arse very firmly. For fuck's sake, do it! After precious minutes were lost, it deigned to provide a measure of relief.

When I finally got back to the DJ box, poor Joan was pulling her hair out, a look of utter desperation on her face. But I'd just made it back before the second track finished. Job well done, so to speak. But Joan was very quiet the rest of the night and I wondered why.

'You all right, Joan love?'

'Yeah fine,' she replied in a slightly shaky voice.

I found out the next day, listening to the broadcast on *Kiss FM*. As I'd been told that my DJ segment wasn't going to be included, I was amazed to hear the following spiel.

'Now we're going over to London's most glamorous DJ, the Very Miss Dusty O in the VIP Room here at Ministry of Sound!'

The next voice I heard, ever so faint and extremely frightened was poor Joan's.

'I'm ever so sorry but she's just gone to the toilet and it takes her ages because of the big dress.'

'Okay cool!' replied the presenter with a slightly perplexed laugh. 'So now let's go over to the main floor with DJ Darren Darling – unless he's in the toilet too.'

Through all those years, I'd just never be able to take DJ work seriously. With me, it was always a means to an end and never any sort of passion. In magazine interviews, I'd often infuriate those dedicated DJs, who simply weren't interested in anything in life that didn't spin at 45rpm.

'Well it's only playing records, it's not hard is it?' I'd sniff.

It certainly put many a nose out of joint when I won 'Best DJ' in the *BOYZ* Readers' Poll later that year. And again four years later.

One night, Boy George came to Ministry to meet up with me after my set and have a few drinks. George had released several mixed CD's for the Ministry record label, one of which was actually in the Top 10 that week. But this night, he wasn't made up and was wearing a simple black jacket and trousers; not the way people pictured him in their mind's eye.

Being George, he went straight to the front of the queue with our friend Amanda Ghost. He was on Dusty's guest list, he told the security guard who replied that he had to wait in line like anybody else. Amanda pointed out who he was, but the guard didn't care. By now, George was a bit upset because people were watching. He pointed out to this cretin that his Ministry record was in the Top 10 and that it was a bit rude to be treated so discourteously. A row began and the guard pushed George to the floor. The fracas was all recorded by the paparazzi who regularly hovered by the club entrance looking for celebs and who now thought their ship had come in. A photo of George face down on the pavement duly appeared in *News of The World* the next morning. George was rightly furious at such a humiliation. The club was equally upset and issued a huge apology that appeared in the press.

But George got the last laugh, as George often does. The next CD mix he made for Ministry also got into the Top 10. And there on its cover was Boy George, all dolled-up, being carried on a throne by four burly security men, one of whom was the guy who'd dared to push over one of the biggest pop stars on the planet. Karma, I guess.

Such incidents weren't the only negatives that could come with celebrity. Not long before, George had published his autobiography *Take It Like A Man* in which he'd 'outed' a former boyfriend. The man in question denied he'd had a relationship with George and claimed that he'd lost his career as a result of the book's contents and therefore wanted financial compensation. The case went to court and the international press was over it like flies on shit. Fighting the case was never really about money for George. He had plenty of it. For him, the issue was personal. He wanted to be able to say openly who he had loved and not to have to pay a hefty sum in compensation for the privilege of doing so. In his eyes, it was his own story as much as that of the guy complaining.

I went along to court with him as support and company. Each day on leaving the building, he was mobbed by the press. In the end, George won the case and was praised by the judge for his honesty. The other man had to carry the legal costs, but swiftly declared himself bankrupt and unable to pay so, in the end, George found himself forking out. All highly unpleasant. How sad it was that somebody with whom he'd once been intimate, and for whom he'd cared, had put him through this.

I was beginning to understand now that the celebrity that I myself had craved and valued was very much a double-edged sword. It was so easy to be blinded by its dazzle and all the nice things it brought and fail to see the flip side which could be very dark indeed. Only a few years later, I'd discover the reality of that when I'd be on the receiving end of a kicking from the *Daily Mail*. Mind you, I'd already been warned. One minute you're dancing in the spotlight high up on the podium; the next you're lying in the skip in the dark, surrounded by empty cans and broken plastic cups.

ere is the number of my wig maker' I said in a broad Brummie twang. *'Yaw need it more than I do.'*

As great lines in drama go, it's not exactly up there with Lady Macbeth ('Out damned spot!') or Blanche du Bois ('Ah have always depended on the kindness of strangers'). But never let it be forgotten that I'd once been the teenage star of the Aldridge Youth Theatre. A child performer on a par with Daniel Radcliffe and Emma Watson. So when an opportunity arose for Dusty to shake off the superficiality of clubland and reassert herself as a 'serious actress', I grasped it.

When I worked at London Lighthouse, I'd got to know the writer Jonathan Harvey. Jonathan had created some very fine plays, including the gay love story *Beautiful Thing* which was made into a successful film. He'd later go on to write many episodes of *Coronation Street*. In 1999, he was casting for a new sitcom called *Gimme Gimme Gimme* about the shenanigans of a gay man who lived with an eccentric female friend. It would star the brilliant Kathy Burke as

Linda La Hughes and the terrific James Dreyfus as Tom, her over-the-top flatmate. Both a bit sad and lonely, both looking for the perfect boyfriend, but both extremely funny.

Jonathan asked me to audition for a small part in a wedding scene, using my Midlands accent and, in his words, camping it up. So no, not exactly Lady Macbeth or Blanche Du Bois, but I got the part. Three days' work for £300. Suited me fine as I wanted to buy a new telly, on which I'd soon be able to watch my performance.

The first day's filming was in a Chelsea nightclub. All I had to do was to get my wig caught on somebody's coat going up a staircase and scream a lot. I was adamant that the wig shouldn't be completely pulled off, as I was very conscious of my appearance and didn't want to be an object of mirth – probably not the best attitude in which to appear in a sitcom. So, even on my first day, I was no doubt pigeon-holed as a 'difficult' actress. But that had worked for Bette Davis, so it was good enough for me.

The second day was on location at Islington Town Hall. The film crew had created quite a buzz in the area and a large crowd had gathered.

'Ere mister, ain't you Harry Enfield?' a little lad asked, holding up a scrap of paper for me to autograph.

Harry Enfield? At this time, Kathy Burke worked a lot with him on his sketch shows, creating such wonderful characters as Waynetta Slob. But had the little lad ever seen Harry in a gold Westwood masturbation suit and a giant crimped wig? Surely not. I was used to lazy comparisons such as Lily Savage or indeed Boy George but, Christ, I'd not spent all these years turning myself into a walking work of art to be mistaken for fucking Harry Enfield.

The third day was in front of a live audience in a studio. Yet again, I had to film the wig being torn off at the wedding reception, this time by Kathy herself. And now came my one immortal line, delivered in a broad Brummie twang.

'Here is the number of my wig maker. Yaw need it more than I do.'

My old friend Dale Winton was also doing a cameo that day. I knew him from The Limelight Club where he was a regular. Dale was a lovely man, very humble and full of fun. I spent many a happy evening with him, after which he'd take me to a nearby café for a full English breakfast at midnight. Not exactly a wise combination after a skinful of booze, but my motto has always been 'if you're going to be sick, be really sick.' On one occasion, we were joined by Dale's best mate, the legendary Cilla Black. Surprise, surprise all right. This caused quite a furore in the little café. The Scouse chanteuse, the Brummie drag artist and the Home Counties queen with the slightly orange face. All eating sausages with brown sauce in the middle of the night. Happy days.

But I digress. When *Gimme Gimme Gimme* finally aired, it got the most appallingly snooty reviews I've ever read. That didn't stop it becoming hugely popular, hitting viewing figures of up to seven million and earning Kathy Burke two BAFTA nominations. Today, it's still a bit of a cult. Fans of the repeats on UK Gold came up to me for years afterwards, quoting my one immortal line. Sadly, my phone didn't ring with offers from the National Theatre or from Hollywood. Their loss. I still feel my Ophelia might have been wonderful.

'Get your make-up on,' said Svengali Philip on the phone one afternoon, when I was lying on the sofa recovering from yet another party.

'Why?'

'We're going out to dinner.'

'I still feel like shit from last night.'

'That's a shame. You'd meet a very special guest.'

'It'll have to be somebody very very special…' I said, 'to shift my arse from this sofa.'

'Only one of the most famous women on the planet.'

'Like The Queen?'

'Better than The Queen.' he replied. 'It's Madonna.'

'Oh yeah, right. Fuck off Philip.'

'I'm not joking Dusty. Tonight we're having dinner with Madge herself. Get your glad rags on.'

A friend of Philip's from his glam days working for Anouska Hempel had become friends with Madge and had invited us to a get-together. And Philip had been right. No disrespect to Betty Windsor but, in my celeb-obsessed eyes, this *was* even better than our beloved monarch. Far better. Like most gay men of a certain age, I considered Madonna Louise Ciccone from Bay City, Michigan as akin to a deity and not even a woman, anointed by God and directly descended from William The Conqueror could compete.

I was off that sofa in seconds, into the shower and in front of my make-up mirror for the next three hours. I chose a long Westwood evening coat with just bra and panties underneath and my highest elevator platforms. My wig was a truly enormous confection made by my mate Stan, which even Marie Antoinette might have considered a bit excessive. But I was determined that Madonna was going to notice me and that I'd soon be her new best friend. Move over Rupert Everett.

Philip came to pick me up and we headed for a very swanky restaurant in Mayfair. This was going to be yet another of my greatest entrances. Or so I thought.

'We're here for dinner with Madonna,' I announced loudly to the door whore.

'Very sorry madam, but I can't admit you,' he said. 'You're not dressed appropriately for this restaurant.'

'You what? We're here for dinner with Madonna.' I repeated.

But the door whore wouldn't budge. He'd not have cared if I'd come for The Last Supper with Jesus Christ and the 12 Disciples. Philip went inside to track down his friend to come and vouch for me.

Oh God. The humiliation was excruciating. There I was, stuck outside on the pavement like Little Orphan Annie, literally freezing my tits off in just bra and panties under a Westwood coat that hadn't exactly been designed for Arctic conditions. Now I knew how the many people I'd turned away from clubs for not being 'appropriately dressed' had felt. I think the ancient Greeks called it nemesis.

Eventually I was allowed in and swished past the pompous arse on the door with as much swagger as I could muster. We were led to a big round table in a semi-private section at the back of the room. I didn't look to see if heads turned, I just gazed straight ahead as if I didn't give a fuck, when in truth I really, really did. I just hoped that passing waiters bearing trays of long-tailed quail didn't catch them in my gi-normous wig and that my scene in *Gimme Gimme Gimme* wouldn't be recreated in hellish reality.

I was introduced to the other people at the table. Madge had not yet arrived. I wondered what she and I would chat about. Hair, make-up and clothes of course; she was sure to recognise Westwood a mile off. Or maybe I could natter about my evening with Robbie Williams and Gary Barlow. Perhaps she'd even been to Walsall. But I was starting to feel increasingly nervous, so I began to down the champers like it was Lucozade and by the time the star arrived I was pretty well bladdered.

As people always say when they see The Queen in person, I was surprised by how small Madonna was. Just a titch of a thing. Somehow, you always expect that world-famous, larger-than-life personalities are going to be physically large too and so often they're not. Yet they'd made themselves imposing by sheer force of will. Her face seemed very furry, almost like a peach. I'm not saying she was hairy exactly, but she certainly seemed to be a stranger to the depilatory counter at Boots.

But the most noticeable feature was how sour and grumpy she was. Oh dear. She acknowledged the other guests with a curt nod and positioned her chair with her back turned to most of us, so that the only person she spoke to was the mutual friend of Philip's who'd arranged the evening. The only time she turned round was to ask us to speak more quietly as she had a headache. Not at all pleasant, not remotely well-mannered. Maybe she was bored with being invited to things where she was the default centre of attention, where besotted fans like me wittered on to her about how much they loved/admired/respected her. Blah blah blah. Maybe she really wanted to be at home in front of *Midsomer Murders*, in old jeans and a T-shirt, with a bottle of beer and her feet soaking in Epsom Salts. God knows.

Only when the party broke up and she turned to go, did her eyes come to rest on me.

'I'm sure I've seen you somewhere before.' she said, giving me a very odd look.

'Maybe on the 73 bus to King's Cross?' I said, by this point as pissed as a fart.

This attempt at humour was quite lost on Madge. She looked me up and down without cracking a smile and swanned off without a backward glance. My mission to be Madonna's new best friend had failed miserably. Rupert Everett was safe.

What a let-down. I did however dine out on it for months and elaborated on it greatly, so that people really did start to think I was her new buddy and would shortly be flying to her mansion in LA to hang out by the pool with her and Guy. If only they'd known the sad truth, which was that I would indeed be on the 73 bus to King's Cross.

The one positive thing that came from the evening was when Dusty was to appear on a TV show called *Lie Detector*. This involved making a startling claim, being quizzed by a celebrity panel as to its truth and finally taking a lie detector test. Mine of course was having dinner with Madonna. The panel asked all sorts of questions which I fudged as best I could. Naturally, I passed the lie detector test, so my street-cred was left intact, even if I'd exaggerated the thing to quite ridiculous proportions. I just prayed that Madge never caught the show, while slobbing at home with her feet in the Epsom Salts.

Even now, some people still ask me what she's like and I always give the same reply.

'A woman of few words, especially to me.'

In the course of Dusty's long career, I'd meet more than my fair share of celebs and usually loved every minute of it. But, now and again, the idols you'd put up on pedestals turned out to have feet of clay. And that had been one of those times. I just couldn't understand why Madge couldn't even show basic politeness to other people. Headache or no headache. And whether she was interested in them or not. As my Nana Edna used to say, politeness costs nothing.

It had certainly been a leap from sausage and egg with Cilla in a transport caff to dinner in a swish restaurant with one of the most famous people in the universe. But I'd take Cilla and the sausages any time.

'Hey Dusty, can I have your autograph please?' somebody shouted.

Wow. It had finally happened. Somebody wanted my signature on a bit of paper. Such an odd phenomenon when you think about it, but accepted the world over as a symbol of somehow having 'arrived', whatever that means.

Where I had literally arrived was at Milan Airport in the company of Boy George, who'd invited me to accompany him to a big Gianni Versace show in Milan for which he was producing the 'runway music'.

He was a big star in Italy at this time, having just had two Top Three dance singles, so a gaggle of his fans were there to meet him and say '*benvenuto*'. George and I had been pictured a lot together by now and the fans knew who I was too. And at least nobody here thought I was Harry Enfield.

Despite my encounter earlier that year with Madonna Louise Ciccone, I hadn't yet gone cold turkey in my addiction to glamour and celebrity.

'Dusty, it's going to be super glitz,' George had said on the phone, 'and all over the press. A spectacular look please, darling.'

No encouragement was needed. By now I could have found my way to Westwood in Conduit Street, blindfolded and off my face on Benylin. This time, I bought a gorgeous, corseted suit in black velvet which I intended to wear with as much Westwood bling jewellery as I could squeeze onto one human body. My wig maker friend Stan had prepped yet another of his vast tonsorial masterpieces; a blue-blonde concoction of curls and knots that was actually no less than three wigs pinned together.

'The higher the hair, the closer to God,' as I always said.

On the day, a sleek limousine had purred its way down my ordinary street in King's Cross, sent by courtesy of Versace. At Heathrow, we'd been whisked into the First-Class Lounge as we were flying Business Class. I'd never turned left at the plane door before and felt quite sorry for everyone who had to turn right. This was all very pleasing and in stark contrast to where I'd been only 12 hours earlier – doing a gig for £150 in a half empty, depressing pub in Chinatown, where the punters had seemed more interested in what was happening in the gents' toilet than in anything I was doing at the decks.

In Milan, we were driven in a big limo to a five-star hotel where George settled into his pop-star-sized suite and I was given a stunning single room along the corridor.

This was the life.

'See you in an hour Dusty,' said George. 'We're going to see Donatella and watch the rehearsals, then dinner afterwards with Naomi Campbell.'

After that, there would be a fitting at the Versace studio for the outfit George would wear tomorrow at the show and at the after-party dinner. As I sat in my ritzy room drawing on my eyebrows, I thought back to the first time George and I had met. Being attacked by that gang of girls at the Anti-Apartheid gig on Clapham Common, being hauled over the barrier by the security guard and ending up in George's trailer, when he was totally wasted and rolling on the grass. Now here I was, with him as a friend, about to go and meet Donatella Versace and Naomi Campbell. Heady stuff.

At the show venue, George introduced me to Donatella with whom he'd worked several times before and knew quite well. She was a bit frightening to look at, with her long poker straight hair and a face that had been, er, modified quite extensively. But she turned out to be charming and kind.

'What will you be wearing at the show tomorrow?' she asked me.

The smile faltered when I outlined my new Westwood outfit.

'Oh, no, no, no!' she said. 'You cannot sit in the front row at a Versace show wearing Westwood. That is totally impossible!'

Like an idiot, this point hadn't occurred to me. It'd cost me a thousand quid in Conduit Street and all for nothing. Shit. My little face must have puckered up and my lip quivered, but Donatella snapped her fingers at some hovering minion.

'First thing tomorrow, you will take Miss Dusty to the Versace shop and give her anything she wants.' said Gianni's all-powerful sister. 'Don't worry darling, we get you sorted out.'

And they did. The stunning Versace shop was in the glass-domed splendour of the Galleria Vittorio Emanuelle III, a sort of retail version of St Paul's Cathedral. A range of outfits and shoes was laid out for my inspection as if

I were Joan Collins herself. The secret truth was that I'd always considered Versace a bit tacky and 'Elton John', which wasn't my style *at all*, but a free outfit is a free outfit so button your lip, girl. I finally plumped for a black leather mini skirt and jacket with a big mink collar and shoes with a matching mink trim. They also gave me a free run of the handbags, make-up and even lingerie, so I returned to the hotel with quite a haul.

The evening before, we'd met up with Naomi Campbell at a gorgeous restaurant, where she'd sat and watched George and I feed our faces on the best Italian cuisine while she just sipped water. This brought home to me just how much discipline could be needed to achieve the goals we really want in this life. Naomi was obviously prepared to make any sacrifice to maintain her appearance and thus her career. Good for her. Like George though, she'd been through the hoops of alcohol and drug addiction and come out the other side. That night in Milan, she and George went for a fond wander down Memory Lane.

'Did he tell you I used to hang around outside his house in Hampstead, just like all the other little girls?' she asked. 'He was my hero.'

'Mine too.' I said.

'Posters on the bedroom wall?'

'Yes of course. You too?'

'Me too.' she smiled.

She and George recalled how Naomi at the age of only 12, a stage-school kid, had tap-danced in an early Culture Club video. By this point in the evening I was pretty tired and didn't say much. But it was fascinating just to sit and listen to these two once-ordinary London kids; the daughter of a single mother from Streatham who'd never known her father and the son of a working-class Irish Catholic family from Woolwich.

Except of course, they'd not been 'ordinary' at all. Quite the opposite. Each had been gifted with a certain talent which they had recognised and respected, developing and burnishing it into something which the world had wanted and thus turned them into superstars. Now here they sat in a posh eaterie in Milan; the focus of every eye and the shy, skinny boy from Aldridge sat with them. Though I wasn't remotely in their league, I totally understood the impulses within them which had propelled their lives and I shared them completely.

On the afternoon of the show, I spent the entire time in my room getting ready. It was a shame that I'd not have time to see the attractions of Milano. The great Cathedral and La Scala opera house would have to wait till next time. For now, I was focused on making the Very Miss Dusty O one of the sights of the city, if only for a few hours.

We were escorted in style to the magnificent Palazzo Versace, a glittering monument to the power of style and wealth. There probably weren't many Labour voters around that night or whatever the Italian equivalent was. Every Versace fashion show attracted stars from all over the world, so there was a huge scrum of press and photographers, shouting their tits off to get the stars to turn their heads this way or that. Until you've stood in the middle of it, you've no idea what it's like when a couple of hundred flashguns go off in your face. Looking back at the press pictures, no wonder I look a bit frightened which, under my super confident drag queen guise, is exactly what I was.

Inside the stunningly decorated hall, the front row of chairs was an A-Z of the fashion and entertainment worlds. Cher, Demi Moore, Karl Lagerfeld, Sting and his wife, Anna Wintour of *Vogue* Janet Jackson and even Rupert Everett, having a night off from being Madge's best friend. And, of course, Dusty O, praying she wouldn't need a pee till the whole thing was over. I couldn't grasp that only the day before yesterday I'd been working in that sleazy London pub to earn £150. The contrast between the two worlds was a total head fuck. I felt like an imposter with no right to be there. God knows how I'd make the reverse transition. Like Cinderella after the ball, once more in the kitchen, the golden carriage turned back into a pumpkin.

George of course knew all the other celebs and swapped pleasantries while I sat there quietly, blinking in the lights of the paparazzi, of whom there seemed to be even more inside than out. As expected, the show was incredible with George's soundtrack brilliantly on the mark. An endless succession of drop-dead gorgeous models swanned or slouched along the runway. Such stunning, other-worldly creatures that you could hardly imagine that they belched or went to the loo like the rest of us. God knows how these types coped if they ever found a pimple on their arse. Of course, I pictured the Very Miss Dusty O up there with them in my £3000 Versace gear. At least I'd have cracked a smile.

After the show, we were led into another part of the palazzo. All the celebs were seated at one very grand table, with me plonked on the end. I had no illusions about my place in the pecking order. But I knew that something like this would never happen again and was determined to enjoy myself as much as I could.

On one side of me was the iconic Cher. On the other, the scary but nice Donatella Versace. What do you say in that situation that doesn't sound either naff or just plain wet? Lovely weather, isn't it? Have you been to Milan before? How's Sonny these days? They were both charming though, like Naomi Campbell the night before, they hardly touched anything on their plates. How did these women even have the energy to walk? I'd love to have taken both of them out to the King's Cross chippie and treated them to battered cod, a saveloy and chips. I got the distinct impression that Donatella was more interested in what went up her nose than into her mouth. But Cher and I had a nice long natter about wigs and make-up, like she was my sister.

I really wanted some evidence of this magical night in my life and eventually I had the confidence to take my little disposable camera out of my handbag. For some reason, George always found this hilarious.

'Oh Christ, she's got her Boots camera out again. Big smiles, everyone.'

'What eez this Boots?'

'It's a chemist's shop, Donatella. Have you never been to Boots?'

But with George's help, I forced them all to have selfies with me (though that word hadn't yet been invented). The great Karl Lagerfeld never allowed his picture to be taken with fans or strangers and it was strictly taboo to even ask him. But nobody had told me that.

'Your turn now Karl dear,' I said.

'Oh, very well.' said one of the most famous couturiers in the world, looking me up and down with a practised eye. 'But only because you're the best drag I've seen in years.'

I took that as a big compliment from a man who had a definite androgynous quality himself. With his black clothing, dark glasses and snow-white hair tied back in a pigtail, he looked a bit like Annie Lennox might when she's a very old lady.

'Wow,' said Cher. 'He doesn't usually do that. He must really like you.'

That night, my face scrubbed clean and the £3,000 suit hanging in the wardrobe, I lay between the thousand-thread-count sheets in my lovely bedroom in the five-star gaff, quite unable to sleep. This time tomorrow night, I'd be back in my basement council flat in King's Cross. Back in the real world. But what a journey from being an introverted, bullied Brummic kid to chatting about false hair with Cherilyn Sarkisian under the chandeliers of an Italian palazzo.

Never underestimate Boots. The photographs taken that night on the crap camera turned out wonderfully. *BOYZ* magazine snapped them up and published a two-page spread of Dusty with the stars. At once, like some magic wand, this propelled me straight to the top of London clubland's A List and I became heavily in demand as a name to have at your venue or club night. The Guardian, no less, asked me to write a column for their style section about my wardrobe and beauty regime. Bit of a change for a dead serious, leftie newspaper more used to printing pics of bluestockings like Clare Short and Shirley Williams; worthy ladies both, but not exactly icons of glamour.

So how had this stuff happened to me? The truth is that I'd never set out to be a drag queen and certainly not a celebrity DJ. As a kid, I'd wanted to be a vet (though I'm not sure that would have got beyond the first time I'd had to fist a cow). Though I was hopelessly addicted to dressing-up and make-up, that glorious process of transformation, I'd never thought it would ever become a career option. But it had.

And that mega-bucks Versace suit? Though not ungrateful to darling Donatella, I'd never really liked it all that much. Versace just wasn't 'me' and never would be. Then something happened that put me off it for ever.

'Mink murderer!' some furious biddy yelled outside a club. 'Do you have any idea what these poor creatures go through, so a fool like you can dress up like a tart?'

The honest answer was that I didn't. But after I'd done some research into how these animals were treated before being killed, I vowed I'd never wear real fur again and I never have.

So I sold it to the designer outlet and got a cheque for £2,000. The moment it had cleared, I was on my way to the Westwood shop. In my experience, there are very few issues in life which can't be cured, or at least comforted, by a trip to Conduit Street.

chmoozing with Cher and Donatella had brought me a new level of fame, but not all of it turned out well.

In the mid-Nineties, the biggest Saturday night party in town was held at the now demolished Astoria Theatre in Charing Cross Road. The event was called, not very imaginatively, *G-A-Y.* Unashamedly camp and cheesy, it appealed to a more middle of the road gay crowd than, snootily, I was now used to playing for. Every week, there would be a balloon drop at 1am on the dot and the DJ would have to play *Better The Devil You Know* by Kylie Minogue, like a gay version of *God Save The Queen*. I'm not knocking *G-A-Y* in itself, because it gave great pleasure to many thousands of people and no doubt there are many happy gay couples who first met underneath all those balloons.

But sadly, I hated every second that I worked at *G-A-Y.* The main problem was the promoter, a man called Jeremy Joseph, then a very big name on the London club scene. He ran a very tight ship indeed and was a tough boss to please.

Jeremy was always keen to link his brand with anything or anyone considered fashionable and, at that point in time, it was the Very Miss Dusty O.

His lord and master Jeremy knew his target audience well and tolerated little deviation from a formula designed to keep them happy. Every DJ, especially newbies like me, were expected to submit set lists for his approval. At *Pushca* and almost everywhere else I'd ever played, I'd been used to a certain level of politeness and special treatment, but Jeremy Joseph didn't really 'do' either of these. Nor did I take to his dry sardonic sense of humour which seemed to be directed largely at me.

But though I disliked him intensely, I was astute enough to know that it was a prestige gig and accepted his offer with the proviso that my name would appear on all adverts, flyers and press releases. But the DJs at *G-A-Y* were never listed in publicity material as *his lord and master* Jeremy saw the club as the brand and never wanted to make stars of his employees or acknowledge the contribution of any one person to the success of his events. This was a step too far for my ego and I said, 'No name-check, no Dusty'. For once he complied, much to the disgust of the other talented, long-standing DJs on his roster, who remained anonymous underlings.

Despite this unheard-of concession, it was a grim experience. In those days, we still played vinyl records and as the DJ box was very easy for customers to access, I'd be plagued all night by requests to 'play Madonna again'. But repeating what had already been played that night, unless it was No 1 in the charts, was strictly against Jeremy's rules. I used to find it depressing always saying 'no' to the punters and seeing their happy faces fall, thinking I was a miserable queen – which of course was exactly what I was in this bootcamp of a club.

My mixing skills were still minimal and the other DJs used to smirk and grin, making me feel very unwelcome indeed. Rarely would anyone even get me a drink. I knew hardly anyone there. The joy that I usually found in my work deserted me almost entirely. I'd never imagined that could ever happen. But it was a useful lesson in a way. However much glitter and fun there might be on the surface of the club world, it could be as bleak, soul-destroying and utterly pointless as working on the bins or on the checkout at Asda. Lesson learnt.

'Oooh, it tickles,' I'd said to the stylist on the shoot, as I eased my bits into panties lined with the feathers of the exotic maribou bird.

'I know...' she said, with a wink.

If you've not felt maribou feathers on your privates, I can't recommend it highly enough.

I was styled as a typical Soho hooker, lounging on a bed in those feathered panties and a baby doll nightie. I wore a dog collar and black contact lenses and looked ever so slightly frightening. As a rule, the Very Miss Dusty O projected a warm, funny, albeit bitchy, persona, but this look was a lot more edgy than that. A darker Dusty. Dusty with a Health & Safety warning.

I'd told them to make of me what they wanted and they'd taken me at my word. It was for the front cover of *BOYZ* magazine; the equivalent of *Playboy* but with cute little gay bunnies. I'd had covers earlier in the year, but this was by far the most important accolade. The occasion was my 28th birthday and a big party was being thrown at The Limelight Club. *BOYZ* had wanted to tempt me out of my *haute couture* comfort zone and it worked a treat. Flyers promoting the party were created to look like the cards the working girls would leave in phone boxes back then and we plastered them all over Soho. The party was a massive success with a huge queue of people waiting to get in. This cover, my other exposure in the mainstream press plus the bits and bobs on TV had made me into something of an 'It Girl', as we'd have said in those days. Today, I guess I'd be called an 'influencer' and have a million followers on Instagram.

Riding high on the success of my party, *his lord and master* Jeremy called to say that Kylie Minogue was debuting her new single at *G-A-Y*. She had asked for three drag queens to be dressed up to look like her and to appear beside her on the stage. Even though it was Jeremy, who could resist? Within hours, I was being styled in a specially made dress.

'You can keep the dress afterwards.' somebody said.

'What?' I replied.

'Well, there's no fee. Weren't you told that?'

'No.'

'Oh dear. Sorry. Well, it'll be good for your career.'

I bit my tongue and said nothing. It was something all performers and drag queens heard all too often. Doing the job for free. It always got on my false tits. Would they ask a police officer or a bank manager to do their job for nothing? I think not, so why ask *me* to do it? But in this case, I relented. It was Kylie after all. Another memory for my old age, when I'm sitting on the commode in the care home.

On the day, I was rehearsed in my moves by Kylie herself. Like Madge, she was a tiny little creature, but that's where the comparison stopped. Kylie was as sweet and charming as you'd hoped she'd be. An international star who knew how to treat 'lesser mortals' with courtesy and respect. I wasn't the world's greatest dancer, but I got through the show in front of three thousand gay fans who were screaming in both senses of the word. The next day's papers all carried shots of Kylie with little old me waving my arms and legs like a lunatic behind her. If Kylie thought I was crap, she was far too nice to say so.

Years later, I got invited to a party at Kylie's house, when I began to wonder if that wholesome image was entirely accurate. In Kylie's kitchen, for all to see, was a large fridge magnet – in the shape of a huge cock.

The next few years were, I suppose, the zenith in the career of the Very Miss Dusty O. I worked up to five nights a week in various venues, either hosting or being a DJ. And now, I had yet another string to my bow. My voice wasn't at all bad and I'd let myself be persuaded by a small indie record label to make some tracks, usually covers or pastiches of well-known songs. It was great fun, though I'd no illusions that I'd ever give Boy George a run for his money. It was just one more way of keeping my face in the spotlight, staying fashionable, making sure I was always in demand. Like everybody else, I had bills to pay: the gas, the electricity, the water, the Westwood shop.

By this time, keeping myself in that spotlight was the focus of my life, the driving force, the reason for getting up in the morning. For a long time now, I'd had little time for gratuitous sex, let alone romance or even love. Then, for a few lovely months, that miraculously changed. I met a beautiful Italian man called Antonio. Drop dead gorgeous and extremely romantic, like all those dishy Italian movie stars. I couldn't believe my luck and decided that, wonder of wonders, I had actually fallen in love and went around with my wig in the clouds. We went on a trip to Rome, where I did a guest slot in a club and threw coins into the Trevi Fountain. I was pretty sure that, as the legend went, the fountain would bless me and I'd return to Rome with gorgeous Antonio again and again. We went to his hometown of Naples too, where we strolled through the ruins of Pompeii and watched the moon rise above Mount Vesuvius. It was good Jackie Collins stuff, though in this case the nipples were all male.

Sadly, but just to make it even more romantic, this was to be a doomed love affair. And guess who doomed it. Like Mount Vesuvius, I still erupted in temper tantrums with monotonous and wearing regularity. Despite all my current success, my healthy income, the magazine covers and the celebrity chums, I still carried inside me that toxic legacy from my childhood in Walsall. The notion that yelling and screaming was a normal and acceptable means of interacting with other human beings. The example of my parents' tempestuous relationship was still bred in the bone. I truly believed it was totally fine to say what the hell you liked. I had no filter. None at all.

I suppose it was ironic that Antonio was Italian. All that shouting and throwing things was something of a Latin cliché. Those old movies with Sophia Loren or Gina Lollobrigida chucking the spaghetti at the walls. But Antonio simply wasn't that sort of Italian and I played the part of Sophia once too often. When we returned to London, he faded out of my life, though not before returning a bunch of flowers I'd sent him as an apology for my latest eruption over nothing. The flowers, of course, were dead. A depressing metaphor for what had happened between us.

But on I went, head held high and false tits out. The busiest boy in town. And the loneliest.

That Christmas, instead of spending it with Antonio in a warm and loving relationship, I spent it on yet another *BOYZ* front cover. Cold comfort, some might say, but I was still so drunk on attention I just didn't see it that way.

Naturally, this particular cover was to celebrate the birth of baby Jesus – and it was something else. It was lucky that Mrs Mary Whitehouse had retired by now, or she might have instigated another blasphemy trial, as she'd famously done against *Gay News* 20 years before. At the very least, it would have made her eyes water.

There was Boy George dressed as Jesus with me as The Virgin Mary. Extremely odd casting to say the least, but of course that was the point. It was shot by George's brother David but, for some reason, George was in a right grumpy mood that day. Not remotely festive.

'Dusty, you're wearing far too much make-up' he told me. 'I doubt there was a fucking Boots in Bethlehem.'

Possibly true, but I'd seen plenty of paintings of The Virgin in art galleries and I swear she's wearing lippy and a bit of foundation in more than a few. Just because she was riding that donkey, didn't mean she wouldn't want to look her best. The *BOYZ* cover was accompanied by a three-page spread about us guest-editing the magazine. It wasn't what one might call challenging journalism, mostly us slagging off The Spice Girls and other low-brow stuff but it was all good Yuletide fun.

But I now worried that I was becoming known too much as a 'sidekick' to George. Somebody had once cruelly called me his 'Madge'; not a reference to Miss Ciccone but to the mute, plain bridesmaid of Dame Edna Everage. I'd laughed at the time, but secretly I wasn't at all pleased and made a mental note to be more careful about that. Nor did I ever want George to feel that I was some sort of 'hanger-on', trying to piggyback on his celebrity, as so many others had done. I loved him and valued his friendship too much for that.

So it was just at the right time that an opportunity came for Dusty to spread her wings and display her gorgeousness on a much wider canvas than that of London W.1.

I'd been approached by an agent from a company called DJs Unlimited who looked after many of the celebrity DJs emerging during this period. Karen dangled the prospect of glamorous gigs all over the world and, to my surprise and joy, she was as good as her word. I was low on technical skills, but high in confidence and I knew I had something special to offer. As always, that something was my appearance. Most DJs wore a back to front baseball cap, grubby jeans and T-shirts that hadn't seen the inside of a washing machine for a month. These dudes looked like they were just popping down to the corner shop to buy bread or to change the tyre on a bike. Whereas the sight of Dusty behind the decks could make jaws drop.

The first foreign gig was at an upmarket club in Prague called Radost. It was very flash, stunningly designed and offering original and imaginative entertainment from all over Europe. Right up Dusty's street. My first trip there went extremely well and they asked me back for a monthly residency. It was a well-paid booking with two flight tickets and accommodation thrown in, so I could take a friend for company.

The first person I invited was that bosom friend of my youth, Curtain Mark. After dear Dids passed away, Mark had moved into the flat in King's Cross and I was very glad to have him. Nobody could have filled the hole left by Dids but, if anyone could come close, it was good old Mark. He was now enjoying his own personal drag journey as 'Maria, the Tart with a Heart'. Maria wasn't at all like Dusty, though the two girls got along fine. She was a statuesque redhead with big boobs, very short skirts and saw herself as irresistible to anything in trousers; a right cock-teaser. Maria also liked a bevy or two and had an acid tongue, ready and willing to take on any detractor. She had a right gob on her did Maria. God help you if you said the wrong thing.

On this occasion, there was to be a high-profile fashion party at Radost and they'd installed a runway right through the room. The event was being filmed for the Fashion Channel, was being covered by *Elle* magazine and would be attended by all the movers and shakers in the Czech Republic and the neighbouring states. It wasn't quite Versace in Milan, but it was nothing to be sniffed at.

Maria and Dusty were looking forward to it especially as, before the fashion show, we were first being taken to the launch of a chic new restaurant on an island in the River Danube. But what sounded enchanting in theory, turned out to be frightening in reality. The place was filled to the rafters with Russian Mafia. Then, as now, LGBT people were deeply unwelcome in Russia and there was a tangible lack of the enthusiasm that usually greets the entrance of fabulously-dressed drag queens at a venue. Instead of whistles and applause, the Russians glared at us with menacing looks. In their eyes, we represented everything they despised about the decadent West.

For the first time ever, Maria's courage seemed to wobble in the face of this passive but definitely scary hostility. She therefore turned to courage of the Dutch variety, hitting the absinthe with a vengeance. But Maria, who'd drunk everything from champagne cocktails to Jeyes' Fluid, had somehow missed out on absinthe and had no idea how strong it was. She soon found out and, within 20 minutes, was as drunk as a Birmingham skunk and brassy as a carthorse on heat. She made Bet Lynch look like Lady Antonia Fraser. Unfortunately, she decided to engage the Mafia in salty conversation.

'Hey boys!' She called across to the scowling faces, blowing them kisses. 'Never seen a hot Brummie bitch before?'

'Stop it Mark, for Christ's sake.' I hissed. 'Stop it.'

But Maria was only just getting going. She started cat-walking up and down the aisle of the place, displaying her endless legs which she rightly regarded as her best asset.

'Look at these legs, boys,' she shouted. 'Gorgeous or what? Legs like a gazelle. A fucking gazelle. Bet you'd like them wrapped round your backs, wouldn't you boys?'

And so on. The owner of Radost began to look distinctly nervous and got us out of there and off the island as fast as Maria's gazelle-like legs could go, which by now wasn't very fast at all. The River Danube was certainly blue that night.

By the time we got back to the club, Maria was almost incoherent. The fashion show was already in full swing, so we were told to sneak in quietly and get to the DJ box in preparation for my set and some pictures with the local press. Stupidly, I let Maria go into the throng ahead of me.

'Keep walking,' I instructed her. 'Just keep walking. And try to stand up straight.'

She proceeded to push and shove her way through the glittering crowd in a most unladylike fashion.

'Come on, move your arse, luv,' she'd say to anyone blocking her zigzag path. 'There's a real lady coming through.'

Half-blinded by the booze and the lights, what Maria failed to see ahead of her was the huge runway platform set up for the show. She duly collided with the said runway, fell over, rolled across it and dropped off the other side, losing her wig in the process. Suddenly, every eye in the room was fixed onto her. Totally unfazed, as only the really pissed can be, she got back onto her feet, perched her bottom on the side of the runway and pulled her wig back on, though not exactly very neatly. Then in a very stately and composed manner, she made her way through the aghast crowd to wait for me in the DJ box at the back of the room.

'Well, that's it.' I said, furiously when I reached her. 'That's my Prague residency gone down the toilet. Thanks a bunch, you old slag.'

It was pointless saying anything else, as she was too stupified to understand anything. So I played my DJ set as professionally as I could, while Maria sat slumped behind me on the floor of the box, looking like a cast-off costume from '*Sesame Street*', her wig now poking out of the top of her handbag and clutching her stilettos in her hand.

Thankfully, the promoter saw the funny side. Apparently, it was to become a legendary moment on the Prague clubland scene and was remembered for many years afterwards. I kept the residency and had many nice trips out there with the various friends I took with me. But that brassy strumpet was never one of them. As the song goes, how do you solve a problem like Maria?

Soon after Prague, Karen the agent got me a gig in Israel. It would be two DJ stints plus a live personal appearance, singing a couple of the tracks I'd recently recorded. The three gigs were all on the same night; two in Tel Aviv and a fast drive over to Jerusalem for the final early morning slot at a nightclub in the Holy City itself. A tough schedule. Bizarrely, this was all to be part of the celebrations for the 50th anniversary of the birth of the State of Israel. Christ on a bike. I didn't know much about Jewish history, although I had seen Babs Streisand in *Yentl*. But back in 1948, I'm pretty sure that the founding fathers of this new country never imagined that, half a century on, some drag queen from Walsall would fly in to join the party. Not that they'd have known what a drag queen was.

So off I toddled to Tel Aviv, with my drag bags (aka 'luggage') stuffed with couture and all my record boxes. In those days, when we still played vinyl, my bags had become so heavy that I ended up buying what I called my 'old lady shopping trolley' to help me get my gear in and out of venues.

'Welcome Miss Dusty O!' said the promoter who met me at the airport. 'I'm the Jeremy Joseph of Israel.'

'I bloody hope not,' I nearly said, but managed to smile instead.

I was driven to a hotel that wasn't very nice and put in a room which, strangely, had a connecting door to the adjacent room. It was locked but it made me feel uneasy. It was extremely hot and the air conditioning minimal, but

I managed to get some sleep. The next evening, as I got ready for the first of the gigs, I did my make-up in the nude, sitting on the floor with the mirror in front of me. Two hours later, I stood up with stiff legs and a sore back, still bollock naked. Suddenly the phone rang, which was odd as I wasn't expecting to be picked up for another hour.

'I wondered if you'd like to join me for a drink at the hotel bar?' asked a softly spoken male voice.

I presumed it was the promoter who seemed to have taken a bit of a shine to me, though I didn't reciprocate and was playing it politely but very cool.

'Thanks, but I've still got a lot of preparation to do, so I'll be down at the time we agreed.'

'That's a shame,' replied the voice. 'You look beautiful.'

'How do you know that?' I laughed.

'Because I'm in the next room and I've been watching you through the keyhole.'

I slammed the phone down and grabbed the nearest towel to cover myself. I pushed a chest of drawers in front of the keyhole. I rang the promoter who came running and got me moved to another room. Some sharp words in Hebrew were soon being shouted and screamed along the corridor. I suppose it was a compliment really, but if somebody's going to pleasure themselves at the sight of my gorgeousness, I'd prefer them to be in the same space and hung like a horse so I can enjoy it too.

The gigs in Tel Aviv went very well, then we headed to Jerusalem. Nobody had bothered to brief me about the difference between these two cities and they should have done. The Holy City was a far more conservative town than the modern capital.

My DJ spot went right on through the small hours and didn't finish till 10 in the morning. After that, I was taken to a hotel to catch a few hours' sleep before flying back to London.

When we got to the hotel, I was bleary-eyed and fairly drunk. Not the best state in which to walk straight into a really unpleasant experience. A massive Jewish Orthodox wedding was underway and the lobby was filled with people in the black hats, long frock coats and the traditional ringlets of that branch of the religion. It was Stamford Hill with decent weather. At the sight of me in my floor-length fur coat, a huge dark wig and feathered tricorn hat, they recoiled instantly in shock and horror.

'Come away, come away from that man!' the men in black said, grabbing their children and turning the kids' faces away from me.

'You're disgusting.'

'Shame on you.'

'What sort of man are you?'

And much more of the same. They literally hissed at me like a group of venomous black snakes. I was terrified and sobered up quickly.

'We've got to get you out of here,' said one of my minders. 'And right now.'

They whisked me up to my room in five seconds flat. How upsetting to think that the mere sight of me could bring forth such hatred and the few hours' sleep I snatched were troubled. Suddenly, all the glamour of coming to Israel had gone. All the applause and appreciation that had come my way just a few hours before in the clubs, had vanished. Suddenly, I was back to being the boy in the school playground with the cry of 'poof' echoing in my ears. Or me and my friends walking through that Birmingham estate in full drag, followed by 40 mocking yobs. It was a salutary reminder of how lucky I was to live in the usually safe space of London's West End. In The Holy City, where any religion should be about love, I'd encountered people who saw me as a lower form of humanity, from whom their children should be protected. It was especially sad that such prejudice should come from Jewish people, who had suffered so tragically in The Holocaust. They seemed to have forgotten, or maybe just refused to remember, that half a million homosexual people had also been exterminated in the camps. Oh well. Hey ho.

But my visit to Israel didn't teach me the lesson which it should have done. Only a month later, I accepted a gig in Beirut in Lebanon. I'd been booked to play DJ at a private party on a yacht. It was to be the same scenario as Israel: business class flight, five-star hotel but, hopefully, this time no wankers at the keyhole or religious fundamentalists. What's not to like? As things turned out, rather a lot.

At first, everything seemed fab. I was met at the airport and whisked through customs by two huge Incredible Hulk types in suits. The car had blacked out windows and sped along the motorway at the most incredible speed as if it were an ambulance and I was about to give birth. I wondered what the rush was and why the car had blackened windows.

The hotel suite was the most gorgeous place I'd ever stayed in. It made my glitzy hotel in Milan look like a B&B in Bridlington. Decorated in faux Louis XV style, it had a big round bed on a raised platform, chandeliers, gilded mirrors and a thick white carpet at least two inches deep. There was a marble bath and even a jacuzzi. The Incredible Hulks said I could order anything I wanted from room service and to rest till tomorrow evening when they'd pick me up and take me to the yacht. I ordered a superb meal and cracked open a bottle of bubbly from the mini-bar, which I knocked back as I soaked in the marble bath. It was all extremely vulgar and tasteless, like one of those old commercials for Cussons Imperial Leather. I loved every second of it.

I slipped into the fluffy white bathrobe and phoned everyone I could think of in the UK.

'You should see me!' I crowed to Curtain Mark back home in our King's Cross council flat. 'I'm like Joan Collins and Imelda Marcos rolled into one.'

By about 10 that night I was getting bored with showing off and decided to go for a wander round the hotel. But when I opened the bedroom door, I got a shock. The two Hulks who'd delivered me here were sitting on chairs right outside and obviously armed. I was under guard.

'Is there a problem?' I asked Hulk 1.

'Not at all,' he replied, 'but where are you going please?'

'Just for a toddle round the place.' I said. 'Have a bit of a butchers.'

'If you wish to do that,' said Hulk 2, 'we will accompany you.'

'Oh, no need for that, luv.' I said.

'I'm afraid we must insist.' replied Hulk 1.

So the three of us went for a stroll round this sparkly new billet, where everything was on the menu except class. For about 30 seconds, I was allowed a swift look at the sunken gardens, dotted with palm trees and pretty little fountains. Though I had no make-up on, I was wearing a Westwood pirate top and matching shorts. This combo plus my razor cut bleached crop didn't exactly blend in with the rest of the locals. I became aware that the two Hulks were uneasy and unhappy about being seen with me. The embarrassment came off them like sweat in the scorching hot night. After 15 minutes, I'd had enough and retreated to my room which, I now realised, was really a gilded cage in which I was expected to remain.

The truth was that I knew next to nothing about the promoters of the event I'd been hired for, let alone who owned the fancy yacht on which I was to do my thing. As always, I'd left everything in the capable hands of Karen the agent. All I'd really wanted to know was the fee and if I'd be turning left at the door of the plane. Nor was I really aware of how dangerous Lebanon was at that point, having just emerged from a long civil war and still riddled with warring factions. It was a country trying to rebuild itself on very shaky foundations.

In the morning, the security men had disappeared from outside my door. Yippee, I'd sneak out and have a look at the town. Beirut, before all its recent troubles, had been a beautiful, cosmopolitan city often called 'the Paris of the Middle East' and I was damned well going to see the sights. Even this early in the day, it was already hot so, to keep cool, I wore a pair of white harem pants, a flowing, off the shoulder white top and white sandals. I reckoned I looked both ethereal and glamorous. What I didn't understand was that, to a lot of people, I was also going to look threatening and even subversive. Despite the cloudless skies, I was about to walk into a storm.

I was so used to being stared at that, for most of the time, I didn't even notice it. But as I wandered down the side streets of Beirut, I was soon aware of hostile reactions. Especially from men, who would literally stop in their tracks when they saw me, either looking angry or making a strange clicking noise as I went past. I suppose the noise was the Lebanese equivalent of 'tut tut', but it was an eerie, disturbing sound, like something an animal might make before it lashed out. Before long, I was being followed by a small crowd of young men whose intentions I couldn't guess, but probably not because they admired couture fashion. Now it was me who felt like the animal, an animal being hunted down. Little by little, I increased my pace and by the time I was back near the hotel, I was practically jogging.

The security guards, in obvious panic, ran towards me.

'Where have you been? Where have you been?'

'Just for a walk,' I said. 'But a load of men began to follow me, so I came back.'

'You must understand,' said Hulk 2, 'that Westerners are not popular here. And your appearance is not what they're used to.'

'What's wrong with my appearance?' I asked, Dusty's hackles beginning to rise.

'It is not what Lebanese people are used to,' said Hulk 1. 'They do not approve of such clothing.'

'Well, that's a shame.' I replied. 'This is Westwood.'

I still found it really difficult to understand why some people couldn't recognise Auntie Vivienne's designs on sight.

'You must understand,' said Hulk 2, 'that you are very lucky to get back to this hotel unharmed. You are not to leave it again unless one of us goes with you.'

Still a bit stroppy, probably as a side-effect of being shaken up, I moaned that I was bored and that I wasn't going to sit in that suite all day. So the Hulks took pity and agreed to take me for a drive and some lunch. At least nobody would see me inside the blacked-out car. And it was lovely. We drove up through the mountains and cedar forests around the city, then up to the ancient Roman town of Tyre where they allowed me a short walk around the ruins, though never out of their sight for a moment. Lebanon was a stunningly beautiful country, which made it doubly sad that it was clearly a dangerous place for anyone who didn't conform to the rigid ideas of local culture.

At six on the dot, I was back in the blacked-out car, whisked to the marina and onto a huge yacht bristling with yet more armed security. I was to do a one hour set from a flower-bedecked grotto close to where the guests would arrive. I was told that the music was to be subdued and not overpowering. The sound man set it at an almost inaudible level and I was instructed never to increase it and swamp conversation. Bugger this, I thought. So I just popped on a pre-recorded CD mix and faked it for an hour. Nobody was very interested anyway. The guests were mostly overdressed women covered in diamonds and chubby men in penguin suits. Since I was never introduced to the host, I still have no idea who spent all that money flying a British drag queen all the way to Beirut, providing him with security and putting him into an expensive hotel suite, just to plonk him in the middle of a fucking flowerbed with the sound turned down. Nowt so queer as folk. I can only guess that I was there just to signal the host's progressive, liberal values or some shit like that. Perhaps only someone of boundless wealth could take the risk of displaying those values in a country that was very socially conservative, even dangerously so.

In the end, I was glad to get out of that sumptuous hotel suite. Out of the black car and back on the plane to London. I said goodbye to the two Hulks who I could tell couldn't wait to wave me off. I wondered what they said when they got home.

'What were you doing today, dear?' I heard their imaginary wives asking.

No doubt they lied. Looking after a drag queen was probably not seen as man's work. But who knows? Maybe, there was an alternative truth. Maybe they were two closeted gay boys, hiding behind their suits, their dark shades and their guns, unable to be themselves.

By now, I was seriously wondering if these trips to foreign climes, however glam and well-paid, were good for my soul. The Orthodox Jews of Israel didn't seem to want me there, nor did the Arabs of Lebanon. Good Old Blighty wasn't exactly a homophobia-free zone, but when the cab from Heathrow took me home, King's Cross had never looked lovelier.

here were three of us in the relationship,' my beloved Princess Diana had once famously said, 'so it was a bit crowded.'

By now, that was precisely the case with the boy called David Hodge from Walsall and most of the human interactions, romantic or otherwise, which entered his life. The third person was of course the Very Miss Dusty O.

For the two decades of my adult years when drag consumed it, I think my personality was quite unstable. My all-consuming passion was myself in the form of the drag diva I'd created. I'm not saying I was schizophrenic exactly, like Norman Bates dressing up as his dead mum in *Psycho*, but there was definitely some degree of conflict going on inside me. How could there not be? Like that actor who's played Ken Barlow in Corrie for most of his life or Charlie from *Casualty*, there must surely be some psychological effect, even if it's relatively minor. Some blurring of the lines where one character ends and the other begins. In my case, Dusty had always been, to some extent, a facet of my own personality. She was never exactly a 'role' I played, she was an extension of myself. The wild, flamboyant, glamorous 'me' that I'd fantasised about being when I was the boy who sat by the window.

But during Dusty's golden period, she was certainly the part of me who dominated. Dusty's appearance and Dusty's needs almost always took precedence over those of David Hodge. She certainly elbowed out much chance of a serious relationship. Since my teens, I'd dreamed of meeting the right man and settling down together in a lovely house with dogs and cats. The whole gay dream. In fact, the dream of most human beings, if only they admitted it.

There were some one-night-stands, even a few fleeting romances. None seemed to last long, though it was never me who ended them. Never once was I the one to walk out. I always hung on in there until they ran for the hills. What some men liked about me initially was often the thing they ended up running away from, as the reality of my lifestyle came home to them. Sometimes, my own physical realities would disappoint. When they woke up beside me in the morning, the glamazon they'd taken to bed the night before was revealed to be a pale, eyebrow-less corseted little man and they would soon move on to someone more conventionally 'cute'. Half a century before, the Forties movie goddess Rita Hayworth had nailed it when lamenting her own troubled love life and broken marriages.

'They went to bed with Gilda,' she sighed, recalling her most famous film role, 'and they woke up with me.'

Some boys used me as a step up the social ladder. As I've described, when I was 'Queen of Soho', I'd become a mini-celebrity, on the 'A List' for clubland's big events. I sometimes appeared on television. I knew the coolest crowd of performers, artists and promoters. Occasionally, some beautiful boy would flirt with me, become my 'favourite' of the moment and I'd delude myself that this Adonis liked me for myself and not for the invitations to the best parties and the free drugs and drink that came with hanging out with Dusty. An easy mistake to make when something that resembles Michelangelo's David is fluttering his eyelashes at you and the lashes aren't false.

Then there were the occasions when things would almost progress to the bedroom door.

'Would you like to go back to mine for a nightcap?' I'd ask, without much originality.

'Oh thanks, I really like you, but I'm just not ready for a relationship,' was the reply. Which meant they liked me but not enough to sleep with me.

Or alternatively...

'I just don't want to spoil what we have.'

Which meant not spoiling it for *them* as they were doing just great out of the arrangement as it was, thanks very much.

Inevitably, these scenarios would end with us falling out or with me deliberately throwing one of my tornado tantrums, simply to disentangle myself from a freeloader who I now realised wasn't really interested in me. It was all rather unpleasant and dispiriting so gradually, over the years, I erected a wall of indifference against the whole idea of having a relationship. My self-protective barriers became heightened and I became less and less trustful of men in general.

'Men!' I'd joke. 'Only interested in one thing.'

But I wasn't laughing inside. Maybe I'd end up like that pervert in the hotel in Israel. Looking through keyholes and using my right hand.

There was, however, one category of guy I was rarely short of. The type who was sexually into drag artists or trans people. For me, the idea of having it off with my drag on was horrific. Since all my drag gear was of the highest calibre, I wasn't keen on that at all. I certainly wasn't having somebody pump one out all over a £500 hairpiece. I didn't like it psychologically either. It was Dusty they wanted to shag, not me. I just wasn't interested in helping somebody live out their fetishes and getting nothing much back in return except a ruined wig.

Within this particular tribe, there was even a sub-group (to use a highly appropriate expression) who first appeared as I nudged into middle-age. This lot wanted to enjoy some kind of maternal domination. You know the sort of thing (though, hopefully you don't). A smacked bottom and sent to bed early with their thumb in their mouth. Or resting their head on mummy's bosom whilst just wearing a nappy. Not my cup of tea at all. Much too Cynthia Payne.

In short, there were very few gay men who wanted a serious romance with a drag queen. Far too embarrassing to explain to their families and friends.

'So what does your new friend do for a living, dear?' somebody's liberal, tolerant mother might ask, expecting a conventional answer. A teacher, a lawyer, an accountant, even a hairdresser. But a drag queen would probably test mother's tolerance a bit too far.

Back then, drag simply wasn't mainstream in the way it is now. We were still seen as bizarre creatures; a fringe within a fringe. And though that fact was the very essence of our appeal, it was also our drawback. From memory, I'd say that 99 percent of the drag queens of that period were single and made do with what they could get, sexually and emotionally. For most gay men, a friendship with a drag artist was all very well; something cool and trendy, a virtue-signalling of your progressive values. But a lifelong relationship? That was something else entirely.

In my own case, the great irony was that drag was never part of my sexual character anyway. It simply had nothing to do with my sexuality. I was essentially just a gay man who liked other gay men. Drag was undeniably my main focus in life; a wonderful creative outlet that had made me a good living and, for both those reasons, I took it very seriously. But that was as far as it went. I never for one second saw myself as a transvestite who wanted to wear women's clothes 24 hours a day. Nor did I have the slightest inclination to change my gender.

But, like everyone else, I had my 'needs' and eventually found my own way of satisfying them. At the start of the Nineties, gay saunas had become very popular and London was soon scattered with them. The biggest of these was the famous Chariots, tucked discreetly under a railway arch in Shoreditch. Behind a small entrance, it was like Doctor Who's Tardis; a huge place, complete with swimming-pool, jacuzzis and a bar; clean, well-run and a lot less seedy than the grim bathhouses of yesteryear.

This was somewhere you went for anonymous sex. Nothing more. Unlike in a gay pub or the clubs where I performed, you didn't have to chat for hours, or even speak at all, before you both got what you wanted. Here, not in drag and with only a skimpy towel wrapped round me, I would never be recognised or gossiped about. I loved the anonymity of it. If somebody rejected you, you just shrugged your naked shoulders and moved on to another possibility. At Chariots, everyone was judged purely on the same simple criterion of sexual desirability. It didn't matter what class you were, what job you did, how much money you had. Everybody here had an equal chance of scratching their own particular itch. For the first time, it provided me with some sort of regular sex life. Above all, Dusty was nowhere to be seen. In those sweaty, steam-filled chambers, she didn't exist.

The one time I ever chatted to somebody over a coffee was the one time I got hurt. I reached home to find that he had plastered 'I just shagged Dusty O' all over his Facebook page and I was inundated with hateful remarks. It taught me a lesson. After that, I was even more careful to keep the different segments of my life in their own neat little boxes and never allow them to mix. Inevitably, that just made me feel even more isolated.

So, for years on end, I was to be completely alone emotionally. I had some much-loved friends like Curtain Mark and Stan and Mr O'Dowd, but always beneath my defiant surface, I longed to find somebody who could love me for me; the person I was 24 hours a day and not just the drag diva, that creature who only came alive in those few tipsy hours on either side of midnight. On so many nights, I staggered home drunkenly, washed off the make-up and fell onto my big golden sleigh bed, crying out of sheer loneliness. An hour before, I'd been the belle of the ball, up in the spotlight, the life and soul of the party and now I lay weeping alone. No longer Dusty, but David again.

Still the busiest boy in town.

And still the loneliest.

asten your seat belts, it's going to be a bumpy night' said Bette Davis as Margo Channing in *All About Eve*.

Though the Millennium came and went, the Very Miss Dusty O went on forever, or so it seemed to me – and possibly to some envious others too. Staying at the top of the trec in what was quite a cut-throat profession needed a lot of determination and effort. There were always a lot of queens chasing not that many jobs and plenty of fresh young faces coming up behind me. I wasn't quite Margo Channing just yet, but there were a good few Eve Harringtons with their eye on the title 'Queen of Soho.'

The drag 'sisterhood' was certainly not notably warm and friendly. Far from it. It was frequently eyebrow-pencils at dawn. In public however, we usually gave people what they wanted to hear. That it was a fun-filled world of self-expression and excitement where barriers were cast aside, where people had each other's back, and which was a community filled with love and cuddly liberal values. I even went onto a crappy Esther Rantzen talk show which was 'investigating' drag and spouted all this bollocks. God knows why. Probably the fee.

By now I'm afraid the cracks were setting in from a life of non-stop parties, alcohol, drugs and vanity. They were still small cracks, hardly more than hairline fissures, but in time they were going to split wide open. I also felt the fun factor slipping away from me and knew that could be fatal.

But on the painted surface, all was well. I was probably the highest-earning drag queen in Britain. I held prestigious residencies in three of London's biggest clubs. The long-running *Gay Tea Dance* at The Limelight Club had closed due to redevelopment, but we quickly moved it to a venue in Leicester Square and renamed it *Sound On Sunday - SOS* for short – and just carried on. Atomic Kitten was our first star turn just before they had their No 1 single *Whole Again* and photos of me with the girls were splashed across the press. I still never missed any opportunity to maintain my visibility. By now, that was a reflex. Probably even an addiction.

As it always had been, keeping myself in the spotlight was a very expensive business. Much of the money I made was consumed by the cost of my clothes, shoes and wigs, when I should have been investing it for my future. At one point, I was £10K in debt but the lure of the lifestyle was still too strong for me to stop spending. Maybe I was psychologically removing myself from the deprivations of my childhood, when the bailiffs had come and taken our lovely house, my sisters' ponies, the big car and everything else we'd taken for granted. I could still remember how small and freezing cold Nana Edna's tiny house had been. How I'd shared a miserable bedroom with my two sisters. How

I'd had to wear my mother's hand-knitted jumpers to school and the laughter of my classmates and Miss Pinchface. But nobody was going to laugh at my clothes now. Nobody ever laughed at Westwood.

SOS was never to become one of the great club nights like *Pushca* or *Bambina*. It always did respectable business, but never pulled in the huge crowds I'd so often won elsewhere. Grace Jones never danced on the bar. Robbie Williams and Gary Barlow never came and sipped champagne inside an Arabian tent. Its profits weren't that great, so I wracked my brains to come up with some big event that would grab attention and put bums on bar-stools. The clubbers of London were like some ravenous beast that had to be constantly fed something new and fresh or they would bare their teeth at you then walk away.

Luckily, I had a Road to Damascus moment. A big star. Almost rivalling Boy George at one point. Been living in semi-obscurity for years, like Greta Garbo. The punters would come just to see what he looked like now. His name was Peter Robinson. Known to the world as Marilyn.

But would he do it? As he was a friend of George's, I'd come across him a few times in the past and not always happily. Marilyn could really play the temperamental diva when he felt like it (yeah, yeah, it takes one to know one). But Marilyn really needed to be handled with kid gloves, so I pulled them on pronto. He was going to be the big star I needed; the rocket-booster to improve the *SOS* balance sheet.

When he was young, Marilyn had arguably been the most beautiful of all the androgynous rock stars who personified the New Romantic movement of the early Eighties. Half Jamaican, with an exquisite face and long blond hair, he'd looked like something out of a Caravaggio painting. But he'd followed the path that so many did. Too much attention. Too much indulgence. He'd had a big hit single back in 1983 but, after a few years in the public eye and a very publicised fall from grace due to drug addiction, had pretty much vanished without trace. A brief meteor that had fizzled out long before its time.

'So, what d'you say, Marilyn?' I asked.

'No.'

'Oh come on, it'll be great,' I coaxed. 'All your old fans would love to see you. And the new kids too. You're still a legend!'

'No.'

This went on for ages. It seemed Marilyn wanted to be courted like some shy maiden. But a bunch of flowers and a box of Cadbury's Milk Tray weren't going to crack it. So I agreed to a driver and a night in a decent hotel and he agreed to a surprisingly low fee. I suspect he was nervous at the thought of a 'comeback'. Worried that it might be a disaster and make headlines for all the wrong reasons.

The buzz started the moment the ads for the gig hit the gay rags, with big pictures of him in his beauteous youth. Would he show up? Could he still sing? What did he look like now? Was he still on drugs and, if he was, would he be fit to perform? It was like that Judy Garland thing in her final appearances; the vultures gathering, half-hoping to see a car crash.

Before the event, Marilyn behaved beautifully and even did a few press interviews by phone to promote the gig. On the night though, we were all a bag of nerves as so much was depending on him. Things didn't start too well.

A particularly dishy driver was sent to Marilyn's house to fetch him. I forget the driver's name, but let's call him Clint.

'I'm at the house, but he's not ready yet.' Clint phoned to say.

'Okay…'

'He's still not ready yet,' reported Clint, half an hour later, then an hour later, then an hour and a half later.

At the club, we were beginning to sweat a little. What was Marilyn doing? Was he just playing the diva? Or was he locked inside his own bathroom, shitting himself at the prospect of an audience after all these years? I started to wonder if tonight was going to be the clubland equivalent of the sinking of the Titanic. Taking not just himself, but me and the *SOS* club down with him. The name of the club suddenly seemed worryingly apposite.

'Here he comes!' called Clint. 'We're on our way to his hotel.'

Phew. We relaxed a little.

'Um, we've stopped off in Soho,' said Clint 10 minutes later. 'He's gone to pick something up from a friend.'

'Pick what up?' I almost yelled into the phone, praying it wasn't a substance I really didn't want him to take before he'd done the show.

'Fucked if I know,' sighed Clint.

The clock was really ticking now. We were due to open at nine o'clock and Marilyn needed a do a sound-check first. Would there be time for that? Oh God. But finally he arrived, was charming to everyone, did a professional sound-check then disappeared back to his hotel (a hotel he didn't really need anyway as he lived fairly close). I was extremely reluctant to let him leave the building again in case he went instead to pick up something else from some other friend.

By now, there was a massive queue out in Leicester Square. All the old disco grandees of the Eighties and Nineties club scene had slapped on the face-packs, squeezed into their clubbing gear and come out to see him. Some fans had come from as far as Italy. The buzz was electric. You could even feel it in the night air.

On the dot of 10.30pm Marilyn arrived back, escorted by Clint. Obviously, he was no longer the breathtaking young man he'd once been. The slim, beautiful body had thickened into that of a middle-aged man and, strangely, he'd lost a few teeth, but overall he looked in reasonable working order. When he walked onto that stage, the applause was ear-splitting. He performed his hits, both big and not so big, and the fans adored it. A blast from the past and nostalgia at its best. And I could see that Marilyn was really moved by his fantastic reception.

So was I. The evening had suddenly become far more than just a gig to fill the club's coffers. I almost forgot that vulgar criterion as I watched one of the great pop icons strut his stuff again and bring the house down. His performance later won an award in *BOYZ* magazine as the P.A. of the Year. Better still, he beat all of Jeremy Joseph's chart-topping kiddie turns from *G-A-Y*, a fact which gave me limitless pleasure. Thanks to Marilyn, *SOS* was now established as a credible club. Bette Davis once said, 'old age isn't for cissies.' Maybe not, but Marilyn had proved that middle-age could still be pretty damn impressive.

None of us was getting any younger. There was no denying that. I was well into my thirties by now and so was George. He went through a period of putting on a lot of weight and, like Marilyn, was no longer the pencil-slim sylph of yore. In some interview, I made the mistake of referring to his 'big body'.

'Better a big body than a no-body', George hit back in another of the gay mags.

Oooh. Bitch. But it was nothing new. George and I quite often had spats. We were both surprisingly similar, which was probably why we'd become mates in the first place. We still both didn't give a fuck what people thought. We both called a spade a spade. As I've said, we both lacked that filter which is a very useful gift if you want a quiet life. Of course, neither George nor I did want a quiet life. So our little tiffs happened quite often. Usually over sod all. And usually, to be honest, started by me.

One day he rang me up after we'd been out for dinner with a bunch of people the night before.

'What was wrong with you last night then?' he asked. 'Face like a funeral.'

'I wasn't enjoying myself,' I pouted back.

'And why was that? I paid the fucking bill, didn't I?' he replied. 'What exactly was not to the liking of the great Queen of Soho?'

'I was stuck at the far end of the table, wasn't I?' I replied. 'Like a poor relation.'

'Oh, for fuck's sake.'

'And it was such a squash on that banquette that one of my arse cheeks was suspended in mid-air for two solid hours.'

'Oh, was that you?' he said. 'I remember somebody blowing off. Very unpleasant.'

'Up yours.'

'Up yours too,' he replied, and the phone slammed down.

We'd then both sulk for a few days till one of us would call the other and it was never mentioned again. Silly queens. I guess part of it was me never wanting George to see me as a typical gushing fan or as one of those sycophants and hangers-on that all stars attract like flies on shit. I couldn't have borne it if he'd thought that. I admired him so much as an artist and would forever be grateful to him for the inspiration he'd been to me so long before, when I'd pinned up his pictures and my mother had gone 'tut tut'.

But my dear old Mom had stopped going 'tut tut' many years ago, finally realising it was a waste of breath. When my next birthday came along, I decided to throw a big party at *SOS* and I wanted my family to come down for it. Obviously, their lives were very different to my own. Walsall and London were only a hundred miles apart but they might have been on different planets. So although the love remained between us, communication was often fairly simplistic and confined to bland generalities. You know the sort of thing.

'How's Dad?' I'd ask my mother on the phone.

'He's fine,' she'd replied. 'Well, fine as he'll ever be.'

'And how's Julie?' I asked.

'She's fine too. Going on holiday soon.'

'That's nice. Where to?'

'I've forgotten. Somewhere hot, I think.'

'That's nice,' I'd reply.

'Did I tell you that fat woman two doors down has had a hysterectomy? Very nasty time, poor thing.'

And so on. My parents rarely asked any questions about my life or my work. Even after all this time, my mother and father remained focused on each other; their marriage as tempestuous as it had always been. There would have been little point in telling them I was known as the 'Queen of Soho', because it wouldn't really have interested them. Soho was a foreign country; its landscape and way of life quite beyond their understanding. Their world remained that of the suburbs with the manicured lawns. A world of narrow horizons.

But there was one exception to that. Even Mom and Julie were tempted down to London for the chance to meet Boy George. For the first time ever, I'd asked him if he'd do a bit of a turn at one of my club nights. At that time, he was performing in his own musical, *Taboo*, to rave reviews. After some difficult times, his star was again in the ascendant, exactly where it deserved to be.

When I met my mother and sister off the train, I had a full head of black and white waist length extensions. Whereas, she'd once have freaked out at such an apparition, Mom didn't bat an eyelid, now pretty much bomb-proof to the way I looked. There had come a moment when she'd realised she'd lost the war and graciously accepted defeat. I'm not sure exactly when that moment had been; perhaps around the time that she had visited Dids at his bedside in those final days. Maybe it had finally sunk into her then that the people I mixed with, and whom I loved, weren't just a bunch of worthless weirdos, but were wonderful human beings who happened to occupy a different world from that which she herself inhabited. The bottom line was that big progress had been made between Mom and me. A truce had been declared and now we could actually start getting along together.

When I took her and my sister backstage to meet George, he didn't look remotely like he usually did. At the party, he was to perform numbers from his musical in which he played the character of Leigh Bowery, a clubland style icon of the

Eighties and the famous muse of the painter Lucian Freud. Consequently, he was dressed in a huge polka dot crinoline with enormous spiked headers and platform-heeled boots. The pop star with the plaits and pink lips singing *Karma Chameleon* was nowhere to be seen.

'You're not Boy George!' she exclaimed.

'Yes I am, Mrs Hodge. I promise you.'

'Oh no, you're not.'

'Oh yes I am.'

Eventually he convinced her and a fabulous picture was taken of the two of them which still stands on her bureau at home. Now, as a very old lady who can't walk too well, Mom has carers to look after her and she loves to tell them about nightclubbing in London once with Boy George and her drag queen son. Mom and I have come a long way from that day when she found my make-up bag and threw it all in the bin. I wasn't the son she expected to have, though I like to imagine she's now almost glad of that. But if she is, she'll never tell me.

Christmas was coming and once again I needed to think of a special guest who might bring the crowds flooding into Leicester Square. I'd already had Marilyn and George, so it seemed like a brilliant idea to invite the last of the Eighties gender-benders to perform at *SOS*.

Pete Burns of Dead or Alive had always been a personal idol. But Pete didn't need the money and would now only do a gig if he wanted to. He was one of those strange people who'd made a fortune as a performer, but who didn't much enjoy performing. Pete far preferred shopping or having yet another cosmetic procedure.

To my surprise, he accepted at once and with none of the diva-esque behaviour for which he was notorious. He did an amazing set to the delight of the army of his hardcore fans who always turned out to see Pete's appearances. Like me, they'd have gone almost anywhere to see him. If he'd announced a gig in Antarctica these folk would have got there on sledges pulled by huskies. That night, he delivered nine great tracks and did no less than four costume changes. When Pete gave a show he gave it his all, right down to his last bead of sweat. He had the big star's knack of holding an audience exactly where he wanted them, then slapping them round the face to get an even bigger reaction. It was one of the most mesmerising performances I've ever seen. Pete could still spin them round.

Poor dear Pete Burns. One of the indisputable greats of the Eighties and Nineties alternative scene, but a name largely unknown to kids today. His health ruined by endless cosmetic surgery, to which he was addicted and which had bankrupted him. If one operation had been botched, he'd have a second one to try to fix what had gone wrong with the first. The once beautiful face was now grotesque. When he died of a massive heart attack in 2016, aged only 57, it upset me badly. He was a fabulous one-off and I'll never forget him. Rest in peace Pete. Hope you're causing chaos in heaven.

Boy George, Marilyn, Pete Burns. All of them had enjoyed fabulous success but also some very dark times. That old showbiz cliché, I suppose.

Though I wasn't remotely in their league, as time passed, I too was beginning to have more and more of what Margo Channing had called 'bumpy nights'.

For the first five years of the new Millennium, I was still working almost every night. Sometimes I felt like a mouse in a cage, running endlessly on a wheel. It was a glittering wheel, but a wheel nonetheless. For the first time, my lifelong enjoyment of dressing-up and turning my face into a work of art was beginning to fade. There were only so many times an artist could paint the same picture without getting bored painting it. Nowadays, what I was doing was most definitely *work*. I didn't hate it, but my joy in it was no longer anything like as existential. My life was consumed by being the Very Miss Dusty O and not David Hodge. An issue of which I was becoming more and more aware.

On top of this weariness and boredom, I began to suffer severe back pain, triggered by years of wearing six-inch heels for eight hours at a time. To cope, I began to drink more heavily, liking it more and more. In the clubs, a large percentage of my customers were usually drunk, so why not join them? After all, a good host should be in the same frame of mind as his guests. Up for it. Ready for fun. Life is a cabaret, blah blah blah. I was also uncomfortably conscious of the fact that the gigs I now got, though still numerous enough, weren't of the same calibre as they'd once been.

I'd gone from playing host to Kylie Minogue, Grace Jones and Robbie Williams to entertaining Joe Average on his weekly night out. Nothing to be ashamed of or embarrassed about, but it had come home to me that I was no longer the bright young thing I'd once been. The drink also meant I was also putting on weight. In Conduit Street, the Westwood gang must have clocked that Dusty's measurements were rapidly changing. I was no longer the Size 12 of my *Bambina* days. Now I was size 14 at a push and with a very deep breath.

So, bit by bit, the booze became an indispensable crutch to ease both the pain in my back and the tiredness in my soul. Incredibly, it seemed I'd forgotten the awful addiction of my father and the hell it had caused in our family life. Except, that wasn't totally true. Some of the grim images from that time were indelibly etched in my memory. The misery. The tears. The remorse. The broken promises. All of it stayed with me, in glorious technicolour, as if it had happened yesterday. So why didn't I try to stop? I suppose because I didn't want to. Neither had Margo in *All About Eve*. Time was passing. I was surrounded by all the young 'Eve Harringtons' of the drag scene. I was no longer quite as pretty as I'd once been. My love life was non-existent.

Fuck it, let's open another bottle.

The Very Miss Dusty O, backstage at Pride 2014

There's a lot to be said for the chihuahua. Small, cheap to run, loyal and loving, don't need lots of walking. For a lonely, ageing drag queen, they might deliver some of the affection he was yearning for.

I got three of them.

By this time, I'd lived for 10 years in my two-bedroom council flat. Curtain Mark (still aka Maria the Tart with a Heart) and I got along fine and it was a happy, cosy place, illuminated by memories of Dids and of the loads of good times holding dinner parties and little get-togethers with fun people. There was a tiny back yard, which I'd transformed into a mini paradise of potted plants and jasmine climbing up the walls. I'd trellised and fenced it in and it was a lovely little oasis of calm slap bang in the middle of King's Cross. *Time Out* magazine had done a shoot, with me sitting in my bower of flowers in a big straw hat and a white suit. The Vita Sackville-West of the gay community.

In this very eclectic, alternative corner of town, my neighbours had always been very friendly. Obviously, I led a very different sort of life to most, but I wasn't noisy and caused no trouble to anyone. We'd stop and chat when I was walking the dogs. I was even invited to join the local residents' committee, a major compliment I guess, but I politely declined. Not really my scene.

Then, out of the blue, everything changed. A new man moved into the flat above us. He was young and loud with a huge English Bull Terrier which terrified my tiny chihuahuas. The peace and calm we'd previously enjoyed was soon shattered. He played music almost non-stop and his dog would bark hour after hour when he left it on its own, sometimes for days on end, and we'd be kept awake half the night. I was more concerned about the poor dog than the noise it made, but our lovely home was no longer such a pleasant place to be.

If I passed him in the street, he'd glare at me and I was conscious of being watched when I went off to work in the evenings. I began to feel very vulnerable every time I left the flat.

'I think he's clocking my movements,' I said to Curtain Mark. 'I don't like this at all. I don't feel safe.'

'Maybe you're imagining it. Relax.'

Perhaps Curtain Mark was right. Perhaps I was being a drama queen as usual. So I decided to try to get this new neighbour on board, to kill him with courtesy. I began saying hello, getting just a grunt in return. Then one day, I found his dog loose outside and returned it to his door. He hadn't noticed she was gone, but he managed to mumble some sort of thanks, as the animal would have been killed pretty quickly on the busy streets.

It turned out that the poor creature was very friendly and not frightening at all. The neighbour appeared to warm to me slightly too. Job done, I thought. He never took the poor beast for walks, so I offered my dog walking services. Mine were walked three times daily and one more pooch wouldn't be a problem. So the bull terrier joined the pack and they all got on well. No doubt we made a strange sight; three tiny chihuahuas each no bigger than a handbag and The Hound of the Baskervilles. But, for a short time, things improved, or at least got no worse.

In my little garden paradise, there was a fire escape door from the internal staircase of the building. No one had used this door in years. Until now.

'That yard is communal,' the neighbour upstairs said one day. 'It's not just for you. It belongs to all of us.'

'That's wrong,' I replied. 'I'll show you my tenancy agreement if you like.'

Next thing I knew, there was a huge washing line going across the space on which he'd hung old blankets, leaving them there for two weeks. I realised he was trying to provoke a reaction and sensed danger. But my little private sanctuary, a space I'd grown to love and value, had been invaded and I wasn't going to take it lying down.

'Dry now,' said the note I pinned to the blankets, leaving them neatly folded in a plastic bag outside his door.

The next thing was the appearance of a large dog kennel at the top of the stairs, in breach of the fire regulations and preventing emergency access. His poor dog was now dumped there, with my little garden as her only toilet and me the only one who cleared up her mess. I was not happy. But I was also increasingly nervous.

'I'm lying low cos I shanked someone in a pub,' he'd told me during one of the infrequent times we'd exchanged sentences. He was clearly a violent, aggressive man.

For a week or so, I escaped from the anxiety of all this, flying to South Africa to perform at their Gay Pride event. It was a wonderful trip. I'd arrived on stage via a crane which lowered me gently down in front of a crowd of 10,000 cheering people and my two-hour set went down a storm. Domestic tensions back in London seemed a million miles away. Pride events are often so full of love and a sense of community that it's easy to forget that the 'real world' is just around the corner, lying in wait.

I arrived home in the middle of the afternoon, exhausted after a 12-hour flight. Curtain Mark had been looking after the dogs, who went bananas at the sight of me. Mark was at work and it was a warm, sunny day, so I opened the back door to let in some air. Unknown to me, the entire time I'd been away, the neighbour's dog had been locked in my garden. From what Mark later told me, she'd howled 24 hours a day and it had become a real problem for the whole house. That morning, after yet another disturbed night, Mark had posted a polite note through the neighbour's door asking him not to leave the dog out at night as he had to work the next day and needed his sleep. That note lit a fuse which, when he'd read it, had exploded in the brain of a dangerous thug. It provided the excuse he'd been looking for.

I heard the fire door slam. He thundered down the stairs, kicking his dog's huge kennel over the handrail and down onto my beautiful flowers. Then he trashed the entire garden, throwing my pots around, ripping up my plants by the root. Years of hard work and loving care smashed and broken in two minutes. Poisonous waves of homophobic bile poured from his lips.

'Fucking queer bastards! Fucking freaks!' he screamed. 'You all ought to be strung up. Have your balls chopped off.'

My instinct told me to flee from the kitchen, but my dogs were barking in panic and I was scared he might hurt them. I gathered them up fast, pushed them into the living-room and slammed the door shut. For a minute or two, it went quiet and I crept back to the kitchen to see what was happening. Big mistake. He was already inside the flat.

'Get out of here,' I shouted.

He grabbed me by the neck, pushing me to the ground, punching and kicking me.

'I'm going to fucking kill you! You dirty fucking queer!'

His hands were now around my throat, trying to strangle me. I could smell his breath as he sprayed me with his venom. Mercifully, I blacked out.

But somebody was looking down and protecting me. At that very moment, Curtain Mark came home. Mark is quite a well-built guy and not one to be easily frightened. He managed to pull this screaming nutcase off me and manhandle him out of the back door. Slowly, I began to come round as Mark called the police. But it wasn't over yet. Outside, the guy finished his task of destroying my lovely garden then went up into the street, where he carried on screaming.

'I ain't done yet, you filthy poofs! I'm coming to get you. You just fucking wait.'

This went on for 15 full, horrible minutes until the police arrived and arrested him. By now, I was in total shock. They took me to the police station where I was seen by a doctor who photographed my bruises and where I gave a statement. The nutcase was charged with trespass, assault, criminal damage and, above all, threats to kill. All of it witnessed, all of it undeniable.

'There's something else I need to tell you,' I said to the police officer interviewing me. 'A while back, he said he was lying low as he'd knifed someone in a pub.'

'Aaahhh,' said the policeman, his eyes lighting up as he made the connection 'We've been looking for this evil bastard for a while. This is two birds with one stone.'

My psychotic neighbour was held in remand. Thank God, because if they'd bailed him and let him go home, I could never have spent another night in that flat with him back upstairs. Eventually, I had my moment in court, as did the man he'd previously attacked in the pub. Our assailant was convicted on all counts and sentenced to six years in prison.

I'd been terrified of having to appear in court that day, looking into the eyes of the man who'd tried to strangle me. I even had melodramatic visions of him leaping out of the dock and getting his hands round my throat again, choking the life out of me. I guess I'd seen too many movies. But it was a very difficult thing to go through. I'd hoped that being a performer might help me cope; the witness box becoming just another stage. After all, I'd only just come back from playing to thousands of people in South Africa and that hadn't fazed me in the least. But in the event, that hadn't helped at all. This stuff was just too serious. If Mark hadn't come back at that moment...

I still live with the trauma of that summer afternoon. I'd seen genuine hate in that man's face. Hate against another human being who'd never done him the smallest harm and who'd reached out to him in friendship. I firmly believe that without Mark, I would have been killed and become yet another hate crime statistic. It was impossible to keep the 'what ifs' out of my head. What if Mark had been delayed at work? What if he'd missed his bus? What if he'd stopped to buy a can of Coke? What if he'd stopped to tie his shoelace?

It's unlikely that my mad neighbour would recognise me in the street these days. I have a beard now and I've aged. But I'm always aware that he's now out of prison and no doubt bearing an almighty grudge against me for having helped to send him there. And after all, I still live at the same address. What if I walked round a corner straight into him and, beard or not, he saw the fear flood into my face and realised who I was. I try very hard not to think of such a nightmare scenario, but it never entirely leaves me.

It is frightening to think that what I wore, the way I looked, the way I chose to love, could ignite loathing in another person. It was a sharp reminder that, even in our supposedly liberal and enlightened times, to some people I was still a freak; still somebody to be punched, kicked and strangled, not applauded and photographed for magazine covers with Boy George. The attack made me feel like that scared little schoolboy again, worried that my mere existence would invoke the blows and the name-calling that had once been my daily lot.

So I'd been wrong to think that my safe bubble of existence in tolerant, progressive London would keep me safe. I'd been wrong to think that the prejudice I'd encountered in a hotel lobby in Tel Aviv and in the streets of Beirut were just the benighted aberrations of two conservative societies. The worst threat to my existence had come from somebody living only a few metres away from me.

But mixed in with all that fear was real anger too. Playing with how I presented myself physically had always been a massive part of me. It had been a way for me to push back against my own boundaries of self. The plain, ginger kid turning himself into something unrecognisable and beautiful. That magical power of transformation. The butterfly emerging from the chrysalis. I was fiercely proud of all that and defiant too.

I lectured myself to remember that and not to let the actions of one deranged individual undermine the confidence in myself which had taken so long to build in the first place. I decided that the best thing was to get on with my way of life and act as if nothing had happened. In that way, the ultimate victory would be mine. While that warped and wicked man was slopping out his shit into a bucket every morning, Dusty would still be up there on stage in the spotlight.

But it was easier said than done. The dark memory of lying on my kitchen floor, defenceless and gasping for breath, remained just under the surface and fed a worry that had begun to seep into my mind. Where was I going? How long did I want to carry on with the life I led? But I didn't have the answers, so I tried to ignore the questions. The show must go on. And it did. Except those questions refused to go away

'*Mirror Mirror On The Wall...*'

That old fairytale question was one of the few for which I definitely did have an answer. Whoever 'the fairest' now was, it sure wasn't me. In the early years of the new century, I was pushing 40. I was still knocking back the booze and had the waistline to prove it. And I was still single as always.

Despite the murderous attack on me and those nagging thoughts about the direction of my life, my addiction to the mirror remained powerful. I was still its slave. I still sat in front of it for two to three hours turning David Hodge of Walsall into the Very Miss Dusty 0, the 'Queen of Soho'. I continued to work my ass off in any club that would have me and to fill my life with the people I met there. It was what I was good at and what I knew so well. I did DJ spots, I wrote music columns for the gay press, I did low-rent TV shows where I dressed to knock their eyes out and delivered the bitchy one-liners they wanted to hear. I filled my world with work and everything connected with it.

Everything else was pushed aside. Shamefully, some old friends who had nothing to do with the scene had been sidelined or even dumped. I felt they didn't 'get' what I was doing. They reminded me too much of my past and maybe too much of the 'real' me as opposed to the one I'd manufactured. The Very Miss Dusty O no longer needed them. These people were no loss to her, but they would become a huge loss to David Hodge, especially in the rough times ahead, when true friends became harder to find.

Being Dusty had opened many doors to me, but they were only ever doors to other corners of that old familiar drag bubble. They were never new or adventurous or challenging. That was a pity because, had I tried to strike out for fresh fields, my name alone would probably have paved the way to make it successful. I had great contacts. Guests I knew in the clubs were frequently people working in the creative industries who could have helped me break into things I'd loved in the past, like writing and art. But instead, I took the easy option and stayed inside that drag bubble, the claustrophobia of which was getting more and more stifling.

The simple truth was that I was getting bored with it. Bored with the same silly clubland conversations with the same narcissistic people. Bored with the music I rarely enjoyed any more, but which I was forced to play in very commercial venues I now worked in. Above all, I was bored with the people who related only to Dusty and not to David. David was desperate for some care and love, but there was no time for him, because 'she' needed to get ready. No time for David's interests because 'she' needed clothes, wigs and make up and all that stuff needed to be earned. Dusty was a very tough and demanding mistress. People reacted to

Dusty in a totally different way to how they did with David. They feted her and made her special; they hardly noticed David. So I put the words in her mouth I knew they wanted to hear and did the things that Dusty would naturally do. Poor little David.

As I've said, I'd always thought of Dusty as an extension of myself, a different side of me. Never as an entirely separate creation. But that was slowly changing. I began to think of her in the third person. Now Dusty was 'she', not 'me'. She was becoming somebody else entirely and I wasn't sure I liked her much.

These days, when I watch *Ru Paul's Drag Race*, a show that has made drag highly fashionable, I hear the young queens declaring that they'd now found 'the real me'. That was never the case with David Hodge and Dusty. By doing drag, I was consciously *hiding* the authentic me under layer upon layer of carefully constructed artifice. And bit by bit, gig by gig, year by year, it was beginning to choke me – almost as fatally as my psycho neighbour had tried to do on my kitchen floor.

Yet still I carried on. And for a time, the drag gods were kinder to me than they had been for a while. Or at least to Dusty. Up on drag Olympus, the gods decided that the old girl was to have one final spell of glory. All the new pretty 'Eve Harringtons' were still snapping at her heels, but the 'Queen of Soho' would be given one last smash hit.

The Raymond Revue Bar had once been a famous, indeed infamous, Soho venue. Like the Windmill Theatre long before it, Paul Raymond's nightclub had been an iconic part of the West End landscape, its name known to people who would never come to Soho in their lives. For a long time, it had been the only place in Britain to offer full-frontal nudity. Since the late 1950s, hundreds of thousands of slightly perspiring men had paid their entrance fee to ogle the strippers and enjoy a twitch in the trouser department.

But by the turn of the century, its cachet had been stolen by newer, cooler places like Stringfellows and Spearmint Rhino and the poor old Revue Bar seemed dated and sad. Luckily, it had now been saved by new owners, who had refurbished it, yet retained much of its old glamour, including the red velvet seating, the gorgeous art deco bar and enormous chandelier. There was now a huge dancefloor and a big stage for cabaret acts, plus two small side stages which had been converted into podiums for pole dancers. Beautiful boys were employed as waiters. Once again, everything sparkled and it was still exactly how people would imagine a decadent Soho nightclub to be. The glittering ghosts of previous decades must have been delighted.

My good friend Walt was now working there, doing PR and programming events, in order to lift the club back up to a premier position in the city's nightlife. He invited me to go along and suss it out as a possible home for a new club night he had in mind for the Very Miss Dusty O. I took one look and fell in love with it. This place would be perfect to host something, but what exactly?

Walt had an awesome idea. In San Francisco, there was a famous club called Trannyshack, which featured innovative, and sometimes controversial, live shows featuring the stars of the California drag community. Walt's idea was to transport the concept to London with Dusty running the show. It would be original, daring and up-market. A place where the fantastic freaks of the Eighties and Nineties could once more strut their stuff, as they had in the glory days of *Pushca* and *Bambina*.

My jaded old heart leapt at the idea. I'd not worked somewhere on that level for such a long time. Over time, many promoters had attempted to recapture the style of nights like *Pushca*, but had usually failed. In the new millennium it seemed that clubbers were more interested in drugs and dancing than in dressing-up. The venues seemed to be filled with Muscle Marys in sweaty vests, covered in tattoos, trying to look like Arnold Schwarzenegger by night, whilst working as accountants or shopgirls by day. There were very few stand-out characters left on the scene. Glamour and style seemed to have dried up.

Walt and I laid our plans and got the approval of the management of the venue. As the place wasn't making a mint of money at that point, the budget would be tight. Not the news you want to hear when you're going for glamour, but somehow we'd make it work.

In homage to the San Francisco club, and with their permission, the night would be called *Trannyshack UK*. In those days, the use of the word 'tranny' was not controversial in the slightest. Later, it would raise a few eyebrows among the more politically correct of the LGBT+ community, something I could never understand as the word 'tranny' was used in an empowering, affectionate way.

I gathered around me a constellation of the current drag aristocracy. Even though I was to be the overall host, DJ and undisputed queen of the castle, I knew I couldn't shoulder this big night all alone. So I was to be joined on the decks by Tasty Tim, a popular drag figure from the late Eighties. She still looked pretty good and her name remained well-known, so she'd bring a bit of extra gravitas to the proceedings. The door whore would be Lady Lloyd, an up-and-coming face on the drag scene. The pretty Shelley Would was to take the entrance money. Inside the club, the hostesses would be my old friends Glendora, Ritzy and Vanilla, all respected artistes in their own right. On the pole-dancing podiums, my friend Steffan would twirl his beautiful body wearing only high heels and tiny pants, his torso painted as a Geisha or even as a zebra. It would be drag wall-to-wall. It would be Drag Revisited. It would be the return of dressing-up in an age of dressing-down. The fantastic freaks were back. *Trannyshack* would be unforgettable.

And it was. On the first night, the queue went round the block. And, most importantly, the 'right' people had come, dressed to kill, faces painted and eyes dancing at the prospect of what we had in store for them.

By this stage in my career, I knew how hard it was to pin-down exactly what it was that would make a club night successful. If it had been easy, no promoter would ever have failed. But often, what looked good on paper simply didn't click with the punters who came in through the door. The décor, the music, the entertainment, the bar prices – all these could be meticulously planned in advance, yet still the thing wouldn't lift off. I guess that what makes a club night work, or not, is the attitude of the punters on that particular night. Actors in the theatre will talk of how much an audience can vary from performance to performance. Sometimes great, sometimes awful. And you never know in advance which it will be until the curtain goes up. It was just like that in clubland, when the doors of the venue were thrown open and the customers piled in. Some nights, the magic would happen, some nights it wouldn't. But that first night of *Trannyshack UK*, with those ghosts from the Revuebar's legendary past floating among the dancers, that magic was certainly there. A brief, glittering sanctuary from the daily grind of the normal world and all the stresses it brings. A sense of excitement, of the joy of being young, alive and on a dancefloor. *That*, I believed, was the business I was in.

But, as I knew only too well, glitzy launch parties do not maketh a successful club. So we continued to advertise heavily, cut our bar prices a bit and slowly but surely we built up a faithful clientele – or as faithful as you'd ever get in clubland. Drag queens and transexuals predominated, but a good enough sprinkling of celebs turned up to gradually build it into a credible 'A List' hangout. I treasure the memory of my adored Pete Burns, wearing six-inch heels, doing handstands in the middle of the dancefloor. No easy feat.

In 2007, my 40th birthday approached. I lost count of the number of people who thought it dead funny to remind me of an old saying...

'Nobody loves a fairy when she's 40!' they'd crow.

'Go fuck yourself,' I'd reply defiantly, but inside my head it was a milestone that brought me up short. As a rule, clubland was not a place for the middle-aged, unless under very low lighting.

I used the birthday party to boost the appeal of *Trannyshack* and keep it in the public eye. I was still making occasional records for my clubland audience and the latest was my own inimitable cover version of Abba's *Does Your Mother Know?* This would be the centrepiece of the evening, but I invited lots of my friends to perform a number or two. Suddenly, the invitation to perform at the 'Queen of Soho's'

40th became like a Royal Command Performance. Half of London's cabaret and performance artists lined up to do their thing and the show was a massive two hours long.

I decided to blow their eyes out in a glorious golden kimono made by my talented friend Dareena. If a fairy really had to be 40, it couldn't have been in a more spectacular way and, in the wake of that evening, the club went from strength to strength. At long last, and not a moment too soon, I'd found the club I'd always wanted, organised the way I wanted it to be. Amazingly, it was to go on for nearly another decade. Dusty's swan song and *coup de grace* rolled into one!

I should have known better.

The success of *Trannyshack* had enabled my friend Walt to use his little black book of contacts to help supplement my income. The unpleasant memories of going to Israel and Lebanon had faded a little so, when a mini tour of Russia was offered, I took it. It never occurred to me that other people would be battered and bruised for that casual decision.

I'd always been a big history buff and the prospect of seeing the great palaces and museums of St Petersburg and Moscow was irresistible. It was a strange visit, faintly disturbing. I was treated very well, put up in lovely hotels and taken on guided tours of these iconic cities. I saw all the palaces and galleries, the gilded domes of the churches, the great buildings of imperial Russia. It was all fabulous, though very hard on the feet.

But all that stuff contrasted fiercely with the general poverty I saw all around me. In the West, it's easy to get the impression that, since the collapse of communism, everybody in Russia had started coining it. Maybe that's because we hear so much about the oligarchs who've flooded London since the turn of the century. But it certainly didn't look like that for the Russian man and woman in the street. For them, things didn't seem that much brighter than when they were under the jackboot of the old Tsarist regime.

Within the general oppression of Putin's Russia, there was one group which was particularly persecuted. Guess which one that was. In St Petersburg, my guide was a young gay man training to be a doctor.

'My family have disowned me,' he said, after we'd got to know each other. 'And I love them, so that is hard to bear.'

'I bet,' I replied, thinking of my own family.

To say we'd had our ups and downs would be an understatement, but we'd somehow got through the worst of that. I may have infuriated them, embarrassed them, frustrated them but they'd certainly never disowned me or kicked me out. My heart went out to this lovely young guy who wanted to live a life helping other people, but who wasn't allowed to be himself.

'I have to be very careful with my neighbours,' he said. 'It would be dangerous for me if they found out. You're so lucky to live in England.'

I didn't know what to say. Did I tell him about the terrifying attack from my own neighbour to show that I understood the fear he felt? Or did I stay silent and allow him the small comfort of believing that there were other places in the world where LGBT+ people could lead safe lives? I opted for the latter.

It was clear to me now that, as a gay man, my visit to Russia exposed me to a small level of risk. But it was really upsetting to discover that other people had suffered for my presence. People I didn't even know. The week before my arrival, an article in the local version of *Time Out* magazine had announced my trip with pictures of me in drag and details of where I'd be playing. This had triggered a protest at one of the venues by a gang of ultra-right wing Orthodox zealots, in which Putin's police had stood by laughing as the patrons were abused and roughed up. The memories of Israel and Lebanon came flooding back, as stark as before. What else might happen? Might I find myself on the ground again, another face full of hatred spitting venom at me, his hands around my throat? I began to wish I'd not been so attracted by the prospect of seeing Red Square and The Winter Palace.

'You must be very careful here,' said the young doctor. 'You really must.'

In the event, the gigs went well enough and, thank God, there were no demos on the nights I played, but there might well have been.

After St. Petersburg and Moscow, there was a third event added on. I was to go to Ekaterinburg, a city in Siberia and a trip memorable for the wrong reasons. Firstly, my case of couture clothes was lost in transit from Moscow and I had to use the make-up and costume that the club promoter could cobble together at five minutes' notice. Not ideal for a perfectionist like me. Dusty was not pleased. This was not at all what she was used to. I didn't quite look like Putin's granny, but it was a close-run thing.

Secondly, I made a pilgrimage to the site of the Ipatiev House where, in 1918, the last Tsar, Nicholas II, his wife Alexandra and their five children were murdered during the revolution. The house itself had long been demolished and a blingy new church built on the spot to commemorate the family, all of whom had now been sanctified by the Orthodox Church. My inner history geek made me buy a bunch of roses and lay them on the spot of the slaughter.

What a shame that the Orthodox Church would gladly give so much respect to the last Tsar, but couldn't bring themselves to show any whatsoever to their LGBT+ citizens. I've thought so often of my guide, the young doctor. No doubt he's slaving away in some hospital in Putin's repressive, authoritarian Russia. Still afraid to be himself. Still scared of his neighbours, just as I had been. Still rejected by his parents. But I'd really love to think that, somehow, there was love in his life. Arms to hold him, a shoulder to cry on, an ear to listen to him when he needed to talk.

'Do you think they'll throw things at me?' asked George.

'If they do, we'll throw them right back.' I replied.

In the summer of 2009, the organisers of the annual Gay Pride celebrations asked if *Trannyshack* would take a float that year. The management of the club coughed up the several thousand quid needed to dress up a lorry in a suitably outrageous fashion. The night before, a gang of volunteers were up till the small hours making the float spectacular. Next day, knackered but excited, we assembled just off Oxford Street. The float. The drag queens, dolled up to the nines. And our very special guest of honour.

Boy George had been, to put it mildly, going through a rough patch. After a few months in prison, for an alleged offence best not remembered, but related to his drug problems, George had been laying low for a while. He was still on a tag and not allowed to be out of his house at certain times of the day or night.

He'd started his sentence in Pentonville then had been moved to somewhere less punitive. I'd never gone to visit him as I knew it would really upset me to see somebody I loved in that situation. Luckily, George understood that and didn't mind. Anyway, the visitor passes were far from numerous and were needed for use by his large family rather than the likes of me. But I'd written almost daily when he was in the nick. I wrote about everyday stuff, gossip and any other trivia that I hoped might take his mind off his predicament. He was showered with support from all over the world, receiving hundreds of letters every single day, so maybe he never read any of mine.

In sharp contrast however, some of the press had been vile to him, throwing all sorts on insults. Which is why he was jumpy about making a public appearance again, especially one as visible as Gay Pride, when the streets of London would be crammed with many thousands of people. But George had never been any sort of coward. His whole life had been about bravery of one kind or another and that attribute didn't desert him now.

'Can I come too, Dusty?' he'd asked, when I told him about our Pride plans. 'On your float?'

'Of course, you can, George,' I replied. 'That'd be wonderful.'

'I could do a few songs too,' he said. 'If you'd like that?'

The daftest question of all time. At the end of the Pride March, there would be a cabaret stage in Leicester Square, where I was to be the compere. It would be a massive coup to have a celebrity of George's magnitude on our *Trannyshack* float, then performing on the stage.

But we kept it a state secret right up to the last minute, in case George got the wobbles and changed his mind. I waited till the night before the parade to press-release all the main newspapers, telling them only that a major star would be appearing on our float. Like casting a fishing-line into the water to see if they bit. And they certainly did.

On the float were no less than 40 drag queens, all dressed in their finest. There was very loud and very camp music blaring out of huge speakers attached to each side of the lorry. When the press saw George, they went mental. For the whole journey through the West End, we were followed by literally hundreds of photographers, desperate to get shots of him on his first public outing since his release from prison. The crowds on the pavements were enormous and no other float in the parade got anything like the reception of the *Trannyshack* extravaganza.

Oxford Circus was the really magical moment. In all four directions was a sea of people as far as the eye could see, kept behind barriers for safety but wildly enthusiastic. We'd placed a big throne-like chair on the float for George to sit on like some deity, but he hardly used it and danced around to the music with all the other queens. And then, in a bright pink fedora, he took the microphone and started to sing *Hare Krishna*. The countless thousands on the pavements went even more bananas as he gave a free concert all the way down Regent Street, round Piccadilly Circus and down the Haymarket. Tourists that day must have thought their ship had come in. One of the world's greatest pop stars performing just for them, surrounded by a constellation of dazzling drag queens, glittering like the fabulous fairies they were. Who needed St Paul's or The Tower of London? This was a sight like no other. Cameras, both professional and amateur, flashed away like demented crickets. The flashguns, the glitter and the sunshine rolled together into something extraordinary and unforgettable.

Despite his rapturous reception on the streets, George got nervous again as he waited behind the makeshift stage in Leicester Square. There were about 5,000 people crammed into the square. He still worried that the moment could go either way. Would there be boos and catcalls or, even worse, mockery? Or would they forgive and forget?

'Listen here you daft queen. I'm going out on that stage right now to introduce you,' I said. 'So just get your arse out there and do it. It'll be fine.'

And it was. It was way more than fine. The crowd welcomed him back with a great roar of joy. The prodigal son of British pop was back. There's a famous self-help book called *Feel The Fear And Do It Anyway* and that was exactly what my friend did that day.

On a day like that, all my daily grumps and gripes with the drag scene, all the hard work and money that went into keeping the Very Miss Dusty O at the top of her game, was suddenly worth it. The path I'd hacked out in my life, the ups and downs, the hatred and the rejection, even the loneliness, were forgotten on that miraculous afternoon. There was no place on earth I'd rather have been than up on that float as it wound its way through the heart of London with George's voice soaring out into the summer air.

 wasn't lying in any more skips. I wasn't lying in a gutter. Or sitting in a shop doorway, begging for coins in a plastic cup. I was still on stage. Still gorgeous in Westwood. Still schmoozing with the celebs who flocked to *Trannyshack*. But by now I was also, without doubt, an alcoholic.

To be precise, I was what they call a '*functioning* alcoholic', which means that though you're addicted to the booze, you're somehow just about holding your life together. Getting up in the morning. Going to work. Holding comprehensible conversations, at least for some of the time.

Looking back, it astonishes me that the sad example of my father and my memories of the hell he inflicted on our family, did so little to rein me in. For years, I'd drunk too much and knew it. For most folk who worked in clubland, it was an occupational hazard; either that or the drugs. I was also intelligent enough to know a slippery slope when I saw one. But I guess it doesn't work like that. The great Elaine Stritch, who suffered from the same illness, once said that for a long time you view alcohol as your friend and believe you can control its role in your life, then one day it suddenly turns round and bites you. That's when you realise that it is now the master and not you. One of Elaine's iconic numbers was *I'm Still Here*, the Sondheim anthem to survival that I'd performed myself more than once. How true those lyrics always were to me. Good times and bum times, I'd certainly seen them all. And I was indeed still here, on the surface at least. Under the surface, I wasn't so sure.

The 'swan song' of the Very Miss Dusty O had turned out to be a very extended play record. *Trannyshack* was to last for almost an entire decade. When its original venue in the old Raymond Revue Bar had shut down for redevelopment, we'd found a new home just round the corner at Madame JoJo's, an equally legendary West End niterie and arguably an even better place for us. A long-established Soho venue with a reputation for eccentricity and glamour, it was not too big, not too small, with a sunken dancefloor and a professionally equipped stage. *Trannyshack* was to thrive there, in its red velvet Art Deco interior, for the next eight years.

It continued to be the place to be seen and a long line of famous guests rolled through the door to enjoy the crazy acts and the Bohemian atmosphere. You never knew who would turn up from one week to the next. Dawn French, Graham Norton, Stephen Fry, Rufus Wainwright and Alan Carr were regulars. One night, I might be snogging (no tongues) the pop star Florence from Florence and The Machine; the next night playing musical chairs on stage with the spunky Freddie Flintoff and eight transvestites. All good clean fun.

One week, Katie Price decided she wanted to perform, subjecting us to an excruciatingly out of tune version of a classic Disney song, which went viral on You Tube, but for all the wrong reasons. Poor Katie. The downmarket version of Florence Foster Jenkins.

It was suddenly very fashionable to hang out with us and my dressing-room would regularly host impromptu parties. I'd not had this level of cult status since the old glory days of *Pushca* and *Bambina*. The press was still calling me 'Queen of Soho', describing me in almost iconic language. But what was meant as a compliment eventually became something of an irritant, and I started to cringe when I read it. Despite running the coolest club in town, it made me feel middle-aged and almost a figure of yesteryear, a sort of gay version of Vera Lynn, whilst in my own mind, I was still young with lots more to offer. When *The Guardian* ran an article on Soho down the decades, its riff on my title was 'Queen of The Nineties.' But to me, the Nineties were already yesterday's news and I wanted to be Queen of *Now*. My looks may have started to fade, but my ego was as big as ever.

This was both a joyous and a frightening time, as I was drinking ever more heavily and feeling less and less in touch with reality. We all do and say very silly things when we're drunk and I was definitely no exception. I was rapidly gaining a reputation for being best avoided if I were in a bad mood or when challenged about anything at all. A bit of an old bitch really.

It didn't help that even more 'Eve Harringtons' were now snapping at my ankles, gagging to grab my hard-earned title. I soon became a bit paranoid about whom I could or couldn't trust. A few unpleasant incidents arose, when I discovered that some former employee or protégé had stabbed me in the back in order to get themselves either work or recognition.

'She drinks, you know.'

'She can hardly stand up some nights.'

'She's piled on the pounds lately. She can hardly squeeze into those frocks anymore.'

'We'll have to buy the old girl a tent from Millets.'

All the probable insults spun round in my head and I began to feel beleaguered and friendless.

And then the actual 'Eve' arrived – and right on my very doorstep.

In King's Cross, Curtain Mark had finally moved out and with him went the last vestiges of my former life, in which people had known David before he'd turned himself into Dusty. As my new housemate, I took in my latest drag queen protégé. No names. Behind a smiling exterior, she began to do me the dirty. Undermining everything I did and offering her services more cheaply to the clubland contacts I'd built up over two decades. She then started to DJ, even adopting my mannerisms and my dress preferences. When I found out about all this stuff, I felt both betrayed and as if I'd been taken over.

The last straw was when a Japanese magazine came to the flat to do a photo shoot about me and my spectacular wardrobe. All went smoothly until, towards the end of the session, 'Eve' appeared from her room, in drag and fully made up.

'What are you doing?' I asked her.

'Just thought I'd join in,' she replied. 'You don't mind do you?'

I was furious but did my best to conceal it. I wasn't going to make a scene there and then, especially as the Japanese were delighted to get two queens for the price of one. And so she eventually appeared in the article beside me. Vanity on my part of course, but I felt totally undermined by someone to whom I'd given a start in the business and taken into my home in good faith and friendship.

'I think it might be best if you left,' I said, after the cameras had gone.

'Why?' she asked.

'I think you know,' I replied.

I didn't fire her from the club as she was good eye candy for the punters and I always tried to put business first and my personal feelings second. At work, I stayed as cordial with her as I could, but I watched my back even more closely after that. The 'Eves' were everywhere.

The years of *Trannyshack* ticked away and I somehow managed to go on living the same nocturnal life as I'd done for nearly two decades. Only I was older, fatter and very much drunker. By now, I was getting truly horrific hangovers which left me in bed all day, riddled with paranoia, self-loathing and guilt. Inflicting the same demons upon myself as my father had done.

In 2011, after years of suffering from other illnesses, Dad passed away. If only he'd found a way to shake off those demons and managed to conquer his addictions, he could have been so much more than he ever was. Underneath it all, Clive Hodge had been a loving, caring, indulgent father. He'd had energy and talent and tried valiantly to pick himself up after the collapse of everything for which he'd worked so hard. In total contrast to my mother, Dad had never once said anything negative to me about my appearance or my career. Nor, once it had become blindingly obvious, about my sexuality. He never ever put me down.

But the booze had got him and had spoiled everything. Both for him and for us. One's reflex is to remember the good times, and that's how it should be. Yet it's impossible to forget the bad times too and the great pain they brought. No young boy should see, as I did, the sight of his own father, the person he worshipped, head in hands, weeping with remorse.

Dad's last days were tough for us all. But they were briefly brightened when Boy George went on the *Loose Women* TV show, said a special hello to him and wished him better. Good old George. Such a wonderful friend. Dad was thrilled to bits but getting 'better' was never going to happen.

My mother, who had spent three-quarters of her life in a perpetual argument with him, was broken by his death. When he was no longer there to fight with, she was completely lost without him. From now on, I'd try to spend as much time in the Midlands as I possibly could. And that did me good. No longer was my main worry in life which wig to wear, but how this old lady would be able to cope. Thank God for my younger sister Julie who always had, and still does, support our mother in every way.

But there was to be a second tragedy to blight our dysfunctional family. One that had been brewing for years. A decade or so before my father's death, my elder sister Karen had entirely cut herself off from the rest of us. I'm still not sure why. Perhaps the rage against her parents, which Karen had exhibited so fiercely in her youth, had never gone away. It was very hard on my mother, especially as Karen lived no more than five minutes away. Mom had never been invited to meet her great-grandchildren, an act of cruelty on my sister's part which is difficult to forgive.

During the writing of this book, we got the news that Karen had died suddenly. Having known nothing of her daughter's illness, my poor mother was obviously devastated. For any parent, having your child die before you seems such an unnatural thing. In this case, the misery of their estrangement made it all so much worse. The place of every mother with a terminally ill child is to be at their bedside, giving comfort and love till their very last breath, but Mom was sadly denied that. As with Dad's alcoholism, the grief of the loss was mixed in with a devastating sense of waste. Mom, Julie and I cried not just for the death itself, but for what might have been in the life that had been lost.

More and more, I also found myself crying for what might have been in my own life. Now that I lived alone again, there was nothing to stop me having as many drunken, self-pitying blubs as I wanted. I'd often get home at four in the morning, pissed as a rat, and lie sobbing on the bathroom floor from the sheer pointlessness of my life. In those deep dark moments I avoided my beloved mirror like the plague. I didn't want it to see me like that.

In the eyes of many, I was now something of a drunken clown and, to some of the younger queens, also something of a joke. The cruel remarks I'd once directed at older performers were now aimed back at me. When social media came along, it only made things worse. Much worse. I used it with bitchy abandon and without inhibition, finding myself embroiled in endless, idiotic online spats. What I gave out, I got back. Torrents of abuse from perfect strangers, especially those on the scene. I soon realised I was now seen as a drag dinosaur with a potty mouth by the cutting-edge kids emerging into the spotlight. As usual, these youngsters had no respect for their elders or any interest whatsoever in Dusty's past glories. I ended up being ridiculed and insulted, only exacerbating things with my drunken retorts when I got home from work and damaging my reputation as a result. Unfortunately, there was nobody to tell me off or to take away my computer.

Most of my old friends had drifted away and I surrounded myself with sycophants and people who were more interested in the free booze that came with hanging out with Dusty or even, once or twice, in stealing things from my flat. They sure as hell weren't interested in David Hodge. I'd never been so isolated, yet so busy at the same time. I had literally nobody to talk to or to trust. I was alone.

Some comfort came from an unexpected source. My adored chihuahuas had long been in doggie heaven and, on an impulse, I bought two Siamese cats. It was a wise move. For the next couple of years they would keep me from tipping right over the edge in my struggle with alcohol. No matter how pissed I was, these two little creatures depended on me to look after them. In return, they offered me a sense of serenity and unconditional affection when I needed it most. During the bleakest times, they became my reason for living. How sad is that? Cue violins.

 part from my pussycats, I suppose that the best thing in my life was that I wasn't skint. Not yet anyway.

My club income was still healthy and a relative left me a very nice sum of money. With this windfall, I decided to redecorate the flat. The style would be faux Rococo and I spent a small fortune on chandeliers and mock Louis XV furniture. I installed bright red carpets and *chaises longues*. My king-sized bed, found in a French catalogue, was a huge golden sleigh with wooden carvings, draped in brocades and silks. The walls were covered in scarlet flock wallpaper and countless little pictures and religious icons. It was Rasputin meets Marie Antoinette. I even put in a dream bathroom in which Marie would happily have done her *toilette*. My ordinary basement flat became even more like a little palace. All it lacked was a Swiss Guard outside the front door.

It all looked quite amazing but, as I soon discovered, was totally uninhabitable. I spent most of my time sitting on one chair as the rest of the furniture was so uncomfortable.

It also required constant dusting and cleaning, something I'd always loathed with a vengeance. In the end, I'd spent £30,000 on what was less a home than a giant stage set. Yet again, when the lolly came in, I did my best to make sure it went right out again.

Despite the damage done by my social media wars and the onslaught of all the young 'Eves', I was still in reasonable demand. To keep my face in the spotlight, I did a couple of reality TV shows. For ITV's *This Morning*, I agreed to take part in a story about Eighties fashion. The comedian Jenny Eclair was to come to the flat to explore my vast wardrobe, followed by a trip to Chelsea fashion market to find Jenny some gear to dress her up in. The witty Miss Eclair was a delight and perfectly at home with me and my eccentric lifestyle. There was only one glitch, when a cameraman needed to move a chair, which resulted in the exposure of my extensive collection of educational DVDs stacked behind it.

'Oooh, what have we got here?' asked Jenny, gazing down at titles such as *All About Steve*, *Briefs Encounter* and *The Magnificent Seven Inches*.

I blushed to the roots of my wig. Not so much for being the possessor of a porn collection that would have shocked the Emperor Tiberius, but for the sad revelation that my sex life involved nobody else except myself. Jenny of course didn't bat an eye, but I was glad it wasn't included in the film that went out.

Trannyshack remained the centre of my existence. One night a week, I tried to park my troubles and go back to being the Very Miss Dusty O. I still worked hard to keep the entertainment as varied and alluring as possible, so that the club wouldn't lose its edge and keep the punters coming back for more. One week we'd have drag strippers, the next it might be our version of *The Golden Girls*, with me of course as the deep-voiced Dorothy, a character I always thought looked a bit like a drag queen anyway. We had drag burlesque shows, drag acrobats, drag knife throwers. We even put together a group of drag dancers, made up of West End chorus boys who'd come to the club after their shows and dazzle the crowds with their point perfect technique. The punters never quite knew what they'd get at *Trannyshack*, which was exactly the idea. There seemed to be no end to the possible interactions of drag and other areas of showbiz. We never found a drag ventriloquist with her hand up the skirts of a drag Sooty, but it wasn't for want of trying.

The diversity of the entertainment was reflected by that of the customers. All sorts beat their way to our door.

'Oh look, soldiers!' cried one of the girls one night, at the arrival of a group of Her Majesty's Armed Forces.

Big strapping lads all of them, and clearly eager to become acquainted with a very different sort of queen. They soon became regulars, one chap in particular becoming highly popular with us all and who'd leave with a different drag queen or transvestite on his arm each week. Probably not the sort of image which The Ministry of Defence would want to project. But the old music-hall song was certainly *almost* true, *All The Nice Girls Love A 'Soldier'*.

Over the years, the club became a fabulous family of misfits, its members bearing exotic or humorous names like Dame Vesta Bules, Rose Garden, Tiffany Kapinsky, Myra Davenport and Barbara Bush (the reference to 'bush' not a horticultural one). All kooky queens with their own gimmicks and ways of doing things. And despite all the bitchery and back-stabbing that I've already described, it was undeniably a kind of family. Like me, plenty of the gay men who'd drifted into drag had had difficult childhoods or been rejected by their birth parents. Often psychologically scarred, they'd been forced to strike out into life on their own, to sink or swim. In the camaraderie of clubland, they encountered similar stories to their own, finding fellowship and understanding and that was never to be undervalued.

Every Christmas, we'd organise a drag pantomime, always a huge hit with the customers. Based very loosely on traditional panto stories, we'd transform them into absolutely filthy, adults-only versions. *(Little Red Riding Crop, RumpledForeskin* etc. You get the picture). Most of us were too drunk to remember our words, so the performances would often descend into chaos, which made them even more hilarious. Most of the hard work for these shows was done by a young drag queen called Vesta. Though only 22 years-old, Vesta liked to transform herself into the character of an old Jewish matriarch at any given opportunity, a persona she kept up for the entire evening. God knows why. But it was very funny to see these cool clubbers being accosted by this old lady, telling them they looked peaky and to drink more chicken soup or urging them to find a nice girl and settle down. Vesta was yet another of the unique personalities for whom *Trannyshack* was a sort of home.

For my birthday one year, I threw a 1940s party. At this point, I was heels-deep in the whole 40s look with a demi-wave wig, evening gowns and suits like Marlene Dietrich used to wear. We hired a trio of female singers in imitation of The Andrews Sisters to perform wartime songs. *The White Cliffs Of Dover, A Nightingale Sang In Berkeley Square, The Boogie-Woogie*

Bugle Boy Of Company B. All that old stuff; strangely moving too, at least when you're several sheets to the wind. For this special night, I had chosen a tuxedo with a dickie-bow and diamonds and a black waved bob wig. It was all very glam and once again I made the cover of *BOYZ*; me sitting centre stage between Baga Chipz of Drag Race fame and Munroe Bergdorf, who later became a well-known trans activist. Even if I say so myself, I looked fabulous that night and always felt that picture deserved more than just the *BOYZ* cover. Like being pasted onto the side of a Spitfire maybe..?

But great parties are sometimes spoiled by the one person who goes too far. And that was one of those times. We'd arranged for a pretty young guy to do a risqué striptease. The usual stuff. A bit of prancing around to the music, then a minute or two of waving his willy in the faces of an eager audience. Nothing to worry about. But then it happened.

'Jesus Christ, what's he doing?'

'He can't be.'

'He is! Oh my God.'

In the centre of the spotlight, in the middle of my meticulously planned party, the stripper was defecating into a Martini glass. But not just that. He was doing it in perfect time to the music. He must have been practising for weeks.

People screamed in horror, then screamed even more when he proceeded to waft the steaming glass around, so that the stink reached their nostrils. In a moment, the whole atmosphere of 40s campery was shattered by a disgusting act of tawdry exhibitionism. *Try A Taste of Martini* ran the old advertising slogan back then. Well, not that night. Though I tried to put a brave face on it, I took it very personally; it almost felt like some sort of insult. In the following days, the word spread quickly and it became the source of clubland gossip for weeks. The stripper who shat in the glass.

I wondered how that guy's sick mind worked. How on earth he thought that could be amusing. Maybe he thought it was somehow artistic or ground-breaking. Clubland wasn't short of pretentious twits like that. Who knows? But the undeniable beauty of his body in no way compensated for, or excused, the putridness of his soul.

Fortunately, that sort of 'shit' was the terrible exception to the rule. Most of the time, the *Trannyshack* nights were a great success. So successful that there were eventual spin-offs at other venues on different nights of the week. *Trannyshack East* in the East End. *Trannyshack North* in Camden Town. *Trannyshack South* in Vauxhall. But the jewel in the crown would always be Wednesdays at Madame JoJo's in the heart of the West End. Where the Very Miss Dusty O still reigned supreme. Where, for a few hours, dressed to impress, her ageing face still a work of art, she could forget that an outside world existed.

That's why I was often reluctant for those hours to end, to go back alone to the flat, wipe off the make-up and face up to the cold blast of reality which would come with the dawn. So, five or six taxis filled with drag queens would regularly descend on my little Versailles and we'd party on till midday, keeping that outside world at bay for as long as possible. It was all kept afloat by booze and though it was great fun at the time, the price to be paid was spending two whole days recovering in bed or cleaning up the horrendous mess after they'd all gone. By the time this herd of glittering bison had left, it was less Versailles and more grubby transport caff on the North Circular.

* * *

And then another woman came into my life. A rival to the Very Miss Dusty O. Her name was Sofonda Cox (think about it).

Those Christmas pantos at *Trannyshack* were to be the unwitting rehearsal for the next twist in my career, a twist as unexpected as it was welcome. An offer came my way from Martin Watts, the impresario who owned the Leicester Square Theatre, one of the big mainstream entertainment palaces in the West End. He was producing an adults-only pantomime in his studio space underneath the main venue and wanted a Dame.

As Sofonda Cox, I'd essentially be playing myself and could dress and look as I wanted. They clearly understood that if they'd required me to wear bloomers and a joke wig, I'd have refused. No way would I ever perform in public looking like some old grotesque with blacked-out teeth. My whole life was about glamour first, glamour last, glamour always.

It was to be an evening of slightly filthy fun, just like the *Trannyshack* pantos, but with one enormous difference. This wouldn't be amateur night, where the more chaotic it was only added to the fun. This was professional. A proper script. A proper West End theatre. The money wasn't great and it would swallow three months of my time with a staggering 74 shows, but I threw caution to the wind and signed up. It would be interesting to put myself out there in something new and different. Look out Dame Judi. Dusty had gone legit.

It turned out to be a wonderful journey. Rehearsals were tough. I wasn't used to being hard at work first thing in the morning. I had to learn my lines and songs and deliver them perfectly. I had to be part of a disciplined team in which other people depended on my professionalism. As a beneficial side-effect, I was away from the clubs, bars and alcohol. I needed to be absolutely sober; hangovers just weren't an option. It was brilliant fun and I became very close to a couple of the cast members with whom I shared a tiny dressing-room. These people were actors; not involved in 'my world' and had no idea who I was or what I did on the gay scene. As a result, they treated me like a normal person called David Hodge and I quickly discovered how much that meant to me.

I had eight costume changes in every show and I really went to town on each one. My wig expenses alone cost nearly as much as I was being paid, but I really felt it was going to be an investment worth making. And it was. Our reviews were all five-star and my personal notices everything I could have dreamed of. For three months, we really rocked that space, sometimes performing three shows a day. It was a huge, sell-out hit and gave me a sense of achievement I'd not felt for a very long time.

Unsurprisingly, the snobby elitists of the drag scene looked down their coked-up noses at 'Dusty doing panto', but most of them would have eaten their own wigs to play in a West End theatre and not in some grubby gay pub that smelt of last night's stale beer. I didn't give a shit anyway, caring less and less what the gay scene thought of me.

This stonking success led to a five-year contract to do panto at a bigger salary and the promise that next year's show would be upgraded from the studio to the main theatre. I couldn't sign up fast enough. I got my own dressing-room with a star on the door. I got my name up in lights at the theatre entrance, which was a truly 'wow' moment. Dusty O twinkling out over the West End.

For the next five seasons, our pantos continued to sell every seat and get sensational reviews. Every year, I was aware that, for the next three months, I'd have to give myself to it completely and work like a trouper. And I did, buoyed up by the realisation that I could do something more than just paint my face and knock back whiskey after whiskey. I could act too. The character of Sofonda Cox grew in strength and personality. Before long, I was performing not as Dusty but as Sofonda. Apart from the same superficial glamour, she wasn't like Dusty at all. Dusty was, as she had always been planned to be, a work of art, a goddess of the make-up box, a creature with a certain stiff dignity as befitted the 'Queen of Soho.' But Sofonda was a living, breathing, three-dimensional being; a cross between Mrs Slocombe and Lily Savage. I had found the courage to leave my comfort zone, break down a few internal barriers and to create a real character. As a teenager, all that time in the Aldridge Youth Theatre had finally paid off. Not for the first time, I really wished I'd been able to track down the outrageous Alain and send him a ticket to the show.

'Darling, you were fabulous!' he'd say in my imagination, swanning into my dressing-room, wearing God knows what camp gear. 'Totally, utterly fabulous. I always knew you had it in you. And I'm never wrong in such matters.'

All through my life, in good times and bum times, the thing Alain had said to the teenage me in a Birmingham street so long ago, had stayed lodged in my soul. Even in my darkest days, it had always represented a tiny glimmer of light and hope.

'David, never be afraid to be yourself.'

In the years to come, that glimmer was to become even more of a lifeline.

 f, as the old joke went, nobody loved a fairy when she's 40, what would it be like when she was 50? I shuddered to think. I was 47 now. Not long to go.

'Judy died at 47,' some silly queen reminded me. 'Mind how you go.'

'Oh fuck off.'

But it was indeed around now that I began to live through a very dark period. As if I were standing square in the middle of a crossroads, trucks coming at me from every direction. Some of them I could dodge or even, as in a dream, pole-vault gracefully over them, but sooner or later, one of them was going to get me.

Soho, that small square mile in which I'd lived most of my adult life was changing. And fast. Many of the smaller traders had been forced out by large rent hikes and the generic high street chains had got a grip on the place, changing its atmosphere completely. What had once been an exciting, bohemian, ever so slightly dodgy place to work and live, was losing its character. Now you had poncey coffee shops and artisan bakeries where a croissant or a bun cost a small fortune. Expensive housing projects and boutique hotels for the rich were springing up like tulips in spring. Many of the affordable little flats that had housed arty, creative cosmopolitan types had been seized back by the landlords, renovated and the rents hiked up till they were beyond the pocket of such folks, who had mostly moved eastwards to newly cool, but still affordable, quarters like Shoreditch.

Worse still, the police were raiding the sex shops and the brothels and increasing pressure on some of the bars and clubs to clean up their acts. The Crossrail project demolished iconic gay venues such as The Astoria and big chunks of LGBT history were being sliced away for the sake of gentrification. Gay venues were closing almost weekly and gradually the edifice of a once vibrant community was becoming sanitised and neutralised. Instead of clubbers and fashion freaks, the streets were filled with gawking tourists and suburban hen parties on a visit to *Mamma Mia*. In short, my beloved, colourful Soho was turning beige.

One day the phone rang. It was Walt, my partner in the *Trannyshack* operation.

'You'll never believe this!' He almost shouted down the line.

'What?'

'The cops have shut down Madame JoJo's.'

'You're kidding. Whatever for?'

'There was some fight on the pavement outside and they've used it as a pretext to close the place down, at least temporarily.'

Despite the gentrification of Soho, Madame JoJo's had remained a profitable venue, hosting several other successful club nights as well as our own. We knew the proprietors would fight tooth and claw to keep it open, which they did. But when it came to court, it was blindingly obvious that both the police and Soho Estates, the landlords of the site, wanted its licence revoked and the place shut down. In the new beige Soho, there seemed to be no place for somewhere like Madame JoJo's.

I had brief visions of a popular uprising. dozens of drag queens occupying the building, barricaded behind upturned tables, fighting off the police. A re-run of the events at the Stonewall Inn in New York in 1969, the event which was the trigger of the modern fight for gay rights. But nothing happened.

At that juncture, Walt and I firmly intended to find a new venue. *Trannyshack* was still a popular night out with a legendary reputation. But that never quite worked out. After 10 years, it was over. A decade of hard work in keeping it afloat, in creating fabulous entertainments, in escorting famous names over the threshold into our dazzling little world. In the blink of an eye, the place that had become a second home to me had gone. I wasn't even allowed to collect some personal property I'd left in my dressing-room ready for that week's show. But it wasn't just some clothing and make-up that I'd lost. I felt as if I'd lost a leg.

The closure of *Trannyshack* was just the first of those speeding trucks that hit me and tossed my life up in the air. Now, I felt forced to ask myself the very real existential question. What is the point of you and what you do? Once upon a time, I'd have known the answer. Now, I wasn't so sure…

I always pictured her as a middle-aged, slightly sad single woman who lived only for her work. In the evenings, she'd sit alone in a colourless flat, eating an M&S single-portion lasagne off a tray while she watched *Gardener's World*. The truth of course may have been quite different. She may have been a young party girl with big knockers and her bum permanently glued to a bar stool as she checked the Tindr messages on her phone. The only thing I knew for sure was that she was a monster, whose one object in life was to ruin my health and happiness.

She was a Tax Inspector.

The letter came, as letters must, quite out of the blue. I was to be investigated about irregularities in my Tax Return, concerning a 12-month period several years back. My accountant was relaxed. We had all the answers ready, he assured me. Don't worry. Wrong. What followed was an investigation lasting for the two whole years, during which they pawed over every bank statement, peering into every single penny I'd earned or spent. Lists of specific questions were sent, the answers to which I'd often long forgotten. But they'd obviously done their homework, interrogating me about long-defunct clubs I'd worked at back in the Nineties.

At this time, *Trannyshack* had gone, my annual panto season in Leicester Square was nearly over and I was basically unemployed with no means of paying any huge sum in back taxes. The main bone of contention was that they refused to accept that my vast spending on clothes was justified as an expense.

'I am *not* a tranvestite,' I wrote. 'I live as a man during the day. My female clothes are purchased for work and are surely tax-deductible.'

'Please explain why you need such expensive costumes,' she wrote back.

'Because I am a drag queen. Drag queens don't dress at Primark,' I replied in words to that effect.

The woman was incredibly suburban and impertinent. I very much doubted she had even *heard* of the Westwood shop in Conduit Street. And if she hadn't, how could she possibly understand what I was talking about? Call me Miss Paranoia, but I also suspected this bitch was more than a little homophobic. It seemed she really wanted to get me into as much of a mess as possible. Again and again, my accountant and I tried to explain the nature of my work, how image was an essential part of it and that clothes were in turn a central part of that image. All to no avail. We went on playing email ping-pong month after month after month. I lost countless nights of sleep, worked myself up into a right old state and imagined myself out on the street with a couple of suitcases and a Siamese cat under each arm.

In the end, after all this drama, I was fined a laughable £200 and the case was closed. It was hard to accept that, at a time when corporations were getting away with billions on tax scams (and still do), that HMRC would go after a 'little person' like me with so much vigour and venom. I'd have paid them five times that sum – even if I'd had to go on the game to raise the money – in order to avoid the sheer stress it caused me.

I hope that woman was satisfied. Just doing her job? I don't think so. Who knows what had maybe happened in her life to make her so vicious? Maybe she'd once fallen in love with a closet case. Maybe she was one herself. I had a fantasy of walking into her boring glass-box office in Shipley, Lancashire in full drag. The security guards would back away speechless at the sight of me. I'd go up in the lift, march to her desk and stand right in front of her, in a floor length ball-gown, sparkling with fake diamonds and furs, dripping in glamour. With my head held high, my tits out and my hands on my hips, I'd face her down.

'*This* is it,' I'd say. '*This* is what a drag queen looks like. Now, go fuck yourself.'

The light bulbs that spelt out my name over Leicester Square were about go dark.

In the middle of January 2014, whilst my tax crisis was at full throttle, it was the last night of my last pantomime at the Leicester Square Theatre. It had been five years of enormous pleasure, of treasured friendships and even a kind of artistic rebirth. I went in early to pack up my costumes and jewellery. Gorgeous, bead-encrusted gowns hung on the rails. Thousands of quids' worth of Butler & Wilson necklaces. A row of stunning wigs, each worth £500. Everything the best that money could buy. While the rest of the cast wore bog-standard Leichner greasepaint, I wore Dior foundation and Francois Nars eyeshadow at £50 a pot.

It had always been the same. I was completely incapable of doing anything on the cheap. Just like Dusty, her alter ego Sofonda Cox had drained the coffers dry. When I did the mathematics, I realised that these five years of panto had made me no profit at all. When the money came in, I'd gone right out and spent it again. I never learned. Yet I'd spent that money joyfully. In my view, the spending had been a creative act. Both these alter egos had seemed, in their different ways, to be the answer to all my problems. They had removed me from the real world and given me access to a far more glamorous one where I no longer had to be the small ginger boy from Walsall and could be whoever I pleased.

But, as the fairy faced 50, it became ever more undeniable that my two creations had now left me high and dry. The Very Miss Dusty O was, to all intents and purposes, gone. And tonight, in Leicester Square, Sofonda Cox would take her last bow.

In the bar after the show, the usual questions were asked.

'So what now, David?' my new friends and fans wanted to know.

'Next stop The Palladium then Dave?'

I blagged it of course, saying I was in talks with various venues and we'd have a big glam relaunch of *Trannyshack* no later than March to which they must all come. By now, I knew this was rubbish, but I couldn't face the heartache of admitting it. No promoter wanted a club night that had already been running for a decade and which was so synonymous with another venue. Nor did anyone with any sense start a club night so soon after Christmas when the punters were staying home and paying off their credit card bills.

When I got home from that last performance in Leicester Square, after all the farewell hugs, kisses and tears, there were more tears waiting for me. The flat had been burgled. They'd nicked every electrical item of value, though that was only an old laptop and a camera. Thank God, they'd been too thick to realise that my clothes and both the Siamese cats were worth far more. No doubt they thought that they'd be a bit conspicuous walking through King's Cross laden down with high-end couture and a couple of slit-eyed pussies. But still, it was a terrifying experience and one which I just wasn't emotionally strong enough to deal with at that moment. My home was the one thing I felt I had left. Like Dusty and Sofonda Cox, it had been my golden creation, an expression of my creativity. And now some strangers had come in and trashed it for the sake of a cruddy laptop. A violation scarcely to be borne.

By now, I knew I was way past my best visually. Creating and inventing looks and images was what I did best, but now the canvas on which I'd created them was heading south. For years, I'd struggled privately with my drink problem. Now, I was also depressed and started having panic attacks during which I could hardly breathe. I went to my doctor and broke down in the surgery. She prescribed a course of anti-anxiety tablets which helped a little, but could do nothing to remove the tax investigation or find me a new job.

My CV was heavy on life experience, but pretty low on everything else. How could my particular skills be transferred to a cosy little office job? Being 'Queen of Soho' wasn't going to find me work and pay the bills. Suddenly, everything I thought I had achieved seemed pointless and futile, gone with the wind. My whole existence had been built around an illusion. My looks were fake. My home was fake. Even the way that people related to me as a human being was fake, because it wasn't me they were relating to, but my alter egos.

Most people didn't even know my real name or what I looked like out of drag. As my looks had faded, I'd done my best to keep that hidden.

So, who exactly was I?

My mind went onto the spin cycle, questioning everything about myself. Was I male or female even? Most people I knew referred to each other by the female pronoun. In truth,

I'd stopped thinking about my gender years ago. That might be strongly applauded in today's 'woke' culture, but I had never especially wanted to be female. Nor, as I've said, did I have the slightest desire to be a transvestite. I was just a gay man who loved dressing-up and that is not transvestism. In the bubble in which I'd spent most of my adult life, I'd never really bothered to think about these questions. In the bubble, I'd been someone a bit special. A famous name, an artistic creation. Now the bubble had definitely burst and I found myself out in the chilly winds of the real world. In that environment, I was a short-sighted, ginger guy pushing 50. The expression 'wake-up call' is overused these days, but this was definitely mine. But it was more than the faint ping on a mobile phone or the buzz of a smartwatch. This was a thousand alarm clocks, all going off at once.

could see sadness in your eyes,' he said, 'and I wanted to make you happy.'

In the grimmer times of life, when those trucks are coming at you, what a relief to discover that one of them is an ambulance. In which you'll be given something to ease the pain. Your wounds will be bandaged. You'll be wrapped up warm and told that everything's going to be all right. In short, your life is saved.

My own 'ambulance' came in the shape of a young man who, with remarkable speed and skill, performed all of the miracles listed above and many more. His name was Marc. A Japanese art school graduate. He was 23 years younger than me, but that didn't seem significant, because in matters of common sense he was easily 23 years older. He was everything I wasn't used to: quiet, gentle, kind, intelligent, romantic. Almost an alien species from so many of those I'd known in clubland.

It had started off very low-key, then drifted into far deeper emotional waters than I'd ever expected. We fell in love. Not the drama-fuelled 'love' that I had always seemed to attract, but something far richer, based on the firm foundation of a deep and growing companionship. Marc encouraged me to drop the barriers I'd built and to be myself. He made me start to think before I opened my big mouth, that toxic legacy from my parents, and to curb the knee jerk reactions that had got me into so much trouble throughout my life. Just by being there, he calmed the waves of my unsteady mental state and, with an infinite wisdom that belied his age, helped me sort through the tangled web of my feelings. For the first time in my life I stopped feeling, essentially, alone.

At long last, someone had fallen in love with David Hodge, not Dusty or Sofonda Cox. All my life, I'd craved the emotional attention I'd never really had from my parents and only ever from one or two special people, such as Dids. Now, in this young Japanese man, it had come to me in unexpected abundance. And at the very moment when I'd never needed it more. Miracle of miracles. Hallelujah. Let the bells ring out.

And thank God, because almost everyone else seemed to have disappeared. When the panto had closed I'd wasted no time in reaching out by phone and email to several club promoters and industry people to test the water about getting some work. But all of a sudden, I seemed to be box office poison.

'Dusty who? Oh, the old girl from *Trannyshack*. Nah, don't think so.'

They didn't say it out loud, but it was obvious that's what they were thinking.

Worse yet, I even approached people who'd started out working *for* me at the club and who now had their own nights in various venues. But to no avail. The bitter truth was that plenty of them revelled in my position. It was payback time for the stuck-up old cow with the tongue like a razor blade, who'd thought she was a cut above the rest. Two of my longstanding employees had started up a night with a similar concept to *Trannyshack* and at a venue just round the corner. But not only was I not included in their new line-up, they blocked me on social media. Insult added to injury. I was tired old Margo Channing, way past her prime, and the 'Eves' had finally won.

The only contact who helped me was Martin Witts from the Leicester Square Theatre. Martin had believed in me from day one and now did so again. A handsome, charming silver fox with great business sense, Martin also owned The Museum of Comedy. Tucked under a church in Holborn, this was a small theatre space with an adjoining exhibition of comedy memorabilia. I was offered the job of Duty Manager. I'd be responsible for floor managing the productions in the tiny theatre, running the bar and staffing the museum space during the day. I'd be mainly working on my own with a couple of support staff when needed. The money wasn't great; a week's pay was about the same as I'd once been able to earn in four hours, but I took it gratefully. I could now pay the rent and the bills and breathe easy, as I tried to map out some sort of future.

And I liked the work. Sitting in on the various shows was fun. On the bar, I learned how to stock-take and cash up at the end of the night. I was less keen on delivering flyers about our events to the many hotels in the area. Provided for this task was a shopping trolley, which was not exactly a glamorous vehicle. But I held my head high, did what I had to do and prayed that nobody I knew would see me doing it. It was all far removed from my previous existence and sometimes I felt a bit insignificant as I stacked the Pringles and counted the bottles of lemonade in the bar. Working at a job with formal hours and with tasks to be completed in a set time came as a major shock to the system after 20 years of doing things pretty much my own way. By the end of the shifts, my back hurt and my feet ached and I'd often return home a bit depressed. But Marc would be waiting with a hug and the words that meant everything.

'Come on, you're doing just great,' he'd say. 'You're fighting back and I'm really proud of you.'

The Very Miss Dusty O wouldn't have been seen dead pushing that shopping trolley through the streets. Neither would Sofonda Cox. But I reminded myself constantly that these characters now hardly existed. It was David Hodge pushing the trolley. A middle-aged man who had now grown a little goatee beard and, after decades without them, had let his long-lost eyebrows grow back. My skin hardly knew what had hit it. What's this? Hair?

But perhaps the transition had been too swift, too brutal, too much for my spirit to cope with. My whole life had changed within six months and I began to pay the price with another tsunami of panic attacks and breathing problems.

'I'm fine,' I'd tell Marc. 'Really, fine. Honest.'

'David, you're not,' he replied. 'You must go to the doctor. You need help that I can't give you.'

I was started on another course of anti-anxiety medication which, in retrospect, helped no end. Slowly, my moods began to stabilise and I started to enjoy small pleasures once again. But with Marc now in my life, those pleasures were of a different kind. Simpler, less showy, less egotistical. In a word, more 'normal'.

'Normal.' A word and a concept I'd always despised and had run a million miles from since I'd been a kid. My whole life had been spent in flamboyant pursuit of its very opposite. Now, however, 'normal' began to seem rather wonderful. Instead of sitting in front of a mirror for three hours, there was time to do some of the things I'd never got round to. Visits to art galleries, museums, the Zoo and the other sights of London. Going out to eat in some small bistro with the person I loved. All that stuff for which I'd either been too busy or I'd had nobody to share it with.

The only aspect of my 'old' existence that I seriously missed was its aspect of creativity. I could easily take off the ball gowns and the glitter, the towering wigs and the six-inch heels. But what was harder to strip away from my daily life was the chance to create, to make something that hadn't been there before. In my case, that had primarily been about turning my appearance into a work of art, but it had been broader than that. My less than brilliant efforts at being a DJ had still been creative. My singing and recording work had been creative. Being a pantomime dame had been creative. As had hosting in a club, curating a great night out, so that hundreds of other souls could leave their troubles outside the door, enter a magical world and feel glad to be alive again. All this seemed to have been whipped away from under my feet. And so quickly that my head was still spinning from the shock of it.

As was now so often the case, the answer came from Marc. A brilliant, imaginative designer and photographer, he 'got' exactly what had happened to me.

'Here you go,' he said one day. 'Try this. Show me what you can do.'

It was a set of paints and three small blank canvases. He knew that I'd tried to paint pictures before, though that had been donkeys years ago. I'd no idea where to start, but I sat at the kitchen table and gave it a go. With my favourite Classic FM playing softly in the background, I blobbed and squished and brushed away for several hours and was surprised by what spilled out of me.

It wasn't exactly pretty. It was never going to be Constable's depiction of *The Hay Wain* or Millais' painting of Ophelia floating down the stream to a watery grave. With hard, determined brush strokes, I painted grotesque figures of neutral gender in violent, acid colours. Angry images, dark images, confusing images. But also glittering with the sequins and sparkle I glued on top. No doubt all a reflection of my self-image at that moment in time. God knows. Yet despite the turbulence of some of the pictures, I found the whole thing incredibly relaxing. A catharsis of my troubles, as good as any prescribed medication.

Never one to hide my light under the proverbial bushel, I posted some of the pictures on Facebook and was delighted by how many people were complimentary. One person even offered to buy them, but I was too embarrassed by these early efforts to take money, so I just gave them away.

But that day was the beginning of an amazing journey into a completely new form of self-expression. Just as the creation of Dusty and Sofonda Cox had been, but in a very different way. Yet the impulse was just the same. To make something new. To express my thoughts and feelings and let them loose in the atmosphere and see what response I got. I wasn't really bothered if they were understood or even liked. My lifelong 'fuck you if you don't like it' attitude still wasn't far below the surface.

The important part was the act of creation. That was the exciting bit, not the outcome. The result dependent on what state my head was in when I picked up the brush. I did lots more pictures and the more I did, the more I loved it. Soon, all my spare time was spent surrounded by paints and glitter with beautiful music filling my ears, submerged in my own emotions, my recollections and that primal urge to create. In short, painting became my therapy, as I suppose Marc had hoped that it might. It carried me away from the tangles of my own difficult situation. It calmed and sustained me. And slowly but surely, I began to come out on the other side.

As my subjects, I painted the things that interested me. These may often have been the same things that other artists had tried to explore in their work, but I tried to make them my own through the colours I used and by letting go of all the narrow-minded ideas I'd always had about art – that it should be representative and that the only 'good' art was the 'old' art i.e. Johnnie Constable and the gang. I became interested in what art meant to me and how my own story was being chronicled in what I painted and how I painted it. Artists call this the 'process', but to me it was just the telling of my tale on a blank canvas and it came easily.

I was grateful that I'd never had any professional instruction, as that enabled me to learn as I went along and in my own time. The end results may have looked a bit naïve and primitive, but at least they were authentic, coming straight out of both my head and my heart. Not a feeble copy of something that had been done better before by somebody else, or derived from some rigid technique I'd been taught at an art school.

Like everything else that had ever mattered to me, I did this alone. It was my own journey, private and intense.

And so, I painted my way out of the old life and painted my way into the new.

eader, I married him (as Jane Eyre once famously said).

In 2015, Marc and I tied the knot. I had never been so sure of anything in my life. I'd have signed up for anything. Love, honour and obey? Yeah fine. Wash his socks and undies? Bring it on. Nothing I might ever do for Marc could repay what he had already done for me. When we were together, the world was okay.

It was my big fat Japanese wedding. Love with all the trimmings. His family flew the 6,000 miles from Tokyo and Mom and Julie managed the 100 miles from Walsall. Despite the language barrier, the families got along just fine. It was a day when words didn't matter as much as feelings.

After the marriage ceremony at Camden Town Hall, we threw a party at a little place nearby. On this unique day, I'd made a conscious effort to reach out to people I'd known in my teenage years, like my college friend Kim who'd been one of the first people in my life who had embraced me exactly as I was. Curtain Mark was best man, giving a speech that managed to be both hilarious and loving at the same time. Most of his jokes were about the age gap and how Marc would soon be changing my nappies. Some cabaret artist friends did a few turns but, apart from them, the characters who had inhabited my life as Dusty, were few and far between.

'I'm so happy that you've found somebody to love you,' said my sister Julie, crying tears of happiness.

And I was equally happy to have her as my big sister. All through the years, though our paths had been so different, Julie had been a rock, an uncritical friend, a peacemaker between me and my mother. From my earliest memories, when she'd snuggled up beside me to shelter me from the family storms, Julie had been one of the great strokes of luck in my life. She still is. She is also the great blessing in her mother's life, especially as Mom has aged and needs more care. So often, Julie puts her own needs on hold in order to give our mother the attention which, as children, our parents had often neglected to give to us. If medals were ever given to carers, Julie deserves the equivalent of the Victoria Cross.

Soon after our wedding, my husband and I (and what queen has never dreamed of using that phrase?), went to Japan. Getting to know Marc's family and friends and exploring his wonderful country was a brilliant experience. We went to a Buddhist ceremony, in which the participants were cleansed of their past sins and permitted to start their lives afresh. Boy, could I relate to that. After the service, my name was transcribed into Japanese, painted onto a wooden baton and ceremoniously presented to me by a monk. It felt like being given the key to freedom. As if David Hodge was being handed back his identity, firmly stamped on the passport to a new existence

When we came back to London, I had one last thing to do before I shed the old life forever. Having assumed that clubland had cheerfully washed its hands of the Very Miss Dusty O, I was very surprised to be asked by the organisers of London Pride to host the main stage that year in Trafalgar Square. As I wrote in the very first pages of this book, that is when I murdered 'her' once and for all. After that *Sunset Boulevard* moment, I went home, got in the bath, washed her off and saw her go down the plughole. Job done. Chapter ended.

That night, I looked again at the baton bearing my real name which the monk had given me in Japan. From now on, in moments of doubt or uncertainty, I grasp it tightly and find the courage to keep going wherever the road is going to take me.

One of the most important steps on that road had already been taken. When I stopped feeling the need to put on a 'show', the need to drink evaporated with it. In recent years, as I'd increasingly felt like an old has-been, it had been the pain-blocker that enabled me to get through the nights in the clubs without losing my mind. But when my circumstances became so much happier, it was just no longer necessary. I now realised I didn't need to be half-cut to be an interesting and worthwhile person. In truth, the booze had masked the best parts of my personality, those very attributes that had brought me success in the first place. It had been a kind of self-sabotage, but no more. Like in some sentimental movie, where the injured person learns to walk again unaided and throws away their crutches as the music swells on the soundtrack, I threw away the booze.

The morning after Trafalgar Square, I started to go through the four, six-feet long rails of Dusty's priceless

Westwood clothing, some of it worn only a couple of times. Not just the frocks, but shoes, handbags and box after box of costume jewellery. Marc photographed and catalogued every single piece, noting the year bought and from which collection it came.

Memories flooded back with each outfit. The white lace catsuit in which I'd been lowered by crane onto a stage in South Africa. The black velvet number in which I'd nearly boiled to death in Naples. The red fur jacket I wore when modelling for Gaultier. It was all there. My life on a clothes rail. The expensive evidence of the addiction to drag that had brought me so much fun but so much chaos, too.

The collectibles were sold to a specialist shop who appreciated their worth and had the contacts to sell them on to. The jewellery went mostly on eBay. The less expensive stuff was exported to a vintage shop in Brighton, where the local fashion-conscious students must have been delighted with the sudden influx of designer stock. Most of the money from this 'sale of the century' paid off the debts I'd run up during my first year without 'her' and the rest was put aside for future emergencies, of which there would no doubt be a few. I kept just three outfits for sentimental reasons. It had taken 25 years of blood, sweat and tears to buy and maintain that wardrobe and it was all gone in a couple of days. Yet I waved bye-bye to it with almost no tears at all, which I knew was a healthy sign. At least now we had the spare room back.

Out of the blue, an old friend called Sean Spence offered me a job working front of house at his hair salon in Hampstead. I became part of a team of mostly young people in a warm, friendly environment. They accepted me at once and showed me so much kindness that, once or twice, I struggled to suppress my tears. Apart from my bosses, none of them knew much about my past; it just wasn't their world. We'd hang out together after work and, for the first time in years, I started to make friends with what you might call 'normal' people. That word yet again. I hesitate to use it, but you know what I mean. Though they were all highly creative personalities, they weren't riddled with ego as most of those in my old life had been. They were centred but not self-centred. They weren't delusional. They fitted their skin better. It was a massive breath of fresh air.

Outside of work, I was still painting as much as I could. Now that I'd found it, there was no way I'd let it go. Sales came in via social media. Some were due to my past notoriety, but certainly not all. A few bitchy remarks were posted by people in my past, but these only spurred me on. Through a colleague at the salon, I was offered a small exhibition at a café/gallery in Belsize Park and sold the lot. To say I was pleased was an understatement. As if I'd planted a tiny seed and could now see it growing.

'You see,' said Marc, at the launch party, 'I knew you could do it. I had faith in you.'

That was such a wonderful thing to hear. In my life, few people had had any faith in me whatsoever. My sister Julie, Mrs Wall the lovely teacher who'd looked like Hattie Jacques, Alain at the Youth Theatre, my college friend Kim, my darling Dids and never forgetting Boy George. But they'd never been thick on the ground. And now there was Marc. Marc above all.

On the back of this first success, I arranged with Sean to take a few months off from the salon. I now had enough money from the clothes sale to tide me over for a while, so that I could produce a lot more work with a view to another, bigger show. A friend had a lovely flat in Sitges, a place I knew well from many holidays, so I went there. It was tough to leave Marc behind, but he encouraged me to take this break from the traumas of the recent past and almost pushed me onto the plane.

Over the next six weeks, on a terrace in the Spanish sunshine, I painted 15 canvases. I painted people I had known and places I had been. Experiences both good and bad. There were simple snapshots of my youth and the more complex images of my later life. Sometimes they were light and fun, others dark and seedy. Some canvases were filled with vigour and hope; others were dystopian and seemingly hope*less*. Whatever. This had been my world and I was owning it again through my paintbrush. I didn't care if the results weren't technically perfect, as long as they were authentic and said what I wanted to convey. In this Catalonian exile, I saw my work become freer, its quality improving and an individual style emerging. Above all, I found great peace in painting them and, for the first time in ages, had begun to sleep well at night. I realised that painting had now become vital to both my mental health and my sense of self-worth, both of which had taken some heavy knocks in recent times. I went back to London in a better state than I'd been in a long while.

'He's back!' my chums at the salon shouted when I walked back in through the door in Hampstead.

I'd now discovered that I quite liked being called by the masculine pronoun and not, as I had been for so long, by the feminine. For all these years, my masculine side had been dominated by my feminine alter egos and it was time the pendulum swung back, so that some balance could be achieved. Where the pendulum came to rest, I didn't really care, but my mental health demanded that some movement should happen. *Que sera, sera*, as Doris used to sing.

But it was my home, with Marc and the cats waiting for me, that mattered most.

'So, did it work?' he asked, as soon as I'd put my cases down and given him a hug.

'It worked,' I replied. 'Thank you.'

I scouted round for a possible exhibition space, but most galleries cost thousands to hire. Dream on, David. Then I chanced on a gallery in the basement of a shop in trendy, cosmopolitan Brick Lane. It was just the right size with just the right vibe and directly opposite the Truman Brewery where a massive art fair was about to be held, so the passing trade would be substantial. But it would cost £4,000 for a two-week gig. Again, dream on.

I was talking to a friend online about it one night. The next morning when I woke, I got a text from him, telling me to check my bank account. He'd paid in the £4,000. A second text arrived.

'Follow your dreams and stay true to yourself.'

I could hardly believe it and cried my eyes out. How wonderful to find one more person who believed in me. I promised I'd repay every penny, but he insisted it was a gift. From that moment on, I believed in angels as well as fairies.

As I'd been exploring both sexuality and gender in my work right from the start, I called the exhibition *We Are All Non-Binary* (a title and a concept that had to be explained to my mother very, very slowly). There would be 20 paintings and 50 pen illustrations. The prices were kept as low as possible, as my prime motivation was to get my work into circulation. I invited everyone I knew to the preview, which overflowed out into the street. Brick Lane was very different to the middle-class Belsize Park of my first exhibition, and it attracted a far more edgy crowd, which was exactly the audience I wanted. It all felt quite Eighties New York, with a mixture of club kids and millionaires crammed into the tiny basement gallery, sipping cheap wine from plastic cups and hearing my friend Paul playing his selection of ancient Vera Lynn records on a portable record player. Bizarre. By the time the show closed two weeks later, I'd sold almost everything.

Hugely encouraged by this success, I began working on new pieces. The inspiration for these derived from my partial colour blindness; something of a handicap for an artist you might think, but which was actually just the opposite. I'd always had trouble telling blue from pink and green from brown, which meant I'd find myself painting a pink sky and brown leaves on trees. So, I decided to explore all that, painting canvases containing green faces and purple horizons. I continued to paint what I was feeling and wanted to express, but just ignored any rules about the realities of colour.

Back in sunny Sitges, where the sea was pink and the sky orange, a local gallery owner I'd got to know, offered me a show. Again, money was the issue. The cost of exporting the work to Spain, and possibly back again if it didn't sell, was substantial. But Marc had the inspired notion of printing all the work onto acrylic tiles which were far cheaper than canvas. The result was great. The exhibition was called *Colour By Numbers*, a nod to Boy George's most successful album and also a two fingers to a bitchy critic from clubland who'd described my work as being like a child's colour-by-numbers book.

By a benign twist of fate, one of the guests at the opening party in Sitges was a friend from Birmingham, who'd flown out specially without telling me he was coming. His name was Wayne Toon, better known by his title of Baron Davenport, the owner of several bars and clubs in Brum as well as a massive brewery and pub chain eponymously called Davenports. Dusty had played in several of his venues and we'd become friends. He'd already bought quite a few of my canvases, even having a corridor in his offices hung entirely with them, which he called his 'Dusty Gallery'.

'What the hell are you doing here?' I asked, when he walked in.

'Aha…' he replied, taping the side of his nose.

The day after the opening, we hung out together and talked about where my art was going. He was interested in how my face had once been the 'canvas' for my creativity and how I'd now made the transference to a literal one and he had some striking ideas about how Davenport's Brewery might work with me on a project. Slowly but surely, my art was being noticed. I still sold it mainly on social media, as none of the mainstream galleries expressed any interest. Good old George had bought a few for the walls of the Gothic mansion. The comedian Julian Clary had purchased a couple of my pieces too and I was thrilled to see a magazine photograph of them hanging in his London house next to an original Keith Haring, the legendary American pop artist.

But I was careful not to let the worm of ambition wriggle its way into me as it had so often done before. At last, I had found some balance and emotional happiness in my life and nothing could be allowed to spoil that. If my art became commercially successful, that would be great. If it didn't, it hardly mattered because, to me, it already was a stonking triumph, in terms of the pleasure and sense of achievement it had brought to me.

The Baron Davenport was as good as his word and soon offered me a 'homecoming' exhibition in Birmingham. He would fund it personally, as part of his wider scheme to bring together local industry and the arts community. For the first time, there was no risk of my shouldering a financial loss; if the show didn't go well, I'd not be eating baked beans on toast for the next six months.

This show was christened *Back To My Roots*. The local media picked up the story and I did various interviews on Brum radio and TV stations. The Baron, bless him, pulled out all the stops to make it a success. The venue was exquisitely dressed with banks of flowers and regiments of flickering candles. A big red carpet stretched out onto the pavement. That night, no less than 400 guests came to sip the free champagne and nibble at the finger buffet served on silver trays by uniformed staff. There was even a DJ booth, so the evening felt like a kind of fusion between my old glamorous life in the clubs and my new unglamorous one at the easel, covered in splodges of paint. It was all a far cry from my first two humble exhibitions.

True to form, my mother made no bones about not being a major fan of my work.

'I'm very proud of him,' she said to anyone who cared to listen, 'but I wouldn't hang much of it in my living-room. Far too rude.'

But that was Jean Hodge to a 'T'. Honest as ever and, despite all our ancient battles, exactly why I had finally come to adore her so much. Unlike so many of the people in my later life, there was nothing phony about my mother. What she said, she meant. What you saw was what you got. It gave me the deepest possible pleasure to have her and Julie there that night, knocking back the champers, far more interested in the buffet than in the art and hearing all these trendy types praise me.

'Oh Mrs Hodge. So nice to meet you. David's pictures are so wonderful. Does he get that from you?'

'I bloody well hope not, dear.'

Everyone made a great fuss of her. At one point, Mom complained of feeling cold and Baroness Cohen lent her a stole, which Mom swanned off in and never gave back. We really must return it sometime...

The venue management was so pleased with the footfall of visitors to my show that they extended the run from one month to four. It was, in short, a bit of a triumph. Up till now, I'd felt slightly embarrassed at identifying myself as 'an artist'. I still thought of myself as a retired drag queen, now a receptionist in a Hampstead hairdresser, who painted a bit on the side.

'And what do you do?' some stranger would ask.

'I'm an artist.' I now replied, at first tentatively, but with increasing ownership of the word.

It was a good feeling. Having been so fragile for so long, my sense of identity grew strong again. I was David Hodge, artist. And nothing had ever made me so proud. Not the schmoozing with Robbie Williams or dancing with Grace Jones on top of the bar. Not chatting to Cher about wigs at the Versace show in Milan. Not even standing in front of 10,000 people in Trafalgar Square. In its time, I'd loved all that and

I was grateful for those memories. But all of it had been, as Dusty was, essentially fake. But the paintings on the walls of that Birmingham gallery weren't fake in the slightest. However good or bad they might be, they were totally authentic, totally 'me'. And what more can you give than that?

One of the guests at the Birmingham exhibition was Kalid Mahmoud, a local Labour MP. On leaving he'd said we should do something together soon. I'd no idea what he meant, but soon after he invited me to show some of my work at the Houses of Parliament. As a Muslim MP, Khalid said he wanted to smash the trope that all Muslims have negative issues with gay people and I was to be the first openly queer artist to exhibit their work within the hallowed walls of the 'Mother of Parliaments'. Wow. The big time.

The instinct for self-promotion that had driven me for so long in my career, had still not deserted me. I got in touch with the London Pride organisers who were instantly keen to get on board, making it the opening event of that year's Pride festivities. They saw it as a landmark event, a celebration of a gay man's work in a building at the very core of The Establishment, a place in which LGBT people had had precious little presence in the past. I even found myself back on the cover of a gay magazine, when *QX* did a three-page spread about the exhibition. But this cover was very different to previous ones. It was the first picture that had ever appeared of me as a male. Not a scrap of make-up; warts and all. Well not warts exactly, but certainly the lines and wrinkles of a 50ish bloke. After so many years hiding behind make-up and costumes, it was a huge step for me emotionally. Like I was saying to my own community, this is who I am now. Dusty is dead. Like it or lump it.

In the months before the show, I'd painted furiously to create a new collection. Sometimes painting till four in the morning, knowing I had to go to work in a few hours but not caring. I lost myself in the maze of my own creativity and it was intoxicating. The exhibition rooms were in the oldest part of Parliament, close to Westminster Hall, where monarchs lay in state and major historic events had taken place, including the trial of Charles the First and the coronation feast of Anne Boleyn. The rooms were grand and imposing. Mullioned windows, thick carpets and oak-panelled walls lined with stately portraits of long-gone royals and peers. Soon they'd be joined by 25 of my own less deferential pieces. I hoped the old royals wouldn't look down their noses too much.

It was a proud moment when I posted the thick cardboard invitations with the Houses of Parliament crest embossed on the front. I imagined the looks on the faces of certain people who'd long since written me off. Some didn't even have the grace to reply, but it didn't bother me. Only confirming my belief that I'd wasted a lot of precious time on people who hadn't deserved it.

On the day of the exhibition, I had my hair bleached and styled in the salon. It was now in an almost monastic bowl cut, like a modern-day Henry V at Agincourt. I'd called this show *Limp Wrist – Iron Fist* from a quote I'd heard describing a camp gay man who was fluffy on the outside but steely on the inside. Exactly how I liked to see myself. Resilient. Resurgent. Steel that had been through the fire and come out stronger.

Over 500 guests turned up at Westminster that day, even though they had to fight their way through a huge anti-Trump demo in Parliament Square. I wasn't allowed to sell any work within these ancient walls, but people could reserve a piece. Within two hours, everything had gone. Not to people who'd known me on the scene but to serious art enthusiasts and collectors. It was a moment of huge validation for me, not just as an artist but as a human being. I felt I'd achieved something of far more value than just disco, DJ-ing and drag. Much of all that had been fun and we all need a bit of mindless frivolity, but it had been ephemeral, insubstantial and blown away on the wind as easily as a dandelion head. But my art was different. Simply on another level. My art might last.

The guest of honour was the unique Mollie Parkin, the brilliant, iconoclastic painter, journalist and major style icon of the Sixties. Now in her late eighties, Mollie hadn't lost an ounce of her originality and verve. Marc and I had met her when I'd approached her on Facebook to ask if he could photograph her. He'd shot the picture at her council flat in World's End, Chelsea, where she'd fed us on crisps and lemonade, then later I used the photograph as the basis for a painting. I loved her at first sight. She had a treasure-trove of risqué stories that could have curled your hair extensions. Years before Boy George, Pete Burns and Marilyn, Mollie had driven a tank through conventionality and ploughed her own dazzling route through life. Good on you, girl. If I can grow old like she has, I'll be happy.

After the exhibition closed, I joined many of my guests at *Circa*, a bar in Soho, where the Very Miss Dusty O had strutted her stuff many times. Among the guests was Damian Hirst's mother, another lovely lady, but her presence felt slightly surreal. Maybe she was checking up to see if her little boy had a serious rival coming up from behind. I should be so lucky.

It'd been a long while since I'd touched a drop of alcohol, but I touched a few drops that night and got fairly tiddly. Yet I knew it was safe to do so, because it wasn't anything like the 'rotten' drunkenness of days gone by, where I'd needed alcohol to mask my inner pain and frustration. That night, my drinking was totally celebratory. And there was so much to celebrate in my life now. Far more than I'd ever have imagined possible just a couple of years before. The next morning, I had a slight headache, but it was worth it. My head might have hurt, but at least I could hold it high again.

f you're going to write a book,' said Boy George, wagging his finger, 'write your truth. Try not to be spiteful, but don't be afraid to tell it like it was.'

So that's what I've tried to do in these pages. Where people have hurt and damaged me, I've said so, though hopefully more in sorrow than in spite, because anger gets you nowhere. There's an old saying that anger is a poison that does more harm to the vessel that contains it, than to anything over which it is poured. So true.

I wanted to write down my story because I felt it might be one that people would relate to. Male or female or not quite sure. Black or white. Gay or straight. I hope so anyway. The details are obviously specific to me, but the themes are surely commonplace.

It is the story of a child growing up into a world where his true self was considered unacceptable. The story of a young man struggling to find that identity in the big city where the streets were certainly not paved with gold. The story of someone prepared to do just about anything to live the life of which he dreamed and not the one prescribed for him.

It's also the tale of the obstacles that rose up along the path to achieving those goals. The hidden addictions, the flaws of character, the inability to recognise and to break free from the bonds that were holding him back.

Most importantly though, it's the story of how hard it was to finally find the person that I really was. Because, so early in life, I'd thrown him away as I didn't much like him and so decided to create a different version. That decision had brought me fame, money, glamour and a whole lot of fun. But it had also made my journey towards peace of mind infinitely harder. There were so many other paths I might have taken to that happier place and got there very much sooner.

But hey, maybe that was just the way it had to be. Without those crazy days, without the drag, without the booze and the falling into the skip, perhaps I wouldn't so much appreciate my ultimate arrival at that happy place. The place in which I had finally come to love David Hodge.

The paintings I create now are the echo of my experiences, the slices of my truth. A truth which I put out into the world for scrutiny and, if necessary, for ridicule. Take them or leave them. It's this fear of ridicule and disapproval that holds people back and stops us from recognising that we are all capable of so much more than we imagine.

That same little boy who sat by the window in Miss Pinchface's classroom wearing his hand-knitted jumper would have been laughed at if he'd ever said he wanted to grow up to be a Goth. In turn, the queer teenage Goth sipping cider on the 51 bus from Walsall to Birmingham would have been mocked if he'd declared that one day he'd go to London to eventually become 'Queen of Soho'. And plenty of people would have sniggered at the idea of that iconic figure, one day climbing down from her pedestal and that she, or rather he, would create yet another self, the best self yet, the self that is hopefully kinder and more understanding. The self that somebody else could fall in love with.

I'm not yet at the end of my journey. There may be many more speeding trucks still to come my way, as there are in the lives of us all. But, as that old Fred Astaire song goes, *I'll pick myself up, dust myself down and start all over again.* That's what my father did and, luckily, it seems to be in the genes. And I encourage you, dear reader, to do the same.

Can you haunt anywhere while you're still alive? I don't know. Does my tiny red-headed ghost perhaps still walk in that bleak classroom in a dull Midlands town? Or if not, is there another young boy or girl a bit like me who is sitting there, wanting to fit in and to be liked, but somehow not quite making the grade? Yes, maybe because they're gay. Or black or brown or yellow. Or disabled. Or dyslexic. Or perhaps just shy, bereft as yet of any sense of him/her/themselves? In short, anyone who is, in some way or other, 'different'. If so, I send him/her/they my love and my encouragement.

In the end, it doesn't really matter if you're the boy who sat by the window. What matters is what you see through it. Not an expanse of scrubby unloved grass, the drab school buildings or the backs of the houses beyond the rusty fence. What matters is that, in your imagination at least, you see a landscape of infinite possibility.

Life after drag – the artist, David Hodge

Two roads diverged in a wood, and I –
I took the one less travelled by,
And that has made all the difference

Robert Frost (1874 - 1963)

ACKNOWLEDGEMENTS

Thank you to mom, dad, Nan, Karen, Julie and Mike and to my gorgeous husband Marc. Also, and obviously, to George and Pete, Sean Spence and all at the Salon. Special thanks to Alan Clarke who helped me find my voice and who was so kind and understanding and with whom it was a joy to work. Iain Mcallum, Mark Farrell, Twiggy and Stan, Kim and Sally Tonge, Andrew Gibbs, Kim and Paul, Keeks, Alan Winter, David Parrish and all at Mardle Books, Nick and Santi, Alain Buxton, David Orr, Peter Cleary, Jane Hutton, Hayden, Jude Bean, Dean Mills, Duncan Marr, Cristiano Basciu, Lee Riley, David Hudson, Stewart Who, Wayne Davenport and everyone who has played a part in my life so far. Good or bad – all is forgiven and I love you. xxxx